MW00862211

HOMES DOWN EAST

HOMES DOWN EAST

Classic Maine Coastal Cottages and Town Houses

EARLE G. SHETTLEWORTH, JR.
CHRISTOPHER GLASS
SCOTT T. HANSON

Photographs by DAVID J. CLOUGH

Tilbury House, Publishers, Thomaston, Maine

The authors wish to thank Hilary Bassett of Greater Portland Landmarks and Abraham Schechter of the Portland Room of the Portland Public Library for their assistance in providing historical illustrations and plans from the original issues of the *Scientific American Building Monthly* and *American Homes and Gardens*.

Tilbury House Publishers
12 Starr Street
Thomaston, Maine 04861
800-582-1899
www.tilburyhouse.com

Text and Jacket design by Harrah Lord. Page layout by Janet Robbins.

ISBN 978-0-88448-349-6

Library of Congress Control Number: 2014949568

Printed in China
14 15 16 17 18 19 SUN 10 9 8 7 6 5 4 3 2 1

To those late nineteenth and early twentieth century architects who created a distinctive residential style in Maine that inspires us still.

CONTENTS

CHAPTER 3

CHAPTER 4

CHAPTER 5

CHAPTER 1

Introduction

Maine Homes for a National Audience

The United States entered an age of expansiveness following the Civil War. Railroads, manufacturing, and the exploration and settlement of the West—all enabled by increased industrial capacity—led to urban expansion and new patterns of living. Suburban housing developments took shape and were served by trolleys and rail; and colonies of vacation homes arose where well-to-do families could escape the heat, congestion, and contagions of the cities during the summer months.

The Maine Coast flourished as a destination for summer vacationers. Starting with boarding houses and hotels, resorts such as Kennebunkport, Prouts Neck, and Bar Harbor developed fashionable cottage colonies. Between the end of the Civil War and the beginning of World War I, architects faced the challenge of creating new house forms for summer lifestyles, varying from informal to grand, depending on the means and desires of their clients. The stone foundations, vernacular lines, and open plans of the Shingle Style were especially suited for coastal locations.

The rise of the Maine Coast as a summer retreat paralleled the development of American architectural magazines that provided architects with opportunities to publish their designs. There had been builders' companions and pattern books since the early days of the republic, but now publishers issued monthly periodicals with house plans and advertisements for all the new hardware, decorative detailing, and appliances that were vying for attention in the marketplace. These magazines give us today a view of what was in the minds of builders more than a century ago.

The first major periodical of this kind was the *American Architect and Building News,* which began in Boston in 1876. Throughout its early years, this magazine and its competitors were restricted to using wood engravings on their pages, supplemented by separately produced photographic and color plates. By about 1890, however, photolithography had advanced to the point that a photograph could be printed directly on a page as an illustration.

The *Scientific American Architects and Builders Edition* was launched in New York in 1885 by Munn & Company as a special trade edition of the *Scientific American.* As it evolved, its name changed first to *Scientific American Building Edition* in 1895, then to *Scientific American Building Monthly* in 1902, and finally in 1905 to *American Homes and Gardens,* which merged with *House and Garden* in 1915. From its first issue, in November 1885, this monthly architectural magazine focused on providing "the latest and best plans for private residences city and country, including those of a very modest cost as well as the more expensive." The format adopted after 1890—black-and-white photolithographed illustrations accompanied by line drawings of floor plans—proved attractive to many architects, who submitted photographs and floor plans of their recent domestic commissions in the hope of attracting new clients.

Portland architect John Calvin Stevens' publishing history with the *Scientific American Building Monthly* is a good example. In 1887 Stevens submitted a pen-and-ink rendering of the Denison Cottage, at Delano Park in Cape Elizabeth, which appeared in the January 1888 issue. Four years later, in January 1892, the magazine illustrated Stevens' Baptist church in Gardiner with a photograph. From that point to its last issue in 1905, the magazine published twenty-two of Stevens' residential designs in photographs.

This book presents all fifty-two of the Maine houses that appeared in the magazine during its thirty-year run. The architects whose Maine cottages were featured in the *Scientific American Building Monthly* represented varied backgrounds. Of the Maine architects, Francis H. Fassett of Portland was the senior figure, having trained John Calvin Stevens, Frederick A. Tompson, and Antoine Dorticos in his office. In fact, both Stevens and Tompson were junior partners in Fassett's firm early in their careers. Fassett, Stevens, and Tompson all enjoyed successful statewide practices, while Dorticos taught French at Portland High School and confined his work to designing summer cottages for the Casco Bay islands.

George Burnham is remembered for planning the Cumberland County Courthouse with Guy Lowell of Boston and the Burnham & Morrill Baked Beans factory, both in Portland. Based in the prosperous Kennebec River city of Gardiner, Edwin E. Lewis was a popular Central Maine architect during the 1880s and 1890s who designed a wide range of buildings.

While Fred L. Savage of Bar Harbor was equally versatile, he was most noted for his prolific design of Mount Desert summer cottages, seventy of which were built in his native Northeast Harbor. Savage also supervised the construction of island summer homes designed by out-of-state architects.

The three architectural firms "from away" who designed Maine summer homes appearing in the *Scientific American Building Monthly* were from Boston: Clark & Russell; Chapman & Fraser; and Richards & Richards.

Clients whose cottages appeared in the *Scientific American Building Monthly* varied according to the demographics of the summer colony. Of the eleven cottage owners in Kennebunkport, nine were out-of-state businessmen and professionals. Prouts Neck clients were from outside Maine: a businessman, an artist, a doctor, and a wealthy Philadelphia socialite. In contrast, the clients building in the Portland-area colonies of Delano Park (in Cape Elizabeth) and Great Diamond and Cushing's islands in Casco Bay were predominantly local business and professional men wanting well-designed, conveniently located second homes for the summer months. Given its cosmopolitan social pretensions, it is unsurprising that Bar Harbor's contributions to the *Scientific American Building Monthly* were built by the president of the Pennsylvania Railroad, a physician from Washington, D.C., and a literary figure from Kentucky.

Although coastal cottages comprise the majority of published Maine house designs in the *Scientific American Building Monthly*, fourteen Maine houses built in urban or suburban settings were also published. Nine of these were constructed in Portland from designs by John Calvin Stevens. The earlier examples, including Stevens' own home on Bowdoin Street, were in the Shingle Style and had much in common with his summer cottage designs of the same period. The later houses were more urban in character, primarily in the Colonial Revival style, like the Franklin C. Payson House, also on Bowdoin Street. Published houses by George Burnham and Frederick A. Tompson were also located in Portland, one near the Western Promenade and the other in suburban Deering Highlands. Three houses were modest middle-class homes located in Augusta and Gardiner.

In July 1905 the *Scientific American Building Monthly* became *American Homes and*

Gardens. By this time the publication had provided architects, builders, and prospective clients with high-quality illustrations, floor plans, and descriptions for nearly two decades. As *American Homes and Gardens*, it proposed to furnish the same material in a more narrative and illustrative format aimed at a broader popular audience, along with a variety of special features of interest to home owners. Throughout its decade of publication *American Homes and Gardens* included several Maine summer homes that appear in this book. While the *Scientific American Building Monthly* had published a wide range of houses, from modest Casco Bay cottages to palatial Bar Harbor retreats, its successor focused on the more expensive properties, reflecting the last phase of Gilded Age life before the dramatic societal changes resulting from World War I. The war in Europe was already more than a year old when *American Homes and Gardens* was absorbed into *House and Garden* in October 1915, signaling a shift back to a more middle-class view of the future that would characterize the postwar America of the 1920s.

But what of the published Maine houses themselves?

They started out as simplified versions of the elaborate Queen Anne style we think of as Victorian. After some flirtations with borrowed styles such as medieval castles, the rise of summer cottage colonies along the coast produced designs for a run of simple but playful small cottages clad in shingles, with intersecting and enveloping rooflines and freely placed windows with varied muntin patterns. The freedom and simplicity of these little houses gave architects an opportunity to experiment with open floor plans, asymmetrical window placements, dramatic rooflines, and a new way of relating to the rugged coastal terrain. These cottages in turn influenced the design of more substantial houses in the new suburbs, houses that departed from the basic boxes of contemporary design to capture some of the freedom of the open coast. Some architecture critics did not know what to make of these shingle houses, using the phrase "odd cottages" to describe them, especially when the style migrated into town.

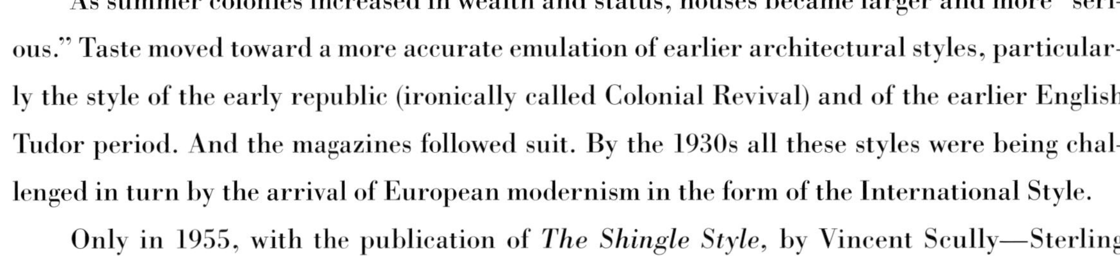

As summer colonies increased in wealth and status, houses became larger and more "serious." Taste moved toward a more accurate emulation of earlier architectural styles, particularly the style of the early republic (ironically called Colonial Revival) and of the earlier English Tudor period. And the magazines followed suit. By the 1930s all these styles were being challenged in turn by the arrival of European modernism in the form of the International Style.

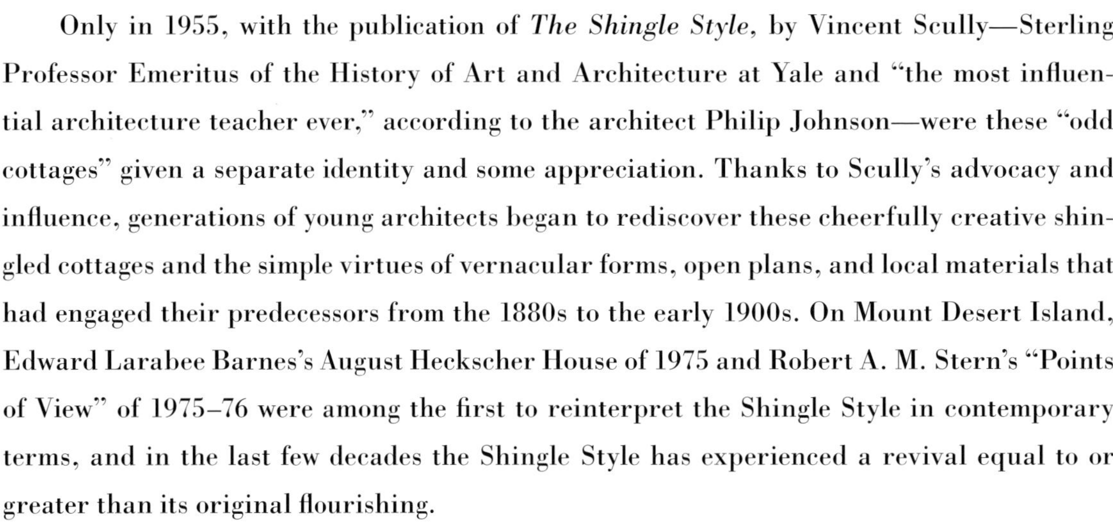

Only in 1955, with the publication of *The Shingle Style*, by Vincent Scully—Sterling Professor Emeritus of the History of Art and Architecture at Yale and "the most influential architecture teacher ever," according to the architect Philip Johnson—were these "odd cottages" given a separate identity and some appreciation. Thanks to Scully's advocacy and influence, generations of young architects began to rediscover these cheerfully creative shingled cottages and the simple virtues of vernacular forms, open plans, and local materials that had engaged their predecessors from the 1880s to the early 1900s. On Mount Desert Island, Edward Larabee Barnes's August Heckscher House of 1975 and Robert A. M. Stern's "Points of View" of 1975–76 were among the first to reinterpret the Shingle Style in contemporary terms, and in the last few decades the Shingle Style has experienced a revival equal to or greater than its original flourishing.

Today, in this postmodern age, the Neo-Shingle Style is a widely accepted form of architectural expression, and many examples can be found on the Maine Coast alongside the Shingle Style cottages of the past. From the vantage point of a century or more, presenting the Maine work of late nineteenth- and early twentieth-century architects through the pages of this book both informs us of our design heritage and guides us toward our architectural future. Thus the original intent of the *Scientific American Building Monthly* takes on a new purpose for our own time.

The Maine houses and cottages published in this magazine were built in a variety of styles, including Queen Anne, Shingle, Colonial Revival, Tudor Revival, and others, between 1883 and 1910. Looking back at them today, they provide a window through which we can glimpse the rise of the original Shingle Style in one of its original locations, Maine. These "odd cottages" have come to be so identified with Maine that they can be considered an iconic part of Maine's image in the twenty-first century. Through the historic images and text reproduced in this book, we can see these houses as they were seen when new, and in many cases we can see them as they are today. More than forty of the fifty-two Maine houses published in the *Scientific American Building Monthly* are still standing—a true testimony to the enduring appeal of these homes as winningly captured by David Clough's photographs for this book. Some of the houses have been enlarged or altered since their original building, but whenever possible, David has taken his new photographs from the same vantage as the originally published ones.

The text that follows consists of essays on each house written by architectural historians Earle G. Shettleworth, Jr. and Scott T. Hanson as well as architectural commentary on each house by architect Christopher Glass. The architectural commentary is in italics to distinguish it from the architectural history essays. The chapter introductions and other materials were written collaboratively by the three authors.

The six "Victorian" houses in the first chapter are in the Queen Anne style, like tens of thousands of houses built across the nation in the last quarter of the nineteenth century. Although some of these examples were built later than many of the Shingle Style cottages and homes included here, they are good examples of the types of residential architecture most common throughout the period and from which the Shingle Style emerged in the 1880s as the first distinctively American architectural style. The Walter G. Davis House provides an example of Queen Anne ~~S~~style by Francis H. Fassett and John Calvin Stevens just as Stevens was about to set out on his own. Stevens continued to design in the Queen Anne ~~S~~style while designing the Shingle Style cottages in the next chapter, as is seen here in the Edward T. Burrowes House of 1885. The last of the six houses in this chapter, the John Kelly Robinson Cottage, was designed by Fassett & Tompson. This was the new partnership formed by Francis H. Fassett and Frederick A. Tompson after the departure of Stevens. The house shows hints of the developing Shingle Style in its use of an open plan inside and fieldstone and shingle siding outside, while largely retaining the form and detailing of the Queen Anne style.

John W. Thompson House

Central Street, Gardiner

1891, Extant

Papermaking was one of nineteenth-century Gardiner's major industries. Mills such as Hollingsworth & Whitney attracted a skilled labor force to the community by offering housing to middle- and upper-level management employees. Thus, a night foreman with the company, John W. Thompson, could rent one of three identical Queen Anne style homes on Central Street within easy walking distance to the mill. Described as "a dwelling of low cost," this company house included both a parlor and a living room as well as three upstairs bedrooms. The $1,900 construction budget fell below the cost of many 1890s summer cottages published in the *Scientific American Building Monthly.*

This house shows the state of the art for 1891. It is a cube with a hipped roof, extended by ells and bays. The underlying shape would become a feature of many mail-order houses that later historians would describe as the American Foursquare. It is as vertical as the three boys on good behavior in the front, and looks as uncomfortable—tall, thin, and angular. The plan is all right angles except the living room bay, which, unusually, is the full width of its room, perhaps foreshadowing future geometric adventures; but each of the rooms is a rectangular box connected to others by simple doorways. There is no bathroom. It is against the backdrop of houses such as these that other architects published by Scientific American Building Monthly *created the new cottages of the Shingle Style.*

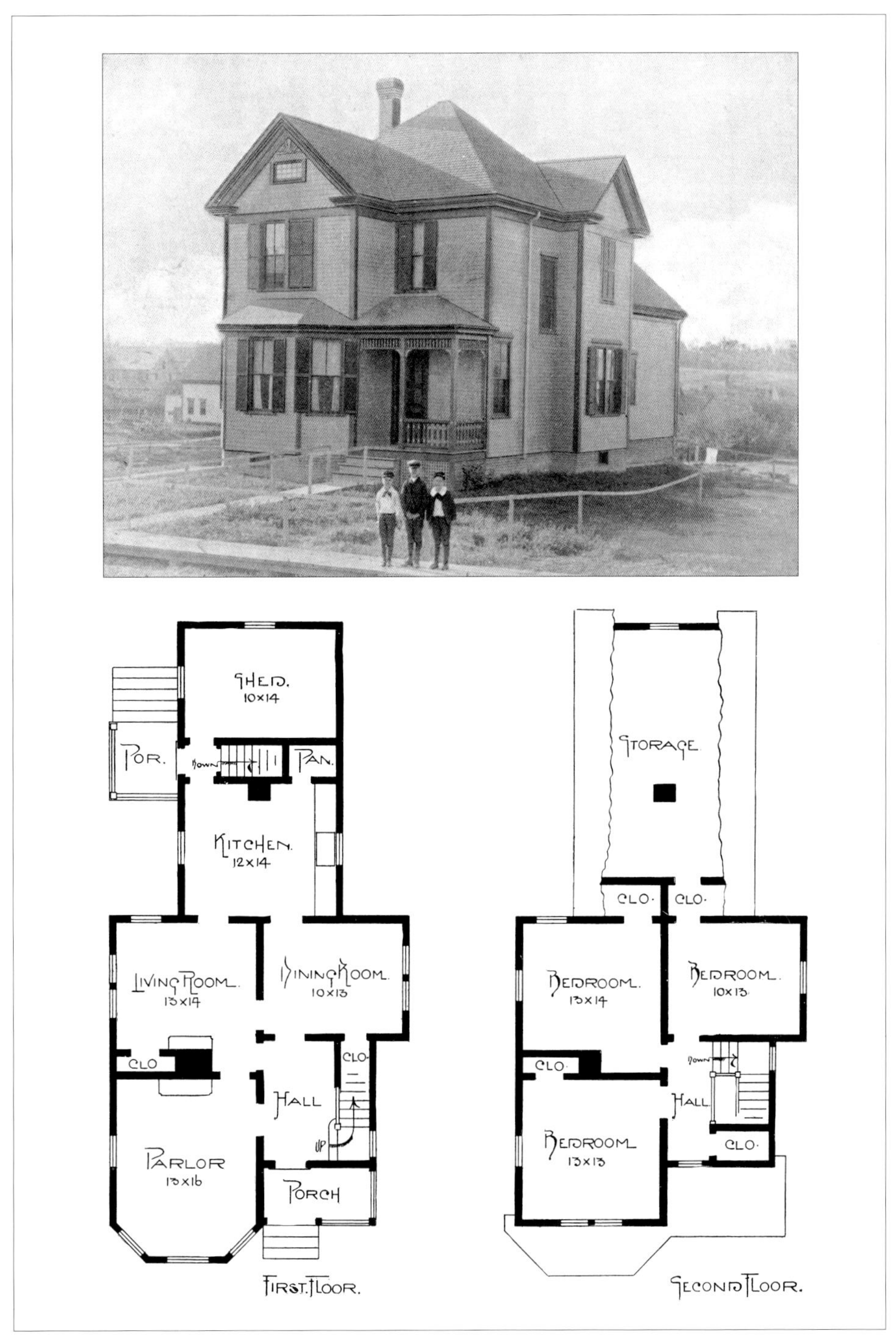
SHED.
10x14
POR.
Down
PAN.
KITCHEN.
12x14
LIVING ROOM.
13x14
DINING ROOM.
10x13
CLO
CLO
HALL
UP
PARLOR
13x16
PORCH
FIRST FLOOR.
STORAGE
CLO.
CLO.
BEDROOM.
13x14
BEDROOM.
10x13.
CLO.
Down
HALL
BEDROOM.
13x13
CLO.
SECOND FLOOR.

D. W. Emery House

20 Columbia Street,
Augusta

1890, EXTANT

D. W. Emery built this trim Queen Anne house at the corner of State and Union streets, Augusta, in 1890. After two decades of operating a planing mill, Emery became a clerk in the state treasurer's office and constructed his $3,200 residence diagonally across from the Maine State House for convenience to his employment. Emery's architect and builder remain unknown. In recent times, the house was moved to a nearby location to make way for a state office building.

This is another upright house, with more conventional bays simply added to the room in place of single windows. The downstairs plan is much more open, with parlor doors from the hall to the dining room and open arches from both to the parlor. The central chimney with three fireplaces creates a focus in the open plan. Compared to the previous house, this plan is considerably more integrated, though all the rooms are still rectangular. The bath, placed strategically between the family bedrooms and the back bedroom, which could be for a servant, is quite sophisticated, with its rectangular toilet seat probably not for a "water closet" but rather a "hopper"—a wooden seat over a bowl, with a vent exhaust through the roof.

There is a foreshadowing of the horizontal organization of the Shingle Style in the continuation of all of the roof cornices across the gables; the porch and bay cornice continued around the whole house as a belt course. Shingles above and clapboards below the belt course try to create an illusion of horizontality in this otherwise vertically proportioned house.

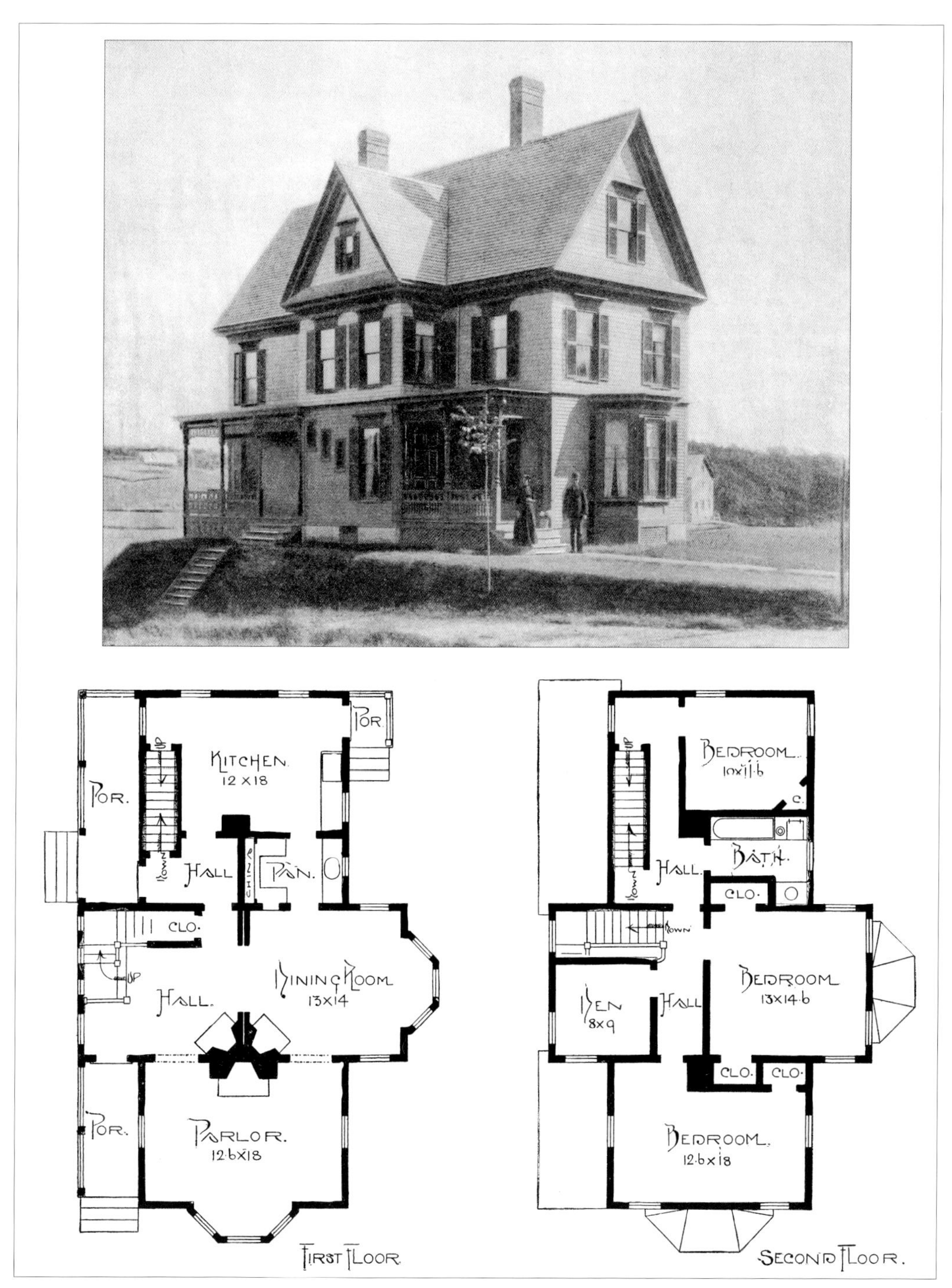
KITCHEN
12 X 18
POR.
POR
UP
DOWN
HALL
CHINA
PAN.
CLO.
UP
HALL.
DINING ROOM
13 X 14
POR.
PARLOR.
12.6 X 18
FIRST FLOOR.
BEDROOM.
10 X 11.6
C.
BATH.
HALL
CLO.
DOWN
BEDROOM
13 X 14.6
DEN
8 X 9
HALL
CLO.
CLO.
BEDROOM.
12.6 X 18
SECOND FLOOR.

First Baptist Church Parsonage

Church Street, Gardiner

Edwin E. Lewis,
Architect

1890, EXTANT

In 1889 the First Baptist congregation of Gardiner constructed a striking Shingle Style church by John Calvin Stevens similar to other Baptist churches designed by Stevens in Skowhegan, Yarmouth, Westbrook, and other Maine communities. The next year the Gardiner Baptists chose the local architect Edwin E. Lewis to design an adjacent parsonage to complement their new church. Constructed during the summer and fall of 1890 for $2,500, the minister's residence was described by the *Gardiner Home Journal* on October 29, 1890, as "one of the prettiest and most conveniently arranged houses that have been built here for some time."

Here the outside gives little hint of an adventurous interior landscape. The geometry of the piazza and the library/study bay are the only exterior indications of the diagonals that energize the plan of the halls up and down. The upstairs hall is especially exciting, with its diagonally organized space lighted by the stairway. But the outside is not as eventful. It is still a rectangular box with added gables and with the small belt course between floors.

Shed
W.C.
Kitchen
16x16.6
Pan.
China Closet
Lobby
Dining Room
12 x 16
Hall
Parlor
13x16
Library
12x12
Lobby
Piazza
First Floor
Bedroom
10x16.6
Clo.
Clo.
Bath
Up
Down
Bedroom
12x12.6
C.
Hall
Clo.
Bed Rm.
8.6x9
Bedroom
11x13
Study
12x12.6
C.
Second Floor

Walter G. Davis House

82 West Street, Portland

Fassett & Stevens
Architect

1884, DEMOLISHED

During the last year in which Francis H. Fassett and John Calvin Stevens practiced architecture together, Walter G. Davis (1857–1918) commissioned the firm to design an elaborate brick Queen Anne house at West and Vaughan streets in the Western Promenade area. When Fassett and Stevens dissolved their partnership in April 1884, Davis became Stevens' client, and the house was completed under his supervision that year. Walter G. Davis prospered as a partner in the Portland Packing Company, a food-canning business his father had founded with Samuel Rumery and James P. Baxter. Early in 1904 he returned to John Calvin Stevens to plan an extensive remodeling campaign for his home. By this time Stevens was being assisted by his son, John Howard Stevens, and the Davis drawings of 1904 to 1906 are among the first to list both their names as architects. The Stevens firm provided Davis with plans that included a new hallway, reception room, dining room, billiard room, and sunroom.

The emerging cottage style Stevens had begun to use on Great Diamond and Cushing's islands is not immediately apparent in this formal brick town house, but the extension of the principal roof down over the entry piazza does recall the cottages then being built on the Casco Bay islands. The plan of the house, with its double parlor and grand entry hall open to the parlor on one side and dining room on the other, provides for generous spaces. The grand staircase, with its arched landing window, leads to an equally generous upstairs bedroom hall. For the first time we see a complete bathroom with tub, sink, and toilet. The bay windows and semi-octagonal dormer soften the rigidity of the brick box. So though this is clearly a grand town house, there are bits of the informality of the cottages to be seen.

POR.
LOBBY.
CLO
PAN
KITCHEN.
13x16
LIBRARY.
15x17
HALL
BUT-
CLO
C
PARLOR.
15x16
HALL.
DINING ROOM
16x16
LOBBY.
NOOK.
PIAZZA.
FIRST. FLOOR.
BATH.
BEDROOM.
15x16
BEDROOM.
13x13
UP
HALL.
CLO·
CLO·
CLO
BEDROOM.
15x21
CLOSET.
BEDROOM.
16x16
CLO
BAL.
CLO·
SECOND FLOOR.

Edward T. Burrowes House

271 Western Promenade, Portland

John Calvin Stevens
Architect

1885, DESTROYED

John Calvin Stevens thought so highly of the Edward T. Burrowes House that he published its design in the *American Architect and Building News* for July 11, 1885, in his book *Examples of American Domestic Architecture* of 1889 and in the *Scientific American Building Monthly* of February 1892. His client, E. T. Burrowes (1852–1918), illustrated the house in catalogues for screen doors and windows, which he manufactured in a large brick factory complex on Spring Street in downtown Portland. In 1885—the same year that Stevens planned Burrowes' house—the architect designed the factory, which took three years to build, contained five acres of space, and housed the largest screen manufacturing operation in the world.

The Burrowes House was a picturesque two-and-a-half-story, frame Queen Anne style dwelling. Stylistic characteristics included the use of clapboards and shingles on the exterior, the corner turret on the façade, and the two tiered bay windows on the side capped by an overhanging roof gable ornamented with decorative panels.

The interior plan was a model of convenience. The first floor contained a central hall that led to a front staircase. A parlor flanked the hallway on the left, with a library and dining room on the right. A kitchen and pantries were located in the rear ell. The second floor was devoted to four bedrooms, a bathroom, and a den. The servants' quarters were in the attic, which was accessed by a back staircase.

In 1889, John Calvin Stevens and Albert Winslow Cobb wrote in *Examples of American Domestic Architecture*, "From the windows of this dwelling the view is superb; since the house is located at the very brow of the Western Promenade."

While at first glance the house seems to be a box with bay windows and a round ell added on, the plan shows that the interior spaces pinwheel around the central stair hall in ways that break out of the box. Parlor and library and dining room all have their own axes, with the space ballooning out from the hall. Again, only the kitchen with its pantries and back stair are cut off from the free flow of space.

Though there is an awkward collision between the second-floor balcony and the round tower, the porch is supported by the clustered columns that make a more formal statement than mere porch posts and look forward to the stricter interpretation of Colonial precedents that Stevens will adopt in his later work.

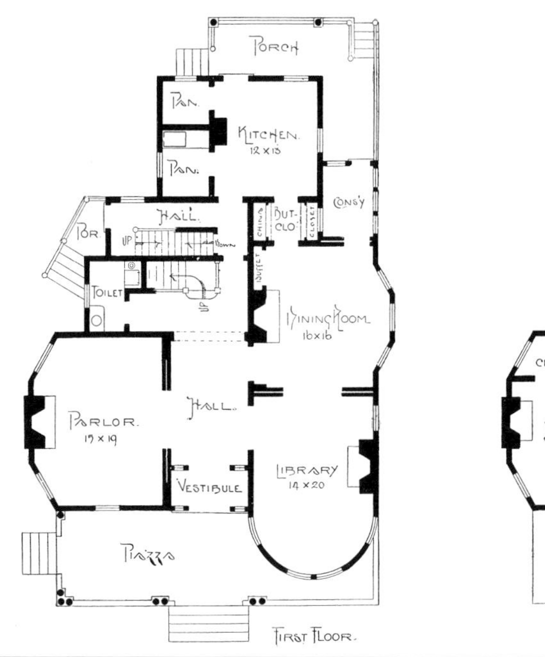

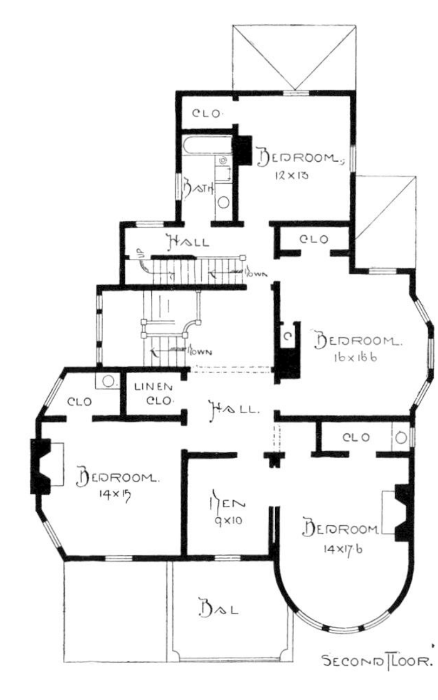

"The Birches," John Kelly Robinson Cottage

Cushing's Island, Casco Bay

Francis H. Fassett & Frederick A. Tompson
Architects

1889–90, EXTANT

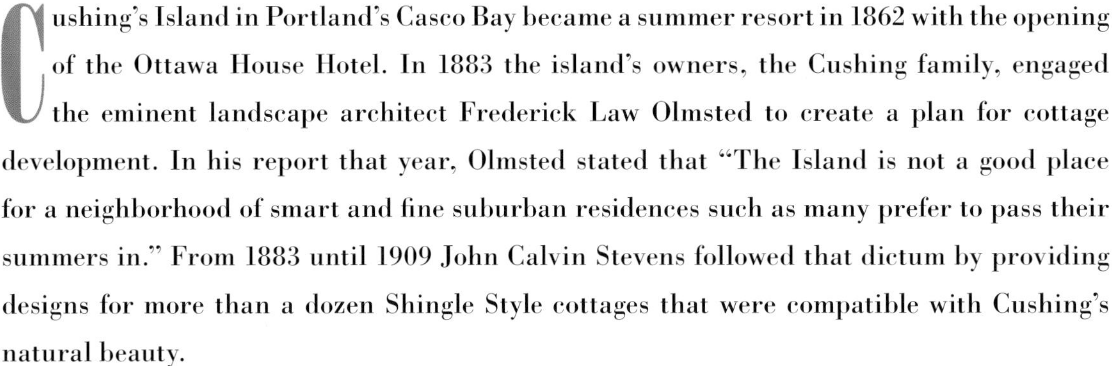

Cushing's Island in Portland's Casco Bay became a summer resort in 1862 with the opening of the Ottawa House Hotel. In 1883 the island's owners, the Cushing family, engaged the eminent landscape architect Frederick Law Olmsted to create a plan for cottage development. In his report that year, Olmsted stated that "The Island is not a good place for a neighborhood of smart and fine suburban residences such as many prefer to pass their summers in." From 1883 until 1909 John Calvin Stevens followed that dictum by providing designs for more than a dozen Shingle Style cottages that were compatible with Cushing's natural beauty.

In contrast to Stevens' approach, Fassett & Tompson's Cushing Island cottages for George H. Knight (1887), William J. Spicer (1887–88), and John Kelly Robinson (1889–90) were in the more ornamental Queen Anne style. The frame construction of the Knight and Spicer cottages reflected the suburban residential architecture of the times, while the rubble stone first story, rounded central bay, and decorative windows and dormers of Robinson's cottage captured the fanciful spirit of summer life.

Known as "Honest John Kelly," Robinson was a self-made man whose industry, wit, and generosity were widely admired by his contemporaries. His fortune resulted from his invention of the diamond-shaped match, which became the chief product of his highly successful Diamond Match Company. Robinson's business stature and his residence in Chicago probably contributed to the design for "The Birches" being featured in the November 1889 issue of that city's magazine, *The Inland Architect.*

Fassett & Tompson's stone cottage shows much greater understanding of the cottage style. It is still a box with a round tower somewhat awkwardly centered on the façade (towers are more ef-

fective on corners, where their military forebears would have been). The roof now comes down to shelter the porch and lower the appearance of the house, and the stone rises convincingly to support the roof. This idea—the stone base supporting a shingled roof structure—is one that will intrigue the cottage architects throughout the period. Walls, which interrupt the flow of the landscape, were always something of an embarrassment.

Here the downstairs has almost no interior walls. Every space opens into every other. Of course this is helped by the absence of a kitchen, which must have been down the steps from the dining room. Upstairs the narrow corridors are almost all gone except for an awkward shortcut to the balcony and a perhaps misleading note labeling the leftover space under the eaves as a linen closet!

Also on this page we see the last holdout of the graphic artists who had dominated magazine publishing in the decades preceding the ability to reproduce photographs. The days of elaborate renderings of highly detailed and ornamented Queen Anne houses are gone, and the artists are still allowed—for a while—to provide decorative frames and borders.

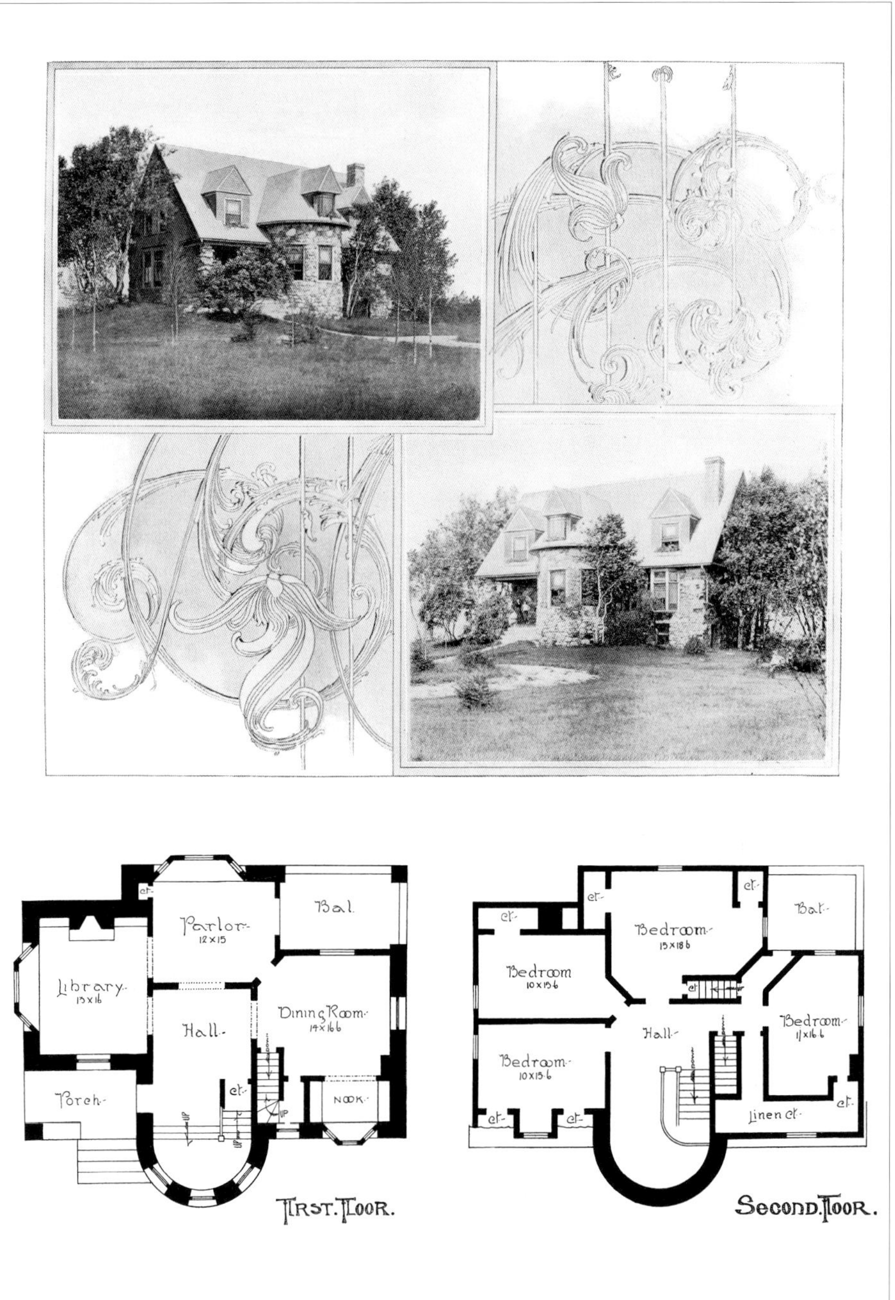

CHAPTER 2

John Calvin Stevens

Development of the Shingle Style in Maine

Since the publication of Vincent Scully's *The Shingle Style* in 1955, John Calvin Stevens of Portland has been identified by architectural historians as a major figure in the development of late nineteenth-century American summer cottage architecture. Scully characterized Stevens' contribution to the Shingle Style as being of "critical importance." While the architect's practice extended from the Maine Coast to the Rocky Mountains, the primary focus of his work remained in the Portland area. This accounts for the Bowdoin Street houses and the cottages on the Casco Bay islands and at nearby Delano Park in Cape Elizabeth that appear in the *Scientific American Building Monthly*.

Born in Boston in 1855, Stevens moved with his family to Portland as a child in 1857. At the age of ten, he witnessed the Great Fire and the dramatic reconstruction that followed. On graduation from Portland High School in 1873, he entered the office of Francis H. Fassett, the local architect responsible for many post-fire structures. Stevens rose within seven years from office boy to become Fassett's junior partner in 1880. That year the young architect opened a branch office of the firm in Boston for the purpose of overseeing the construction of the Hotel Pemberton at Nantasket Beach. His eighteen months in Boston were critical to his professional growth, for he was exposed firsthand to the work of Henry Hobson Richardson and developed friendships with such influential designers as William R. Emerson and Robert S. Peabody.

John Calvin Stevens returned to Portland in 1882 and left Francis Fassett two years later to establish his own practice. With the exception of a brief partnership between 1888 and 1891 with Emerson's former assistant, Albert Winslow Cobb, Stevens operated a closely knit family office until his death in 1940. Younger brother Henry Wingate Stevens served as his chief draftsman for forty-six years. Son John Howard Stevens became his partner in 1904, and grandson John Calvin Stevens II joined the firm in 1933. Great-grandson Paul Stevens continues to practice in the firm of Stevens, Morton, Rose & Thompson, now known as SMRT.

John Calvin Stevens established a national reputation by the distinctive nature of his work and his promotion of it in the professional journals of the time. In *Rameses to Rockefeller,* Charles Harris Whitaker commented in 1934 that beginning with the published designs of William R. Emerson in the late 1870s, "one comes across inklings of architects on whom it had dawned that America was a land of its own, that it had its own needs, landscapes, contours, and materials." According to Whitaker, Emerson's houses had "a new flavor" and struck "a new note. . . . Then," continued Whitaker, "the new note becomes a little more frequent" with the publication of designs by Thomas Hastings, C. Howard Walker, Bruce Price, Wilson Eyre, and John Calvin Stevens.

Beginning with his 1880 sketches for paper mill workers' homes in Berlin, New Hampshire, in the *American Architect and Building News,* Stevens frequently published his designs in that journal and others, including *Architecture and Building,* the *Brickbuilder,* the *Sanitary Engineer,* and the *British Architect.* With the exception of the technologically advanced *Scientific American Building Monthly,* much of this work appeared in the form of pen and ink sketches. However, by 1900, most magazines had replaced the graceful art of freehand illustration with the precision of the photograph.

The rise of American architectural periodicals in the 1880s coincided with the beginning of annual exhibitions by architectural clubs in Boston, New York, Philadelphia, Washington, D.C., Chicago, London, and elsewhere. John Calvin Stevens was a frequent contributor to these shows, and renderings and photographs of his work were often included in the catalogues that accompanied these exhibits. But perhaps the single most important promotion of his career was the 1889 publication by William T. Comstock of *Examples of American Domestic Architecture,* a book that consisted of Stevens' sketches of his work accompanied by his partner Albert Winslow Cobb's socially progressive text. This defining statement of the Shingle Style probably resulted in Stevens' being named a fellow of the American Institute of Architects in 1889. Here, on page after page, are the captivating drawings for a new, distinctively American domestic architecture, one especially suited to the rugged coast of Maine, which caused a noted watercolor artist to exclaim to Stevens, "Oh! I know your work! You are the man who designs summer cottages that we can paint."

Sidney W. Thaxter Cottage

Cushing's Island, Casco Bay

John Calvin Stevens
Architect

1884–85, EXTANT

One of the first of John Calvin Stevens' designs for Cushing's Island was the Sidney W. Thaxter Cottage of 1884–85, which occupies an elevated site with a commanding view of Portland Harbor and the city. A Bangor native and Harvard graduate, Thaxter (1841–1908) served as a major in the First Maine Cavalry during the Civil War, winning the Congressional Medal of Honor. In 1874 he established the Portland branch of his family's flour and grain business, which he managed until his death.

The Thaxter Cottage ranks as a significant early Shingle Style work by Stevens for its skillful articulation of the complex forms of a sloping roof, an arched wraparound porch, and a double saltbox roofline on a side elevation. Moreover, the first-floor space flows easily from a large open living room into a smaller dining room, both benefiting from warming fireplaces provided by a central chimney. The *Scientific American Building Monthly* described the living room as "a unique apartment":

> The studding to walls and the ceiling timbers are left exposed to view, and are stained cherry, the space between being plastered and treated in olive yellow. All woodwork is finished in cherry. The newel post at staircase extends to ceiling, and the space between is provided with a screen filled in with spindle work. The nook is a special feature, with corner seats and an open fireplace built of brick, with hearth laid of same and a mantelshelf of wood.

Sidney Thaxter's cottage is a basic box with a bay, not very adventurous in plan, wrapped on three sides by a shady piazza, which by the time of publication had already been covered in a romantic drapery of vines. The living room has an interesting plan in that it is the whole width of the house but without a central door facing the side steps. This presumably allowed furniture to be placed facing the fireplace and forced a visitor into an indirect path to the door on the side, thus reinforcing—or possibly destroying—the privacy of the cottage.

The plainness of the box shape is relieved on the exterior not only by the corner bay but also by extending the pyramidal roof down over the dependencies in back and over the piazza in front, cutting into the piazza roof to create the typical inset balcony. How roofs extend down to mitigate the verticality of a basic plan will be the "game" these cottages play. Porches, ells, gambrels, and dormers will all be deployed to disguise the plain fact of the two-story box.

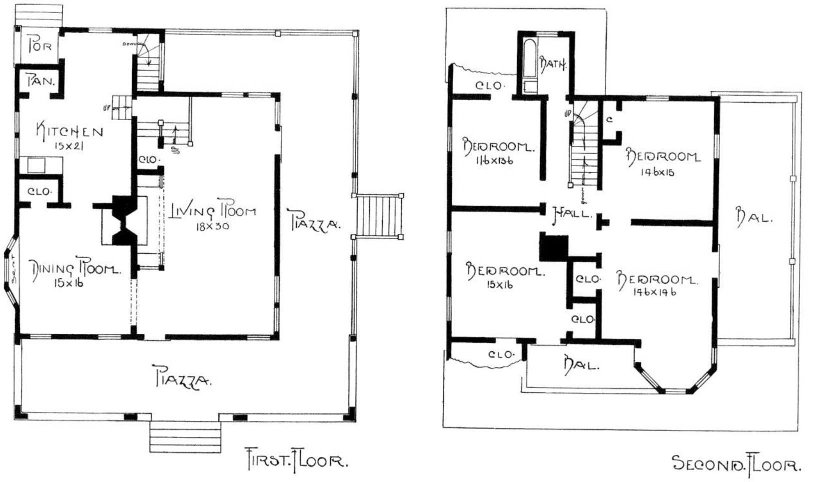

First Floor.

Second Floor.

Ottawa House Cottage No. 1

Cushing's Island, Casco Bay

John Calvin Stevens
Architect

1887, DESTROYED

Opened in 1862, the Ottawa House hotel on Cushing's Island burned in October 1886. In planning its reconstruction, manager Montgomery S. Gibson included three cottages that could be rented to affluent guests seeking the privacy and space of a separate dwelling along with the amenities of the hotel. Gibson commissioned John Calvin Stevens to design three distinctly different Shingle Style cottages in the fall of 1886, and they were built early the next year by A. D. Smith for use in the 1887 summer season.

Ottawa House Cottage No. 1 featured a high-pitched gable roof, the front slope of which extended over a porch with a fieldstone base and rustic log posts. Punctuating the roof slope at the right was a turreted dormer that served to light the master bedroom. The interior consisted of eight principal rooms: living room, parlor, dining room, and kitchen on the first floor and four bedrooms on the second. The *Scientific American Building Monthly* described Stevens' design as "unique and picturesque and an ideal model for a summer home."

As the three Ottawa cottages were all designed and built at once, it is tempting to compare them to see how they differ. This house is in many ways the simplest, though the heavy stone piazza rail gives it a more substantial appearance than the other two. The placement of the fireplace in the corner of the living room—but not at an angle to the corner—is awkward at best, as is the door from the living room to the kitchen. All three

cottages share an ingenious passage under the stair landing from the kitchen to the dining room, and two of the three experiment with a toilet on the stair landing. This house provides closets for only two of the bedrooms, and they are arranged as long, thin rooms rather than the wide, shallow closets we have come to expect. Only the bedroom with the round dormer has windows on more than one side, and the back bedrooms are severely restricted by the slope of the rear roof. Of the three, this one seems the least well worked out.

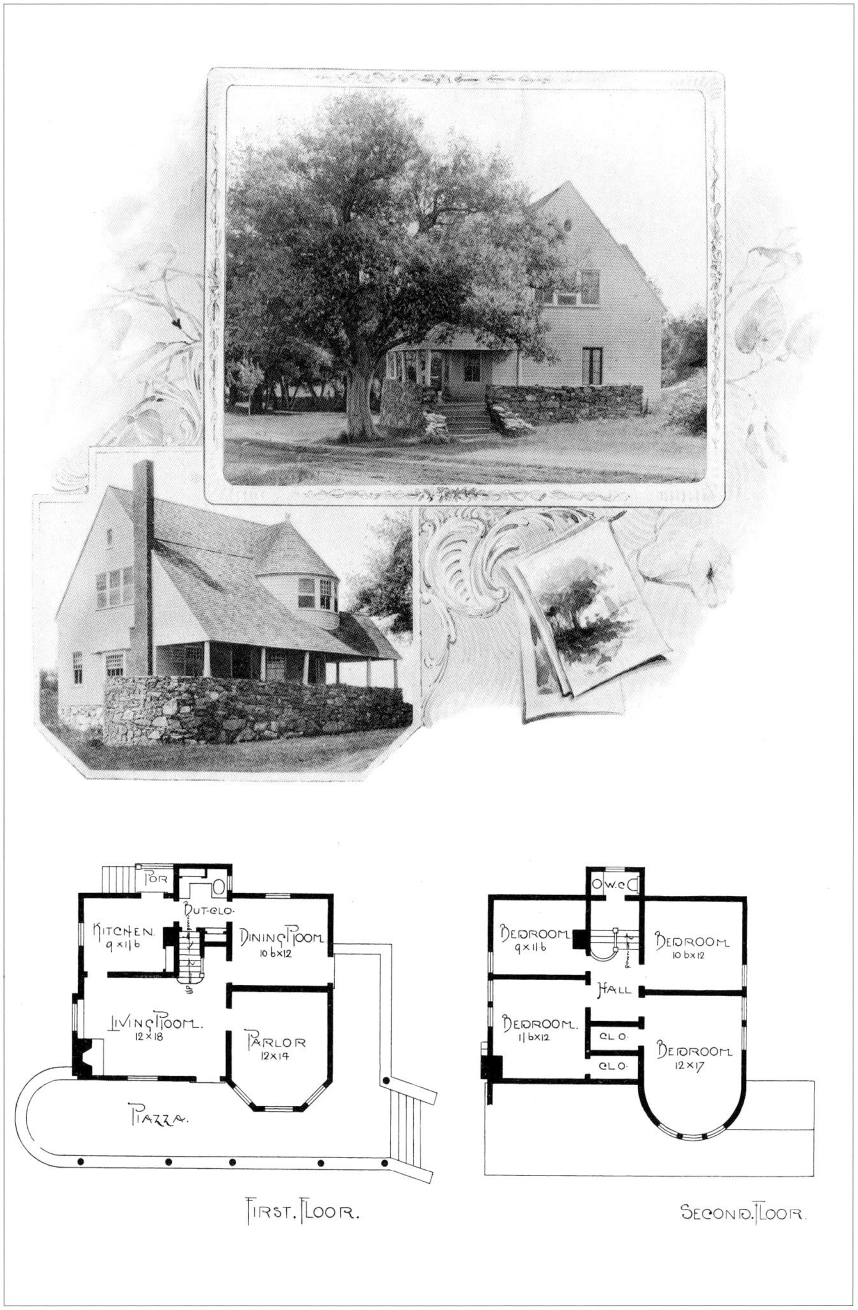

POR.
OUT-CLO.
KITCHEN. 9x11 6
DINING ROOM. 10 6x12
LIVING ROOM. 12x18
PARLOR 12x14
PIAZZA.

FIRST FLOOR.

O.W.C.
BEDROOM. 9x11 6
BEDROOM. 10 6x12
HALL
BEDROOM. 11 6x12
CLO.
CLO.
BEDROOM. 12x17

SECOND FLOOR.

Ottawa House Cottage No. 2

Cushing's Island, Casco Bay

John Calvin Stevens
Architect

1887, EXTANT

Ottawa House Cottage No. 2 is reminiscent in form of Greek Revival capes in which the sloping roof extends beyond the house to form the front porch. There the comparison ends, for the playfully eclectic exterior features rustic porch posts, a pair of stylized Georgian roof dormers, and a projecting two-story side bay with multi-paned sash, rounded corners, and a triangular roof in the English Arts and Crafts manner. The interior contains a traditional central hall plan with the living room and kitchen on the left, the parlor and dining room on the right, and four bedrooms on the second floor. Like Ottawa House Cottage No. 1, No. 2's shingled exterior was painted yellow with a green roof, making for "a handsome little seaside cottage," according to the *Scientific American Building Monthly.*

This house differs from Cottage No. 3 by pairing the chimneys on the outside walls and by recentering the upstairs porch, this time bracketed between the two dormers. This motif of a shed dormer with its flatter roof pitch hidden by two gable dormers is one that Stevens will use in many projects, including his own house. The window seats on the second floor of Ottawa No. 3 have extended now to the first floor, where they form an inglenook on either side of the fireplace. The toilet on the stair landing has disappeared, but has not been replaced by any other space designated as a toilet. This at least allows the central stair hall to be lighted by a window at the landing level, and the upstairs hall now runs through from the balcony to the stair. This device restores privacy to the front bedrooms and provides the back bedrooms with shared access to the balcony.

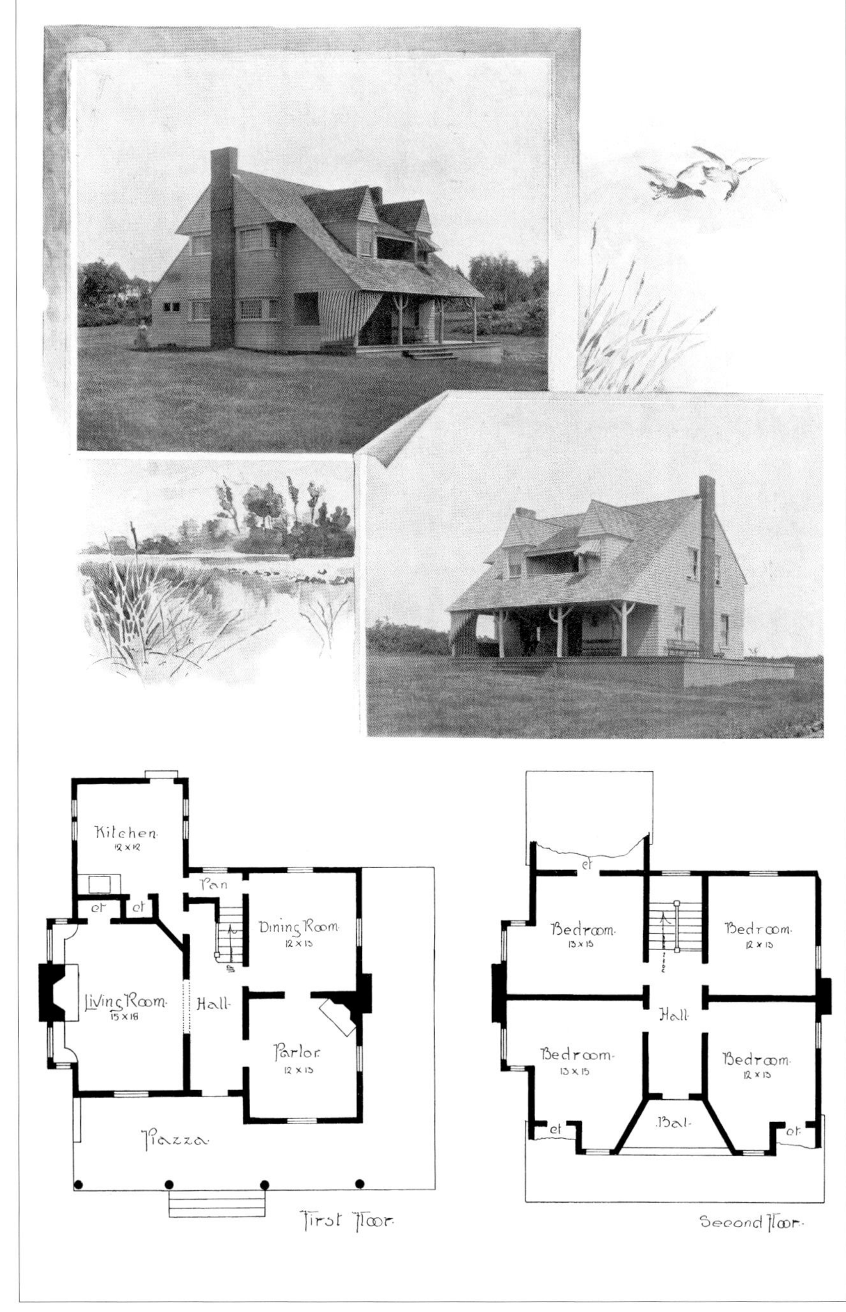

Ottawa House Cottage No. 3

Cushing's Island, Casco Bay

John Calvin Stevens
Architect

1887, EXTANT

Of the three Ottawa House cottages that Montgomery S. Gibson built in 1887 from plans by John Calvin Stevens, No. 3 is the most vernacular in the simplicity of its exterior design. In keeping with its two counterparts, this cottage features a broad sloping roof that encompasses a front porch supported by rustic posts. These posts also appear on the balcony that projects from the right half of the roofline. A fieldstone chimney subdivides two pairs of second-floor bay windows. No. 3 is entered through a reception hall that leads to a stair hall, off which are a parlor, dining room, and kitchen. On the second floor the balcony is accessed through a small den, with the remainder of the space devoted to a hallway and four bedrooms. Sheathed in William Morris tones—green shingles with a red shingled roof—Cottage No. 3 was characterized by the *Scientific American Building Monthly* as "a unique example of a summer home, containing pleasing elevations, well shaded piazza and balcony, and an interior arrangement conveniently fitted up."

Stevens' contribution to this island project introduces variations along with some disciplined proportions. The chief variation here is the off-center, cut-in porch in the roof, but along with that is the compensating mass of the stone chimney on the opposite end. Bracketing the chimney on the upper floor are two window seats under a projecting gable. The piazza has solid rails and clustered round columns that give it an almost classical dignity, while the upstairs porch set to one side offers a wraparound corner window, but no apparent way to drain the floor of the balcony.

Inside the entry is what is called a reception hall, from which a large opening leads onto a stair hall with the house's only toilet on the stair landing.

A SUMMER COTTAGE AT CUSHING'S ISLAND, ME.—See page 34.

"Mizzentop," Captain John W. Deering Cottage

Cape Arundel, Kennebunkport

John Calvin Stevens
Architect

1888, ALTERED

The first cottage John Calvin Stevens designed at Cape Arundel was for a prominent Portland man, Captain John W. Deering (1833–1904). Deering acquired his lot from the Kennebunkport Seashore Company in November 1887. Perspective sketches by Stevens for the Deering Cottage, known as "Mizzentop," are dated January 19, 1888, and a contract for the construction of the house was signed with the Fairfield, Maine, Kennebec Framing and Lumber Company in June of that year.

"Mizzentop" was one of Stevens' most widely published designs. Even before construction began, the architect exhibited a small perspective view showing the house from the landward side at the Seventeenth Exhibition of the Portland Society of Art in May 1888. The ocean side, along with the stable, was featured in a perspective study published in *Building* in December 1888. This view, including the first-floor plan as an inset, also appeared in the 1889 book *Examples of American Domestic Architecture*, by Stevens & Cobb. *Scientific American Building Monthly* for November 1896 featured the house on two pages, with three exterior photographs, one interior photograph, and two floor plans.

The house, designed in the Shingle Style, is compact and efficiently planned, providing the rooms with generous views in each direction. In the typical style of summer homes of the period, the plan is in the form of a main block with a kitchen wing angled off. This composition minimized obscuring scenic views from the rest of the house. An entrance into the center of the principal elevation opens directly into the living room, containing a corner fireplace, a staircase to the second floor, and two broad window seats. To the right this main room opens into a small den or reception room with its own corner fireplace. On the left, also connected by a large opening, is the dining room. The arrangement of this room fully illustrates the freedom the open plan afforded, which is expressed on the exterior in the flowing lines of the shingled skin. In plan the dining room balloons out between the main block of the house and the kitchen wing, maximizing its exposure to light and air. The kitchen wing, with a butler's closet, pantry, and servants' porch, is joined to a back service hall. On the second floor were five bedrooms for the family, two for servants, and a bathroom, each room with at least two windows positioned for views. The third floor contained a billiard room in the tower, a studio in the gable end, and another bedroom.

The wood-shingled exterior is the unifying feature of the design. The house is covered by a gambrel roof extending down to the first floor, with broad overhanging eaves. The dining room is part of a round tower linked to the main block and capped by a third-floor lookout with a conical roof. Twin dormers, connected by a balcony with a shingled railing, overlook the steps leading to the main entrance. The house features a fieldstone foundation forming an open piazza on one side, with a shingled railing, that extends from the corner tower across the principal elevation. The piazza continues beneath the second-floor gambrel roof overhang above the reception room, reemerging in the open to extend across a portion of the rear façade. This masterful composition was a perfect solution for a compact yet architecturally distinguished summer cottage.

When John W. Deering built his Cape Arundel cottage, he had already lived an extraordinary and active life. Born in Saco in 1833, Deering went to sea at the age of sixteen, rising to become a captain of merchant ships that sailed to Europe and China. In 1867 he settled in Portland, where his firm, the Deering Winslow Company, imported southern pine. He

served as an alderman and mayor of Portland, first as a Republican and later as a Democrat. As mayor he played a major role in the creation of the city's park system. "Mizzentop" was his summer residence for nearly fifteen years before his death in 1904.

Here Stevens takes advantage of a substantial commission to pay homage to the architect who was his inspiration, William Ralph Emerson, of Boston. This house has features that closely resemble ones Emerson incorporated in his own house in Milton, Massachusetts, built only two years prior to this house. The angle of the plan, the double-height gambrel, and the two-faceted bays all are directly imitative of Emerson's work.

On the first floor the wonderfully bulbous dining room looks as if the air pressure in the building has split the house and caused a great bubble to bulge out at the point of rupture, forcing the kitchen wing to bend away from the straight axis of the "original" idea. This is far beyond simply inserting a round room into a square plan. The straight walls of this strange dining room are, on one side, the wide opening to the main hall (a more modest phrase than great hall, but more descriptive than stair hall), and on the other a formal fireplace flanked by an inglenook whose back curves to complete the energy of the curved outer wall and make the transition to the grid of the kitchen, and a clever butler's pantry with a hatch to the kitchen. The main hall itself has a picturesque composition of a nook tucked under the grand stair and an angled fireplace sharing a chimney with the one in the square reception room.

Upstairs the curved corner tower becomes the master bedroom, with a broad fireplace and not quite so successfully placed nook set in a wide arch opposite the bed wall. The ingenuity comes at the other end, where a diagonal corridor divides and connects three bedrooms, the most strangely shaped being the one to the right of the loggia. Even the small servants' bedrooms over the kitchen have a cleverly angled hall that departs from the more expected rectangular grid. All together, the plan offers stimulating interior vistas, with surprises waiting around every bend.

The exterior is dominated by the high gambrel punctuated on its gable end by the trademark Palladian window that Stevens will retain long after his Shingle Style days end. This is the first appearance of this device in the Maine houses published in Scientific American Building Monthly. *In his hands it will be manipulated in scale and proportion to express the needs of the façade it occupies. Here it is shortened—deprived of its lower sashes—to serve as the enhanced attic window it is, rather than the principal focus of a primary room.*

The corner tower's detailing is derived from another Emerson house, "Thirlstane," in Bar Harbor, published in The Builder *the same year (1886) as Emerson's own house was built, two years before the Deering House was built in 1888—in other words, freshly in Stevens' mind as a consumer of the trade magazines.*

So in plan, general massing, and detail, the Deering Cottage is Stevens' homage to the man whose work he and his partner Albert Winslow Cobb (who had worked in Emerson's office) had said was "a delight to all who know it."

John H. Davis House

62 Bowdoin Street, Portland

John Calvin Stevens
Architect

1883, EXTANT

After the death in 1881 of Portland's wealthiest businessman, John Bundy Brown, his family subdivided the land on the south side of Bowdoin Street, from Vaughan Street to the Western Promenade, into small house lots. Between 1883 and 1888, seven homes were designed for these lots by John Calvin Stevens. The double house for Ashbel Chaplin and William T. Small facing the Western Promenade was Queen Anne, while the other six were Shingle Style, the year-round urban equivalents of the seasonal cottages that the architect was planning for the new summer colonies on the Casco Bay islands and at Delano Park in Cape Elizabeth. The James Dakers Cottage of 1883 on Cushing's Island was Stevens' first Shingle Style summer cottage, and the John H. Davis House of the same year was his first Shingle work on the Portland peninsula.

Responding to the narrow rectangular lot running perpendicular to Bowdoin Street, Stevens designed the Davis House to present its gable end to the street. The bold simplicity of this New England Colonial saltbox roof as well as the cross gables on the side walls are character-defining features of the Shingle Style. So too is the use of local materials such as stone, brick, and shingles. As the *Scientific American Building Monthly* reported in its August 1893 issue, "The underpinning and first story are built of various kinds of rough stone, laid up at random, with brick trimmings. The second and third stories are covered with shingles and painted a dull red."

The plan of the Davis House is compact and efficient. A small entrance lobby leads to a stair hall, which connects to a parlor and a dining room. Both of these rooms have fireplaces, and the parlor featured a five-sided bay window that was replaced by a later side addition to the house. The kitchen is located at the back corner of the house adjacent to the dining room. The second floor contains four bedrooms and a bathroom.

A native of Portland, John Hobart Davis (1843–1918) was educated in local public schools and served in the Thirteenth Maine Regiment during the Civil War. Following the war, he went to work for the Casco Bank, where he was employed until his death at the age of

75. Davis's obituary in the *Daily Eastern Argus* of November 12, 1918, described him as "one of the trusted and most honored employees of the Casco Mercantile Trust Company."

In this early town house for J. H. Davis, Stevens is experimenting with extending the rooflines to reduce the vertical boxiness of Victorian houses. The entry porch is an extension of the front gable, and the eave of the porch carries around as a projecting belt course defining the division of the lower and upper floors. This division is furthered by the fact that the lower floor is brick, while the upper is shingled. The corner octagonal bay is not extended into a tower as in a Queen Anne house, but is kept as a flared roof limited to the "hem" of the skirt. The subtleties combine to bring the two-story box down to earth. One other cottage reference is the use of small-paned upper sash over large-paned lower sash. In this case, the window is a "16/2"—sixteen panes over two panes. Known as a cottage window, this device allows the grace of the small panes along with the expansive view at eye level of the large panes. It also creates a horizontal division of the façade along the sash lines, which helps lower and extend the house. The plan shows some sophisticated amenities. The front door opens into what we now would call an airlock

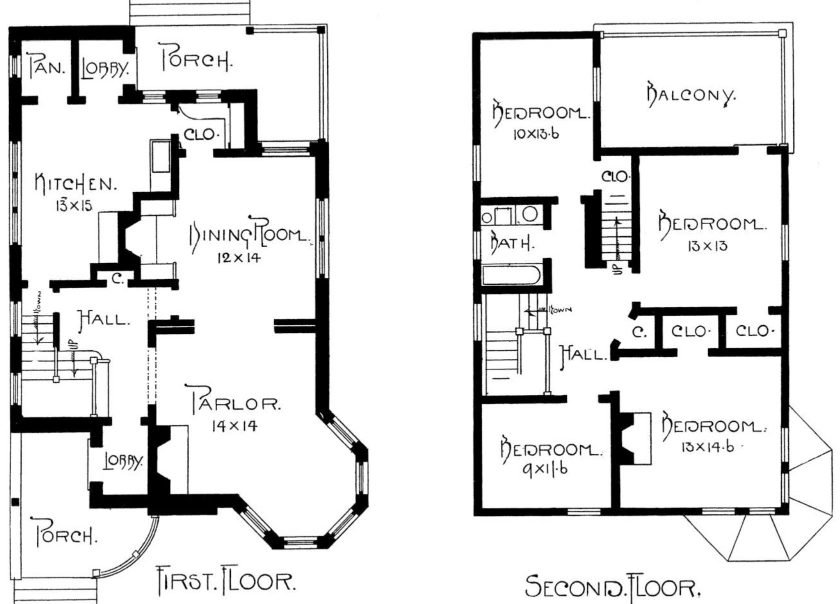

vestibule, and the stair in the hall has a bench in front of the landing. The dining room has a deep inglenook, which recesses the hearth, thus reducing the tendency of a dining room fireplace to toast the diners seated with their backs to the fire. So, while working within the constraints of a narrow town lot, Stevens is tweaking the roofline and adding interior features that are more suggestive of the country cottage than the town house.

John Calvin Stevens House

52 Bowdoin Street, Portland

John Calvin Stevens
Architect

1884–85, EXTANT

The year 1884 was a turning point for 29-year-old Portland architect John Calvin Stevens (1855–1940). In April, Stevens established his own architectural firm after four years of practice with Francis H. Fassett. That summer he purchased a lot on the south side of Bowdoin Street to build his own home, one of the seven houses he designed there between 1883 and 1888 in what the *Portland Daily Press* for August 6, 1884, termed "the present odd cottage style." Stevens was issued a building permit on November 3, 1884, and construction was completed the next year. The result was a masterpiece of the Shingle Style, a simple brick first story surmounted by an equally simple shingled gambrel roof.

For his own home, John Calvin Stevens put his personal philosophy of domestic architecture into practice, reflected in his comment in a period newspaper article that "the new style has a big gambrel roof and wide windows, like the old homestead of colonial days." At 52 Bowdoin Street, Stevens first stated a design program that he employed frequently throughout his career: ordering the volume of a house through the use of an all-encompassing gambrel roof. The architect's unifying solution for 52 Bowdoin Street immediately found its way into the pages of the *American Architect and Building News* (December 20, 1884), followed by publication in the *British Architect* (March 19, 1886), the *Sanitary Engineer* (September 17, 1887), *Examples of American Domestic Architecture* (1889), and the *Scientific American Building Monthly* (January 1892), So popular was the design that it appeared in trade catalogues for building products ranging from screen doors to wall plaster.

In his book *The Shingle Style,* Vincent J. Scully assessed the importance of the John Calvin Stevens House:

> As in the early Emerson houses of the late 70's, in which the roof became a plastic entity uniting the volumes of the house, so here the roof goes a step further toward drawing all subsidiary volumes under the dominance of one main volume. The house becomes one sculptured unit, three-dimensional but contained. The varied equilibriums of the cottage style are resolved into a single unit, and while there is still an indication of the movement of the various spaces within the main volume, they are all eventually drawn in under one sheltering roof.

The Stevens House became the prototype for several gambrel-roofed houses that Stevens designed from the mid-1880s through the 1890s. These included the James Hopkins Smith House of 1884–85, on Falmouth Foreside; S. D. Warren Company workers' cottages of 1886 on Cottage Place, in Cumberland Mills, Westbrook;

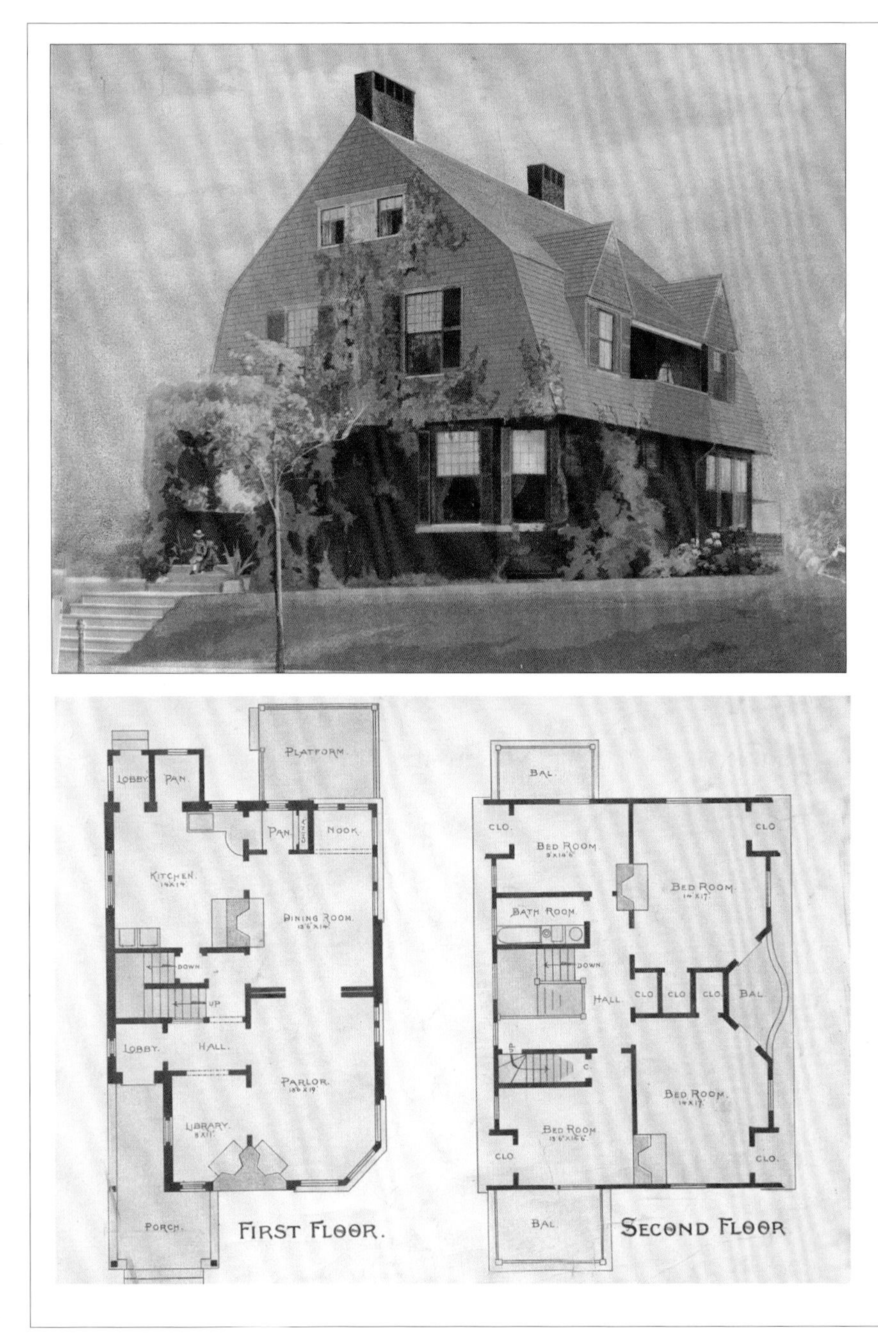
PLATFORM
LOBBY
PAN.
KITCHEN
PAN.
NOOK
DINING ROOM
DOWN
UP
LOBBY
HALL
PARLOR
LIBRARY
PORCH
FIRST FLOOR.
BAL.
CLO.
BED ROOM
CLO
BED ROOM
BATH ROOM
DOWN
HALL
CLO
CLO
CLO.
BAL.
BED ROOM
BED ROOM
CLO.
CLO.
BAL.
SECOND FLOOR

the Frederick Cony House of 1889, on Stone Street in Augusta; and the Jesse D. Wilson House of 1890, at 25 Bramhall Street in Portland. The Smith House earned Stevens a place in George Sheldon's *Artistic Country-Seats* of 1887, with the author commenting, "Effect has been sought by strength of mass and simplicity of form."

John Calvin Stevens resided at 52 Bowdoin Street from 1885 until he moved in 1919 to a new home on Craigie Street, in the Deering suburbs, to be near his son and daughter. In 1905 Stevens remodeled and enlarged 52 Bowdoin Street, and prior to 1924 the main entrance was changed from the north side of the house to the west side.

The house John Calvin Stevens designed for himself shows how the cottage style he was experimenting with on the islands influenced the shape and feeling of this town house. The gambrel roof is the obvious cottage idea, and he uses the inset balcony framed by two gable dormers, even though in this case the roof of the balcony is simply an extension of the upper slope of the gambrel, and he does not need to disguise an unequal roof pitch. The gambrel roof slopes at each corner are taken advantage of to provide closets for the bedrooms.

The entry hall is a scaled down version of that of the John H. Davis House, with the same tiny lobby buffering the entry and the stair hall with its landing window bringing light to the stairwell and the entry hall as well as lighting the upstairs hall. While the downstairs has an open, flowing plan with everything but the kitchen visible, the upstairs has a clear, disciplined arrangement with an axis of symmetry through the main stair.

Only the chimney placement is asymmetrical, and the two chimneys are arranged with flues in a row instead of a compact rectangle and emerge like a rooster comb from the ridge. Stevens solves the problem of placing windows in a gable with a chimney by adding an ornamental panel bridging the two windows on either side of the chimney, thus creating greater horizontal unity and avoiding the anthropomorphism of the two-eyes-in-the-face look.

Montgomery S. Gibson House

44 Bowdoin Street, Portland

John Calvin Stevens
Architect

1885–86, EXTANT

The Montgomery S. Gibson House was the fifth of the seven residences that John Calvin Stevens designed for the south side of Bowdoin Street in the 1880s. In form, plan, and exterior finish, the Gibson House draws upon the John H. Davis House and Stevens' own home, both close in location and time.

The Gibson House shares the gambrel-roofed form of the Stevens House with its gambrel end facing the street and its entrance at the left. Balancing the entrance porch is a two-story corner tower, the first story of which resembles the five-sided corner bay window on the Davis House. While its gambrel-roofed form and shingled exterior define the Gibson House as Shingle Style, the corner tower gives a Queen Anne touch, which led the *Scientific American Building Monthly* for March 1892 to describe the home as "quaint and picturesque." An earlier, more direct comment appeared in the October 23, 1885, issue of the *Industrial Journal* of Bangor, characterizing the house as "of the same odd style as those already reared in that attractive neighborhood."

Adjacent to the Gibson House, John Calvin Stevens designed a gambrel-roofed stable to accommodate a carriage, two horses, a driver's quarters, and a hay loft. Published in the August 1892 issue of the *Scientific American Building Monthly,* the 23- by 34-foot building was described as a "carriage house of low cost"—$700 to be exact. By 1924 the stable had been attached to one side of the house, creating an ell for the main dwelling.

Born in the Canadian province of Quebec in 1843, Montgomery S. Gibson came to Portland in 1865 to work at the Ottawa House on Cushing's Island. Soon he became associated with the United States Hotel and the Preble House. In 1883 he leased the Ottawa House and commissioned John Calvin Stevens to draw plans for remodeling the hotel. Stevens' alterations to the Ottawa House were destroyed when the hotel burned in 1886. Surviving, however, are two of the three cottages that Stevens designed for Gibson that year as hotel rental properties. Gibson presided over the opening of a new Ottawa House in 1888, operating it until 1891.

The Gibson House is a variation on the house that Stevens designed for himself. Here the corner bay evolves from octagonal to circular as its exterior material moves from clapboards to shingles. A V-shaped projection, centered on the back bedroom upstairs, punctuates the dining room rather eccentrically, leaving a windowless wall all the way to the front corner tower. The front chimney straddles the ridge on the diagonal. These elements add to the feeling that they are intentional deviations from his own house.

The front piazza now includes an unroofed section with a dramatically curved perimeter. The entry hall has been widened to include a bench and fireplace, possibly because of his experiences with his own narrow vestibule.

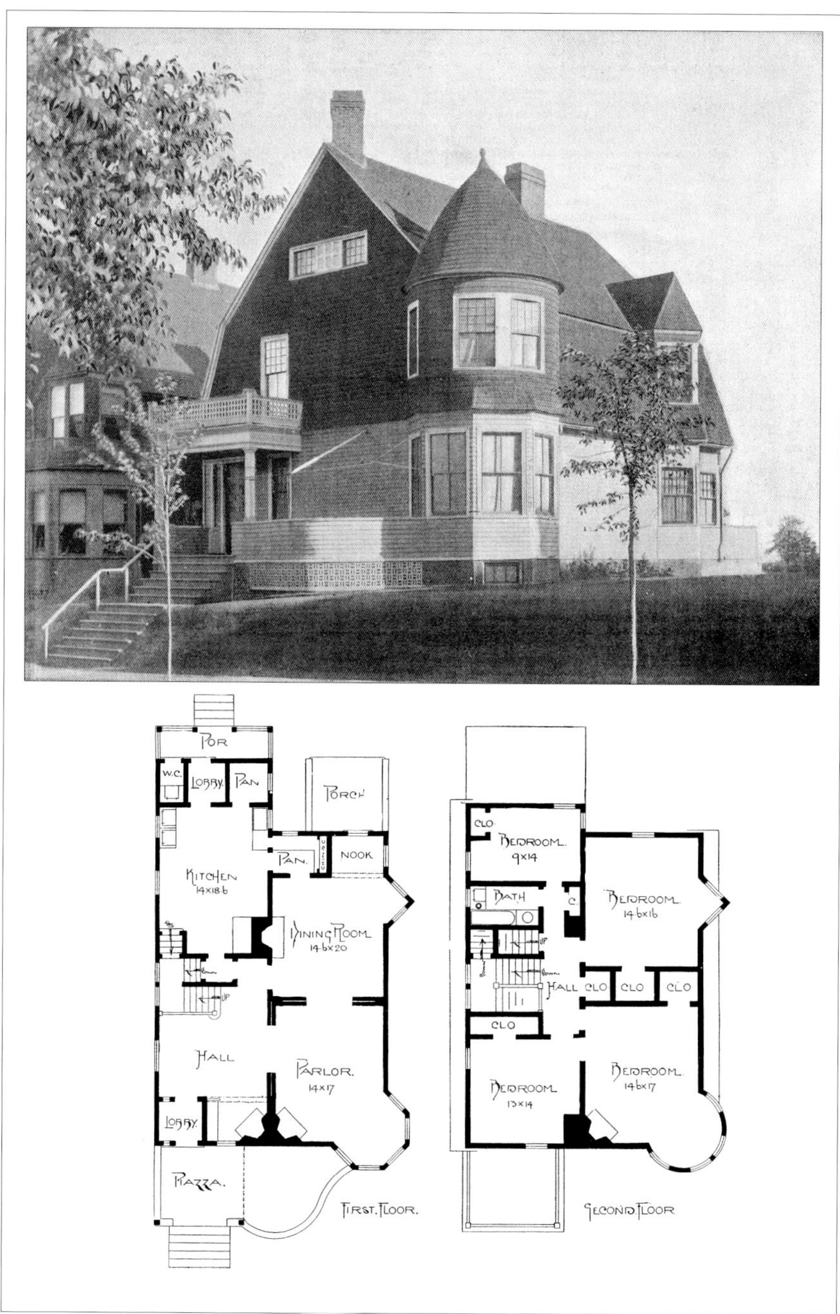

Arthur L. Bates House

95 West Street, Portland

John Calvin Stevens
Architect

1890–91, EXTANT

After using the gambrel roof on his own home in 1884, John Calvin Stevens employed this popular Shingle Style form for several other residential commissions in the 1880s. Thus the form was well established in 1890 when Arthur L. Bates (1851–1938) approached Stevens and partner Albert Winslow Cobb to plan his residence in the Western Promenade area. At that time Bates was the secretary of the Union Mutual Life Insurance Company. He would later serve as its president, from 1914 to 1933.

Completed in 1891 at a cost of $3,800, Bates's home was entirely of frame construction in contrast to the brick first story of the Stevens House and the stone first story of the Smith House. The Bates House was featured in the March 1892 issue of the *Scientific American Building Monthly*, which described it as follows: "The underpinning is built of local brick, while the superstructure is built of wood, with the exterior framework sheathed, shingled and left to weather. Blinds painted bronze green. The design has the appearance of comfort and convenience, while the interior contains many large, well-lighted rooms, that are varied in their treatment."

Last in the series of town cottages, the A. L Bates House shares many features with Stevens' own house and with the Gibson House. The entrance is on the side, entering past parlor doors to dining room and parlor to a stair hall with what must have been a "cozy den" under the lower ceiling of the stair landing, above which the dramatic curve of the upstairs landing enlivens both the downstairs and the upstairs stair hall space. Other than that, the plan is straightforward almost to the point of being perfunctory, foreshadowing the surrender to the symmetrical Colonial Revival that would characterize Stevens' later career. There is one nice touch in the kitchen, where the sink sits on a splendidly sweeping curved counter accessing both the pantry and the backyard window.

On the exterior Stevens repeats the device that we have seen in his own house of disguising a long side dormer by sandwiching it between gable dormers, in this case without introducing a built-in porch. The protruding porch below connects rather awkwardly to the gambrel eave.

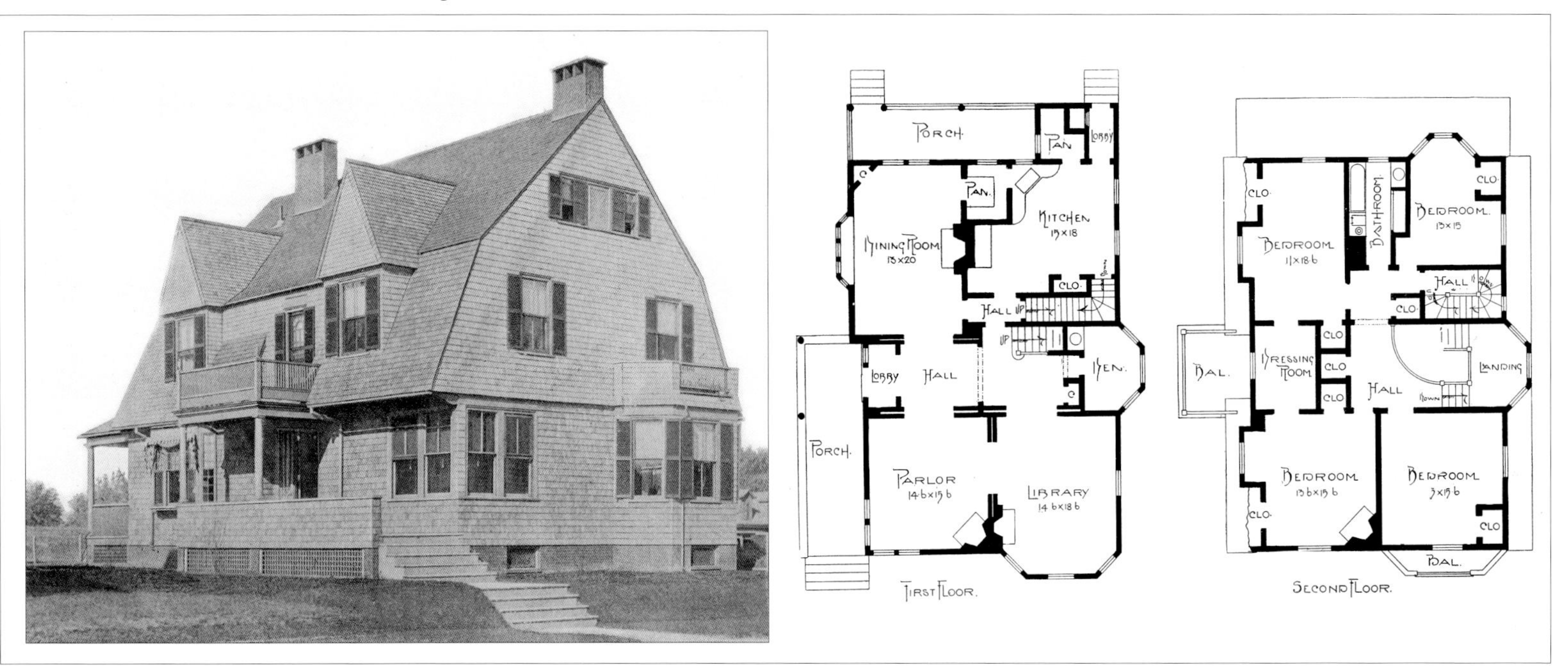

Herbert M. Bailey Cottage

Great Diamond Island, Casco Bay

John Calvin Stevens
Architect

1892, EXTANT

In 1892 Herbert M. Bailey (d. 1930) built this Shingle Style cottage on Great Diamond Island from designs by John Calvin Stevens. At the time Bailey was a partner in the Doten lumber, planing, and molding mill on Fore Street in Portland. He would later become the firm's president.

Standing on an elevated foundation, Bailey's cottage features a wraparound porch and a sloping roof with a dormer and a corner turret. A connecting dining room and living room occupy the front of the first floor, and each is accessed by a door from the porch. Behind these are a kitchen and a servant's bedroom. Four bedrooms are located on the

second floor. The picturesque qualities of Stevens' design were heightened by a sheathing and paint scheme that consisted of a clapboard first story painted olive yellow, a shingled second story stained sienna, and roof shingles painted red.

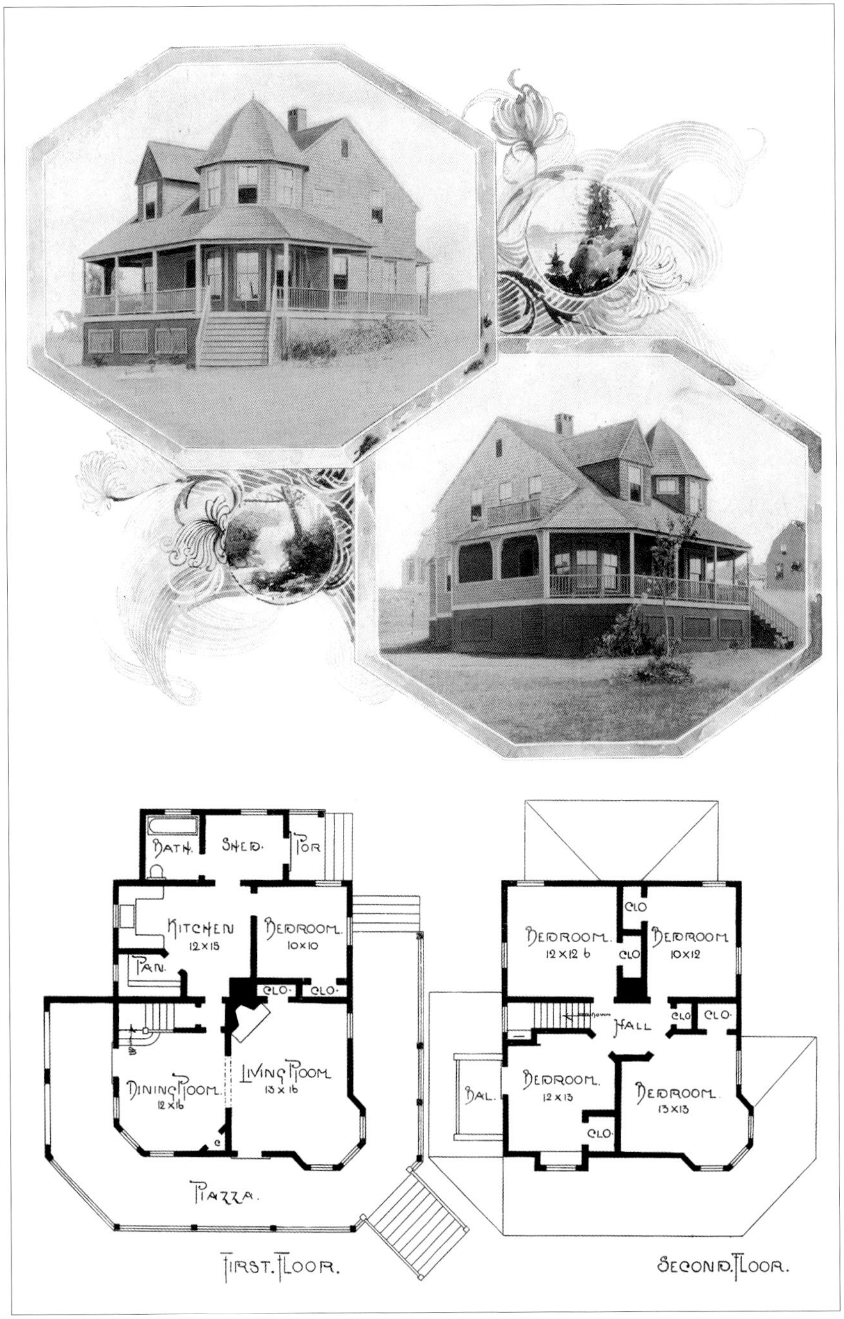

A couple of island cottages were built in 1892, this time on Great Diamond instead of Cushing's Island. Stevens emphasizes the porch in this design, which otherwise has the compressed floor plan of the earlier cottages, with the door entering directly into the parlor and the stair coming down into the dining room. Upstairs the only touch of whimsy is the angled walls for the doors to the front bedrooms, which provide a bit more space than the minimum. There is a rare error on the floor plans, where two of the porch roof hip lines are omitted.

"The Towers," Charles J. Chapman Cottage

Great Diamond Island, Casco Bay

John Calvin Stevens
Architect

1892, EXTANT

Of the many Shingle Style cottages that John Calvin Stevens designed for Portland-area summer colonies, Charles J. Chapman's on Great Diamond Island ranks among the most distinctive. A biography of Chapman in the 1897 book *Men of Progress* noted, "Among the foremost in appreciating the great beauty and value of Casco Bay as a summer resort, he has done much to promote the development of Diamond Island, on whose highest point he erected in 1892 a handsome summer residence, 'The Towers.'"

The design of "The Towers" reflects the intent of both architect and client to maximize the "highest point" on Great Diamond Island. An open piazza wraps around the front and sides of the main block of the cottage, while two-story corner towers are joined by a second-story front loggia supported by Craftsman style posts. Additional second-floor balconies are located on each side wall of the cottage as well as on the rear elevation.

Charles and Anna Chapman's sizable family of four sons and a daughter was accommodated in the principal rooms of the cottage. The open first-floor plan allowed space to flow easily from the reception room, the living room, and the stair hall into the dining room. The living room featured hardwood floors, an arched brick fireplace with adjacent inglenook, and a beamed ceiling that formed deep panels. Light poured into the room through large windows in the corner tower. The kitchen, pantry, bathroom, and servant's bedroom were in the service wing. One family bedroom was located on the first floor and five on the second floor.

Born in Bethel in 1848, Charles J. Chapman (1848–1898) graduated from Bowdoin College in 1868. Two years later he began a successful career in the flour and grain business in Portland. In 1890 Chapman branched out into banking, founding the Chapman National Bank. Active in local politics, he was elected mayor of Portland, 1886 to 1888. He also served as president of the Diamond Island Association.

The other island house of 1892 is considerably more ambitious. The two corner towers serve the same function as gable dormers in disguising the flatter roof pitch of the upstairs "loggia." The loggia is supported by double square-timber posts with heavy brackets, while the downstairs "piazza" is held up by shingled posts of the same width as the double timber ones above. This stacking of different systems is a reference to the classical practice of using different "orders" of columns, with the lighter, thinner Ionic stacked above the heavier Doric or Tuscan, or columns stacked over solid pilasters. Both express the job of supporting weight, with heavier posts handling heavier loads.

The great hipped roof flows down around the towers and dormers to a uniform eave line broken only by the sleeping porch over the back right bedroom. It is possible that the sleeping porch was a late design change. The dormer off the stair landing breaks through the main roof the way the front ones on the smaller cottages do, with solid cheek walls curving to allow for the slope of the roof. The upstairs plan has another of the rare instances of the magazine's draftsman getting something wrong: he fails to show the hip roof breaks on the rear roof.

One peculiarity of the plan is the grand corner stair to the piazza, which does not lead to the door. The strong symmetry of the plan, with rooms on either side of the wide central stair hall, would seem to demand an entry stair on the same axis. Site conditions must have made the side entry more functional, even though it upsets the balance of the front. Altogether this is a strong design, succeeding in containing all of the varied demands of the program..

Frederick L. Jerris Cottage

Delano Park,
Cape Elizabeth

John Calvin Stevens
Architect

1902, EXTANT

In 1885 the Delano Park Association was formed by a group of Portland businessmen to establish a summer colony on the Cape Elizabeth shore. Among the original twenty-five lot owners were George F. Morse, the Reverend Frederick Houghton, Charles A. Brown, and Elias B. Denison, all of whom built Shingle Style cottages between 1885 and 1887 from designs by John Calvin Stevens. In 1901 the park was expanded by a fourteen-lot annex, which resulted in new cottages, including four more by Stevens. Of these, three were built in 1902 for Frederick L. Jerris, Harvey S. Murray, and Dr. George B. Swasey, and a fourth was constructed for Frederick E. Gignoux in 1905–06. A Portland attorney, Jerris (1869–1918) was provided by Stevens with the plans for a one-and-a-half-story summer house that embodied the Shingle Style attributes of simplicity and functionalism.

In 1906 Frederick Jerris returned to the Stevens firm for the addition of a façade dormer and a south-facing second-story bay window. Carefully grafted onto the cottage, these changes did not diminish the force of the architect's original design.

The Delano Park houses are among Stevens' later Shingle Style cottages and have a kind of nostalgic look back at the simplicity of the style as he turned more and more to the more formal Colonial Revival. The Jerris Cottage has an almost schematic simplicity. The piazza appears to be a perfect square, and the house follows the broad gable roof plan, punctuated by an odd dormer that is half porch and half windows and that sits uneasily off axis on the roof. A back bedroom has a similarly unintegrated balcony cut into the shed roof sheltering the side steps. The lower floor is the ultimate expression of the open plan: there is no distinction between living room and dining room. Upstairs the effort to provide access to the six bedrooms results in a tight network of narrow corridors.

The grand piazza of rough posts braced by ships' knees creates a generous platform for summer life.

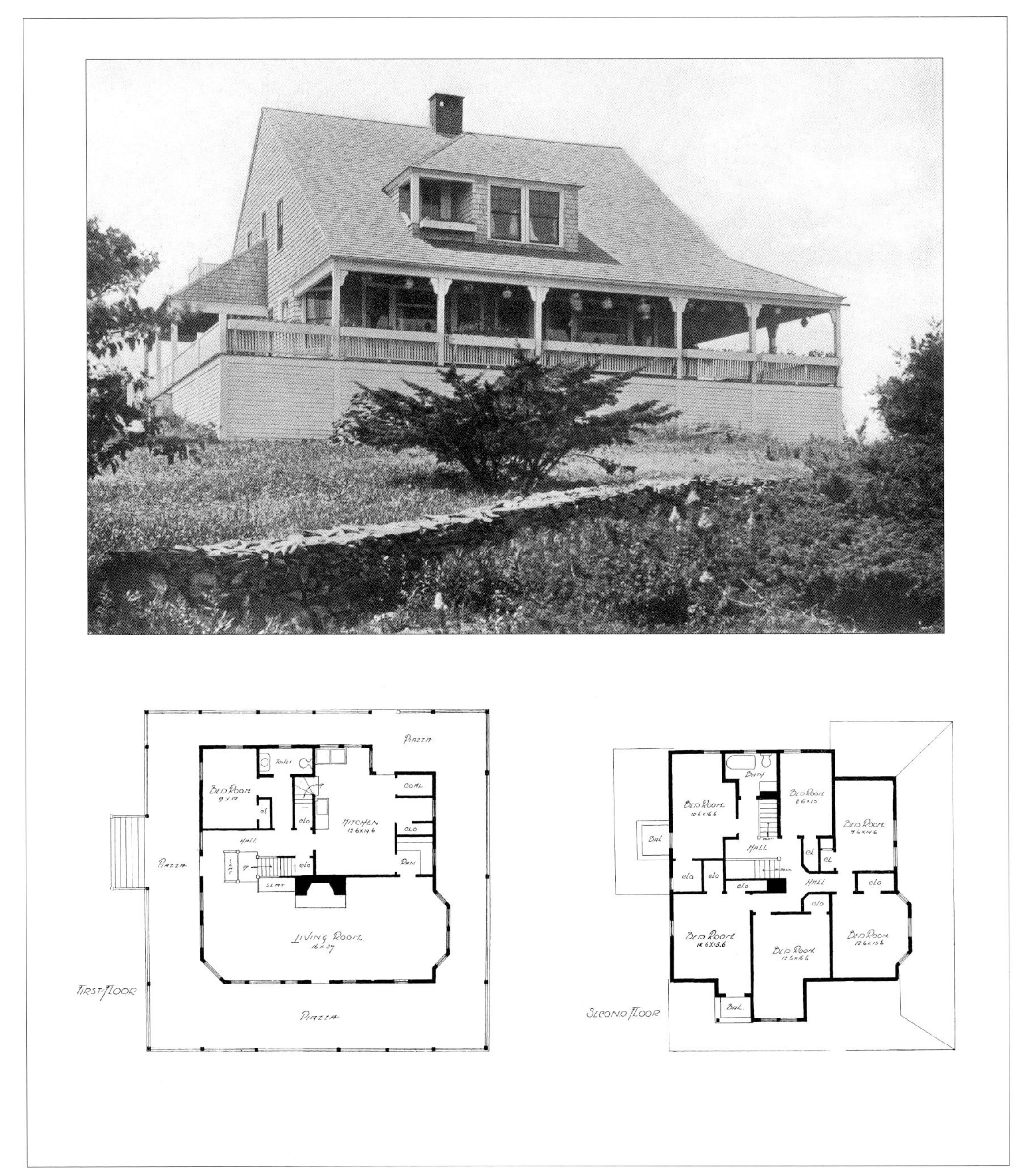
PIAZZA
TOILET
BED ROOM
9 x 12
CL
CLO
COAL
KITCHEN
12 6 x 19 6
CLO
HALL
PIAZZA
SEAT
UP
CLO
PAN
SEAT
LIVING ROOM
16 x 37
FIRST FLOOR
PIAZZA
BATH
BED ROOM
10 6 x 16 6
BED ROOM
8 6 x 13
BED ROOM
9 6 x 14 6
BAL
HALL
CL
CL
CLO
CLO
CLO
HALL
CLO
CLO
BED ROOM
12 6 x 13.6
BED ROOM
13 6 x 16 6
BED ROOM
12 6 x 13 8
BAL.
SECOND FLOOR

George B. Swasey Cottage

Delano Park,
Cape Elizabeth

John Calvin Stevens
Architect

1902, DESTROYED

This Shingle Style summer home, which John Calvin Stevens planned in 1902 for Delano Park, was built for George B. Swasey (1852–1932), a Portland physician. The Swasey Cottage shares several features with the Jerris and Murray cottages of the same year, but has its own distinctive design. This one-and-a-half-story house is elevated on an enclosed foundation of cedar posts. Its broad gable roof ends in a porch on the north side, the east façade, and the southeast corner. The balance of the cottage is surrounded by an open piazza. The porch posts have decorative brackets. From the front of the roof projects a wide hip-roofed dormer with a balcony supported by porch posts. A similar dormer is repeated on the rear without the balcony. A pavilion for the interior staircase is located on the south wall.

As in the Jerris and Murray cottages, the interior plan calls for a living room and dining room at the front of the first floor, a bedroom and kitchen behind them, and several bedrooms on the second floor. All three cottage interiors have the same unfinished appearance. However, as the following description from the *Scientific American Building Monthly* for June 1904 indicates, Dr. Swasey's summer house is slightly more formal, especially in its staircase treatment and in the partition that divides the living room from the dining room: "There is no plaster throughout the interior of the house—the walls, partitions, and ceilings are sealed up with yellow pine; the floor beams are exposed to view, and also the underside of the upper floor. The living and dining-rooms are wainscoted, and the partition between the two rooms is built of battens to the height of seven feet, and the opening above is filled in with ornamental brackets. The entire woodwork is stained and finished in Flemish brown. The open fireplace is built of rock-faced gray stone. There are two paneled seats and an ornamental staircase rising out of the living room."

The Jerris, Murray, and Swasey cottages of 1902 represent a continuation of the architectural program begun by John Calvin Stevens at Delano Park in the mid-1880s, the purpose of which was defined in *Examples of American Domestic Architecture:* "To design structures of a somewhat transitory character is no ignoble task for the Architect. If it be even a mere shell of a wooden summer cottage that he is called upon to contrive, he need not despise the work; he may well give his best thought to making the house graceful, to grouping its rooms effectively and conveniently, and to inventing bits of pretty detail here and there...."

The Swasey Cottage is a smaller-scale version of the Jerris plan with a broad gable sitting on a nearly square piazza platform, partly roofed and partly open. It distinguishes the living room from the dining room with an open screen but allows the stair to interrupt the flow of the living room space. Oddly, the steps to the piazza are not placed opposite the entry door, although several of the cottages in this book seem to share this arrangement. Though most of the porch posts are exposed posts with long tapering knees, one end of the piazza is supported by shingled piers, presumably to give a slightly greater sense of enclosure.

Upstairs the plan is simplified by including only five bedrooms. The dormer is more carefully related to the scale of the roof and includes windows from all three of the front bedrooms, but only allows access to the balcony from the central bedroom..

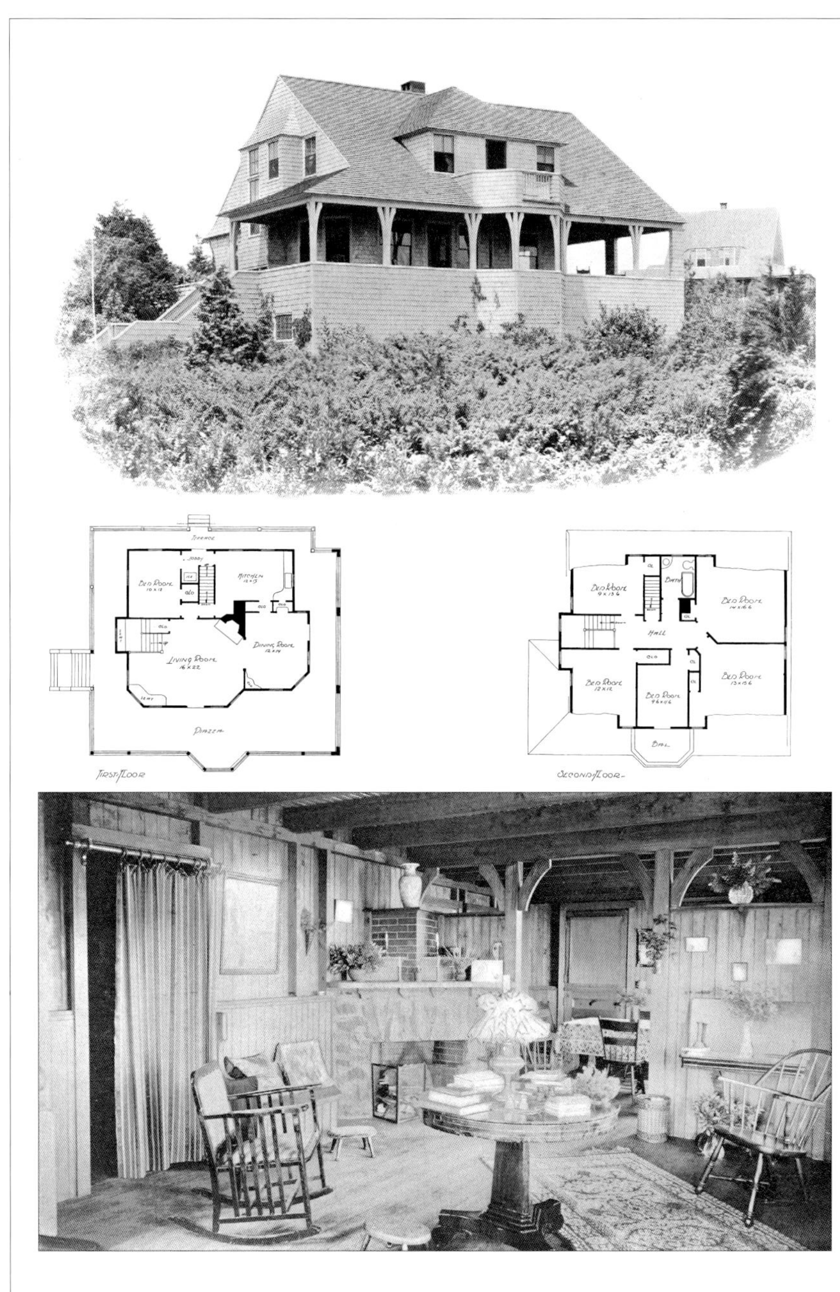

"Bird's Nest," Harvey S. Murray Cottage

Delano Park,
Cape Elizabeth

John Calvin Stevens
Architect

1902, EXTANT

No project was too modest for John Calvin Stevens to apply his talent for creative design. By 1902 Stevens had two decades of experience in planning Shingle Style cottages. That year the Washington, D.C., musician Harvey S. Murray approached the architect about a $1,500 summer cottage at Delano Park in Cape Elizabeth. He responded with the "Bird's Nest," which, as its name implies, was so admired for its low-cost, compact design that it was published in the March 1904 *Scientific American Building Monthly*, the May 1907 *American Homes and Gardens*, and the May 1907 *Pine Tree Magazine*.

Because of its sloping site, the Murray Cottage has an elevated basement high enough for one bedroom at the northeast corner. The cottage itself stands one-and-a-half stories high and is of frame construction with a shingled exterior. On the façade, the sloping gable roof is pierced by an off-center dormer and breaks at an angle to define the depth of the front porch. At the rear, the roof has a large dormer and ends in an overhang supported by gracefully curved shingled brackets. The south elevation features a second-story balcony with a shingled hood, while a saltbox-roofed pavilion projects from the north wall.

POR
Lobby
KITCHEN
9X15
DOWN
BED ROOM
9X13.6
PAN
UP
HALL
CLO
DINING ROOM
11X13
LIVING ROOM
12.6X17
PIAZZA
FIRST FLOOR
CL
BED ROOM
8.6X9
BATH
BED ROOM
8.6X13.6
BAL.
CLO
HALL
CLO.
BED ROOM
12.6X12.6
OPEN
WELL
SECOND FLOOR

The interior plan is similar to the Jerris Cottage in its placement of a combined dining room and living room across the front, with a kitchen and bedroom behind them. A dramatic space is created by opening the living room to the second floor. A staircase at the rear of the cottage provides access to three second-floor bedrooms and the gallery overlooking the living room. The simple décor is described in the following passage from the *Scientific American Building Monthly:* "The interior throughout is trimmed with white pine, and the studding, floor joists, and all partitions are dressed and exposed to view." The brick living room fireplace has an adjacent built-in seat, above which is a spindle-work partition that provides the only division between the living room and the dining room.

In the words of his son, John Howard Stevens, in the *Pine Tree Magazine*, the architect achieved for Harvey S. Murray "an inexpensive summer cottage, having a certain quaintness in its exterior effect which gives it an individuality at first sight."

Certainly of all the small cottages this one is the most cheerfully eccentric. From the curved knees supporting the rear overhang and the pointed window plan of the front dormer to the protrusion of the rear roof element to allow for corner windows for the bedrooms on each floor, the house is playing with the normal shapes in a much freer way than in most of the others. One especially significant departure is the open ceiling of the living room rising up to follow the roof and punctuated by a round window high on the wall. The stair hall upstairs opens into a balcony overlooking the living room in a way that we are used to from the late twentieth century but do not expect in a small house of this period. Even the way the side balcony is treated, with a bulging shingled roof and a partially inset exterior wall, is a departure from everything we have seen.

One possible explanation for this is the obvious difficulty of the site. From the photographs it is clear that this cottage is built into what is, in effect, a pile of rocks, so even though the plan is the same rigorous square of the other two Delano Park cottages, the site encouraged greater freedom in the deployment of the shapes.

Charles S. Homer Jr. Cottage

Prouts Neck, Scarborough

John Calvin Stevens
Architect

1900–01, EXTANT

Like so many locations on the Maine coast, Prouts Neck in Scarborough became a fashionable summer resort after the Civil War. The great painter Winslow Homer vacationed there with his brother Arthur in 1875. Arthur Homer was the first family member to build a cottage on the Neck, followed by his brother Charles S. Homer Jr., who engaged Francis H. Fassett and John Calvin Stevens to design "The Ark" in 1882. The following year Winslow Homer decided to make Prouts Neck his permanent residence and turned to Fassett & Stevens to convert a mansard-roofed stable into a studio and home. During this period the Homers acquired extensive holdings on Prouts Neck, where they

would play a central role in developing a summer colony over the next three decades. In 1900 the Homer brothers—Arthur, Charles Jr. (1834–1917), and Winslow—each commissioned John Calvin Stevens to plan a rental cottage. Of the three, Charles S. Homer Jr.'s cottage best exemplifies Stevens' Shingle Style work at the turn of the century.

Completed in 1901, the two-story C. S. Homer Cottage features a gracefully designed gambrel roof that is penetrated on the façade by a loggia flanked by gable-roofed dormers. This broad roof encompasses a first-story porch on three sides, of which the façade has a

bowed projection enframed by two pairs of columns. On the land-facing end of the house, the roof is extended by a gambrel-roofed pavilion, while a gambrel-roofed service wing projects from the rear. On the first floor, the interior space is planned in an informal manner. A large living room runs across the front, interrupted only by a brick fireplace and an unobtrusive corner staircase. Behind the living room is a dining room as well as the kitchen and service wing. Six bedrooms are located around a second-story hallway, which has the unusual feature of a fireplace. The service wing provides two upstairs rooms for servants.

The February 1905 issue of the *Scientific American Building Monthly* described the walls of the living room and dining room as having "a high wainscoting, and the ceiling joists are dressed and exposed to view." In the opening lines of this article, the magazine spoke approvingly of the Homer Cottage as "a very happy combination of interesting outlines, the whole is most artistically treated."

The final group of Stevens cottages to appear in the Scientific American Building Monthly *is located on Prouts Neck. These are more sub-*

stantial and more conventional than the ones on the islands. In many ways they are town houses visiting the seashore. Certainly this house bears a strong resemblance to Stevens' house for himself, in the gambrel roof punctuated by gable and shed dormers. In the plan, the public rooms—living room and dining room—wrap around the two sides facing the sea. The kitchen and other dependencies are cleverly arranged to share the one chimney while being kept separate from the public rooms. The upstairs is practically a hotel, with six family rooms reached by the main stair and two bedrooms identified as servants' rooms using the back stair.

The piazza is a complex mixture of shingled piers at the corners and along the side, with paired classical columns on the primary side opening onto a curved projection with an open railing instead of the low shingled wall. It is a subtle way of differentiating the areas of the piazza.

Winslow Homer Cottage

Prouts Neck,
Scarborough

John Calvin Stevens
Architect

1901, EXTANT

The artist Winslow Homer (1836–1910) had known John Calvin Stevens since the firm of Fassett & Stevens had designed his brother's cottage at Prouts Neck in 1882 and his own studio the following year. On December 21, 1900, Homer wrote to his brother Charles that he "went to Stevens the architect to consult him on plan for house." Already the designer was at work on rental cottages for brothers Charles and Arthur Homer. Winslow noted in a January 1, 1901, letter to Arthur that "Charlie building corner of (lots) B & C. I am getting land cleared on which to build." Homer's two-story Shingle Style cottage was located on the east end of Prouts Neck overlooking Kettle Cove. The artist told people that he was building it for his retirement, but he would never live there, choosing instead to lease it. Nevertheless he took a personal interest in the project, as is reflected in his fifteen letters to Stevens that

document an intense level of concern for every aspect of his new cottage. Covering the construction period from February through October 1901, the letters range from venting frustration over the contractor Alonzo Googins to providing his own sketches for door and gutter details. As the work progressed, John Calvin Stevens sent his client a bill that requested as payment "Any production of Winslow Homer." The idea of exchanging architecture for art delighted Homer, who responded warmly on June 26 that Stevens was "a brother artist" and that he would receive "this sketch of mine that I think is appropriate & will please you." The "sketch" turned out to be a major oil, *The Artist's Studio in an Afternoon Fog*.

The exterior of the Homer Cottage features a dramatic juxtaposition of gable and gambrel roofs that encompass both open porches and interior spaces. In its July 1904 article about the cottage, the *Scientific American Building Monthly* described the principal rooms: "The living room occupies the entire length of the house, and is provided with an ingle nook, containing an open fireplace built of brick. This room, and also the dining room, is wainscoted from the floor to the ceiling, the latter having beams which are dressed and exposed to view." In contrast, the five bedrooms and one servant's room on the second floor are finished in plaster.

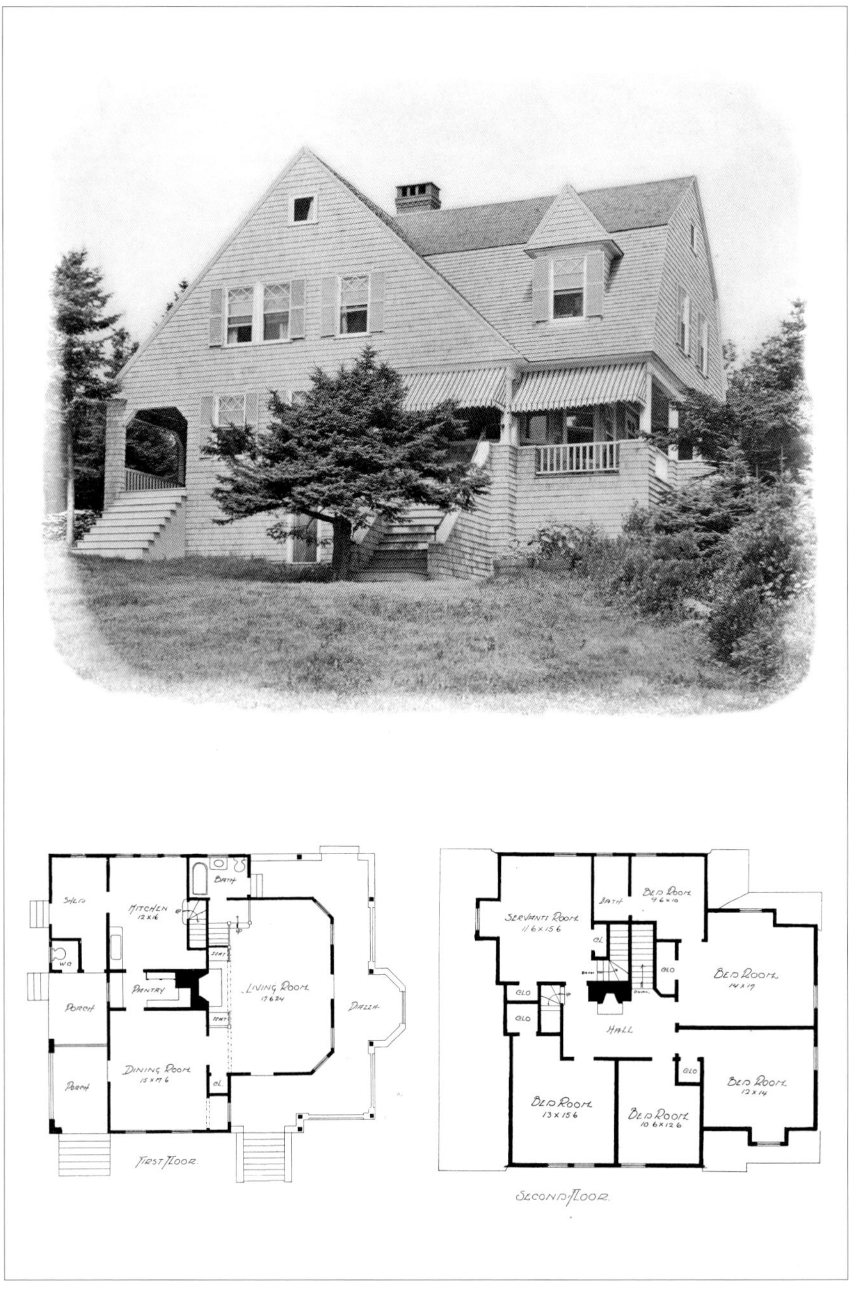

Here the editors nodded. The plan shown was not of the Homer Cottage. Instead, they were the plans of Mrs. Stevenson's cottage, and on her page in the same issue, July of 1904, are the plans of this cottage. For the sake of legibility we have shown the cottages with their correct plans.

The plan is quite similar to the one for Charles Homer, with living room and dining room with windows presumably toward the view. A small bath at landing level on the stair is reached also from the porch, and, unusually, there is a second toilet off the kitchen back porch. That porch has the shingled piers consistent with a more enclosed area, and the front piazza has short columns on shingled rails. The combined gable and gambrel give an impression of a compact mass.

CHAPTER 3

Shingle Style Cottages

Great Diamond Island and Kennebunkport

The cottages in the first part of this chapter were nearly all built on Great Diamond Island in Casco Bay between 1883 and 1889. The construction dates of these cottages overlap with many of the Shingle Style cottages by John Calvin Stevens seen in the preceding chapter. The earliest of these Great Diamond Island cottages started as a Fassett & Stevens cottage, built for James P. Baxter in 1883, and was first expanded by Stevens in 1889. The cottage achieved its published form after a second round of remodeling by the firm of Richards & Richards for new owner Walter Woodman in 1891.

The influence of Stevens is particularly seen in the cottages by Portland architect Antoine Dorticos, who designed six of the thirteen cottages in this chapter. Dorticos was born in Cuba in 1848, the son of a wealthy planter. When his family's estate was destroyed in a political upheaval, he was sent to study in Paris, France, and then came to Portland in 1866 to continue his studies at Gorham Normal School and Westbrook Seminary. Private schools in greater Portland had been educating the sons of wealthy Cubans for decades, the result of important commercial ties between Portland and Cuba. The May 2, 1878, edition of the *Educational Weekly*, a national publication, reported that the spring term at Eaton School in Norridgewock, Maine, had recently opened with Antoine Dorticos, "a graduate of the 'school of engineers' of Paris," teaching French and mathematics. He subsequently returned to Portland to work as a draftsman at the Portland Company. He received his training as an architect working in the office of Francis H. Fassett, Portland's leading Victorian architect who also trained John Calvin Stevens, Frederick A. Tompson, and others. He later attended and subsequently taught mechanical drawing classes at the Maine Charitable Mechanic Association.

The annual *Maine Register* documents that "Antoine Dorticos, Architect," had an office in Room 29 of the First National Bank building at 57 Exchange Street from 1888 through at least 1892. The 1895 edition of the same publication shows his address changed to 107 Clark Street, which was also his residence. In 1887 he advertised as an architect in the French language *Guide Français de la Nouvelle-Angleterre*, published for French-Canadians by Société de publications françaises des Etats-Unis, in Lowell, Massachusetts, perhaps hoping to design cottages for the increasing number of French-Canadians coming to Maine in summer. In spite of his obvious talent as a designer, Dorticos was unable to attract sufficient business to make his living as an architect and taught French at Portland High School for twenty-five years while designing buildings on the side.

Dorticos was credited during his lifetime with introducing Portlanders to the concept of spending their summers on the islands of Casco Bay, which he himself did beginning in the 1870s, first camping on Cushing's Island and then renting a room in a home on Peaks Island. A late nineteenth-century Portland newspaper claimed that:

> . . . the first Portland citizen to suggest and enjoy a sojourn in a cottage at the islands was not a native either of this city or the country. It was nearly twenty years ago that Prof. Antonio (sic) Dorticos, teacher of French at the Portland High School, but then a student here, suggested to friends the idea of making the islands a place of summer residence. They began camping on Cushing's Island. They were not the first campers in the harbor, of course, but when about seventeen years ago they hired rooms in a private house on Peaks they were the first Portland people to do such a thing.

The article credits Dorticos with the concept of renting rooms and influencing Charles Parsons to build two cottages on Peak's Island: "They were occupied by Mr. Dorticos and his wife and her relatives. It remained therefore for a foreigner to start the movement among us to enjoy the unrivaled opportunity for summer homes. Mr. Dorticos brought from France the appreciation of the French for such delightful resorts as our islands afford, and when he came here expressed surprise that Portland people did not live down the harbor during the hot weather. He immediately began to do so and has done so ever since."

Dorticos built his own cottage on Great Chebeague Island in 1885. As his *Scientific American* cottages show, he designed cottages for many Portland residents who took his advice and followed his example. Although inspired by the work of Stevens and other early developers of the Shingle Style, the cottages designed by Dorticos exhibit characteristics that often make his designs identifiable as his unique work, particularly in his treatment of roof forms, balconies, and porches.

Following the Dorticos cottages and the Walter Woodman Cottage in this chapter, the F. H. Morse Cottage on Great Diamond Island, by Fassett & Tompson, was a relatively typical example of the style, which might have been built in any suburb of the period. This chapter concludes with five cottages by Boston architect Henry Paston Clark. They were all built in his ancestral home town of Kennebunkport, where he was the leading architect working in the Shingle Style.

Ansel R. Doten Cottage 1

Great Diamond Island, Casco Bay

Antoine Dorticos
Architect

1891, DESTROYED

Businessman Ansel R. Doten (1841–1916) built his Shingle Style cottage on Great Diamond Island in 1891 for $800. Perhaps the reasonable construction cost was due in part to Ansel and his brother Samuel's ownership of a lumber mill on Fore Street in Portland. Doten's trim gambrel-roofed design was provided by local architect Antoine Dorticos. After only one season of use, the Doten Cottage burned in an island grass fire in April 1892. This fire may have been the impetus for the formation of the Portland Lawn Sprinkler Company, which, the *Oswego Daily Palladium* in New York State reported on December 13, 1892, had been organized at Portland, Maine, with president, Ansel R. Doten; treasurer, Elmer A. Doten; and a capital stock of $150,000.

Ansel Doten's father was a cabinetmaker in Poland, Maine, where Ansel and his brothers were born. Ansel and Samuel Doten had moved to Portland by 1869, when both worked at D. Winslow & Company, a steam planing mill at 246 Fore Street, and resided at Woodford's Corner. The following year, both were working in the Stevens Planing Mill in the Saccarappa section of Westbrook and living next door to each other with their wives in Westbrook. Ansel Doten was back in Portland in 1873, when he was one of the founding members of Odd Fellows Encampment No. 19 in Portland, along with Franklin H. Morse, who would later be a summer neighbor on Great Diamond Island. By 1883, the Doten brothers owned their own steam planing mill at 496 Fore Street as well as the Paris Flouring Company at the same address. Ansel Doten resided at 463 Cumberland Avenue, in a brick double house with wood Stick Style detailing, and Samuel H. Doten resided in the other half of the house. A third brother, Roswell F. Doten, lived nearby in one half of a smaller brick double house at 1 Deering Place and was involved in his brothers' businesses. The Doten brothers' business interests were varied and later involved their sons and other relatives. Several of Ansel Doten's businesses involved other summer residents of Great Diamond Island, including the Maine Real Estate Investment Corporation, incorporated with islander Franklin H. Morse and others in 1893, and the Portland and Yarmouth Electric Railway Corporation, formed with islanders Edwin L. Goding and Franklin H. Morse and others in 1902. In 2014, the remaining portion of the

S. H. and A. R Doten Planing and Molding Mill complex houses the Fore Street restaurant and the Standard Baking Company.

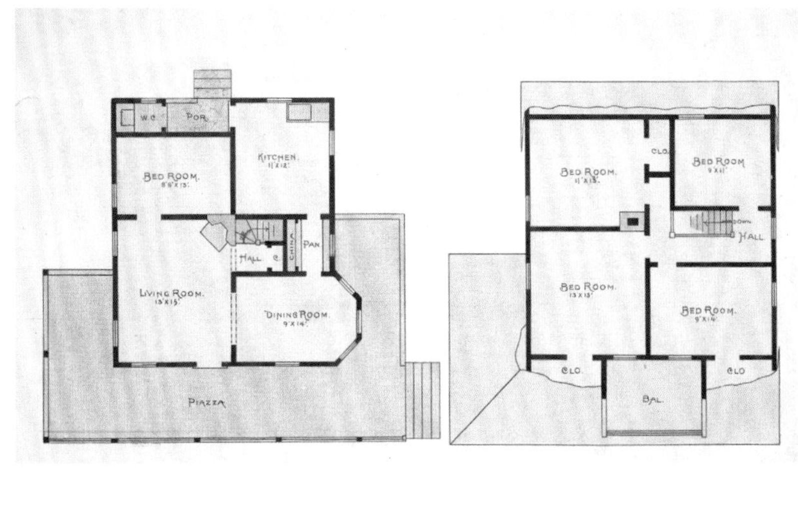

This first cottage for Ansel Doten seems like a relatively simple gambrel-roofed box, with a covered piazza tucked under its skirts and a balcony cutting into the front slope of the gambrel. The plan is simplicity itself, with a room in each corner and a central fireplace. What makes it innovative is the overhang of the second floor on the right-hand side, which brings the gable wall out to the face of the bay window in the dining room. The free end of the roof is supported by a triangular shingled bracket.

The cut-in balcony is deftly handled: the cheek walls on either side are shaped to be above the roof plane and to form the sidewalls of the balcony, while the balustrade allows for drainage along the front.

Ansel R. Doten Cottage II

Great Diamond Island,
Casco Bay

Antoine Dorticos
Architect

1892–94, ALTERED BEFORE 1912

Having lost his Great Diamond Island summer home to fire in April 1892, Ansel R. Doten returned to Antoine Dorticos for a cottage design of similar scale, this time favoring a saltbox roof over the previous gambrel. Once again Doten constructed a handsome Shingle Style cottage for a modest $800. While it would seem logical that he rebuilt in 1892, he was not taxed for his lot until 1894, indicating that there may have been some delay in replacing his earlier cottage with this one. Ansel Doten spent the balance of his summers here, enlarging the second-story porch into an arched loggia prior to 1912.

Dorticos is little known today, but was credited in his lifetime for playing a critical role in persuading local residents to summer on the Casco Bay islands. It is appropriate that the majority of the buildings that can be attributed to his hand are located on these islands, particularly Great Diamond Island. In 1906, at age 58, Antoine Dorticos committed suicide by shooting himself in the head at the intersection of Federal Street and Monument Square.

The steep central stair exaggerates the height of the porch, but is handier to the only door than in the previous scheme. This design has a three-sided covered piazza in front of a two-story house with a gambrel rear slope to house the service ell. On the front, a small gable shelters doors opening onto a large balcony. The hipped porch roof, large balcony, and projecting bracketed gable do not relate well to each other. Each element is "doing its own thing" and reads as a plug-in addition to the main house. The interior has tiny rooms and a tight spiral stair. The most significant plan change has been the elimination of the downstairs bedroom.

It is tempting to interpret this house as a somewhat hasty revision of the house that burned. But some of the problems may be the results of the enlargement, which presumably was done after Dorticos' death.

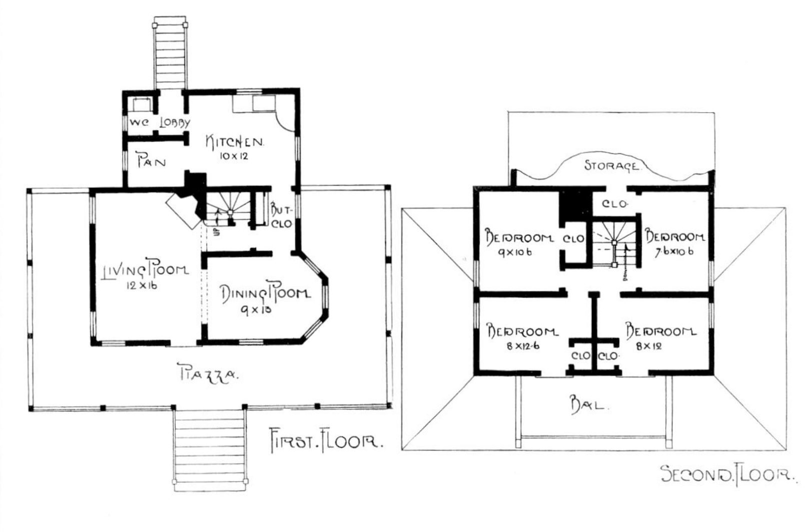

Charles Talbot Cottage

Great Diamond Island,
Casco Bay

Antoine Dorticos
Architect

1885, EXTANT

The cottage of Portland dentist Charles M. Talbot (1850–1937) on Great Diamond Island is the earliest known Shingle Style design of local architect Antoine Dorticos. Here a predominant feature is the dramatic sweep of the saltbox roof, punctuated at the second story by a cross gable and an open porch. An arched loggia on one side provided a sleeping porch for warm nights.

On April 22, 1885, the *Portland Transcript* reported that Dr. Charles Talbot intended to build a summer home on Great Diamond Island that year, and the newspaper followed up with a May 20, 1885, article noting that Talbot had submitted his architectural plans to the Diamond Island Association for approval. Talbot's $900 cottage was completed in time for the 1885 summer season. Talbot resided with his wife, Evis, at 120 Emery Street, and his

office was at 260 Middle Street when he had this cottage built. He later moved to Stroudwater and relocated his office to the Libby Building in Congress Square, where he remained in practice until 1921.

Here Dorticos tries to have both broad gable and gambrel roofs and, for good measure, an arched cutout for an open "loggia." The arch looks as if it is forcing the roofline to break into the gambrel shape.

Dorticos cuts the balcony into the roof but does not relate it to the dormer gable. Outside steps lead directly to the French doors of the living room, which in turn opens to the dining room and the stair so as to feel more spacious than the small dimensions could allow. The shed, containing the "necessary" WC, feels like an afterthought, even though it continues the line of the stair and living room. It is almost as if it is trying to escape out from under the main roof.

George W. Beale Cottage

Great Diamond Island, Casco Bay

Antoine Dorticos
Architect

1887, EXTANT

In October 1886, George W. Beale (1824–1910) asked Antoine Dorticos to design his summer home to be built on Great Diamond Island the following spring. As a superintendent at the Portland Company, which manufactured railroad locomotives and marine engines, Beale was in a position to afford the $1,470 budget for this gambrel-roofed Shingle Style cottage, which featured a spacious porch and a large second-story balcony. Five years after its construction in 1887, Beale's cottage was described as "very picturesque and the plan is excellent."

George W. Beale was born in Monmouth, Maine, in 1824. By 1850, he was working as a machinist in Portland and was a superintendent in an unidentified machine shop by 1870. The 1877 Portland city directory documents that he was a superintendent at the Portland Company. His residence was nearby at 23 St. Lawrence Street. From 1879 through 1890, the directories indicate that he resided at 47 St. Lawrence Street and continued to be a superintendent at the Portland Company. In 1885 Beale served on the Portland Common

Council, representing Ward 1. From 1896 through at least 1905, he was a manager for Morse & Guptill, insurance agents on Exchange Street, owned by Franklin H. Morse, who also owned a cottage on Great Diamond Island. Through these years, Beale lived with his son, Arthur, a bank clerk, at 40 Atlantic Street on Munjoy Hill. The final two years of Beale's life were spent living with the same son at Loveitt Heights in South Portland.

In the Beale Cottage, Dorticos experiments with moving the gable porch to the side of the piazza. While this creates a nice bay on the downstairs corner, it causes an awkward transition above, where a tiny triangle of the gambrel peeks out from the balcony roof. Also, the hipped roof of the piazza projection is not well integrated with the straight roof of the balcony.

The arched opening off the piazza is somewhat arbitrary. Presumably it was intended to create a more sheltered nook in contrast to the open piazza, but the way it blocks the dining room window feels a bit forced. But overall the plan has a nice flow, and the house opens to the views.

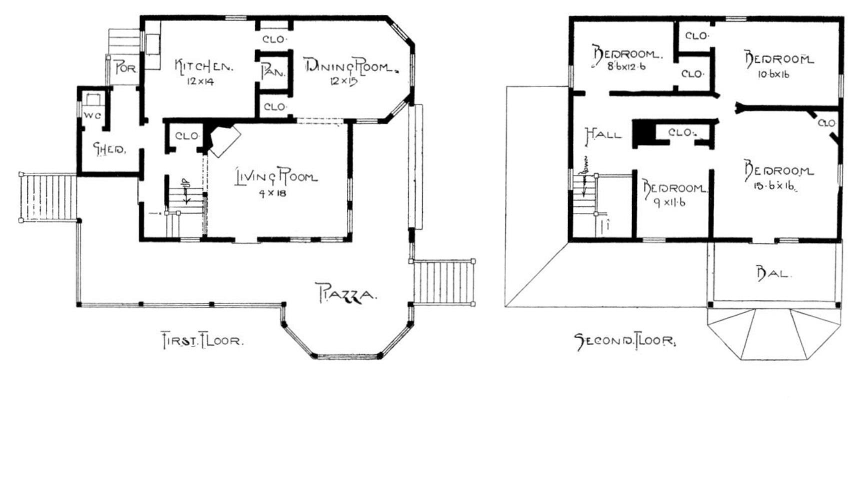

Alfred A. Kendall Cottage

Great Diamond Island,
Casco Bay

Antoine Dorticos
Architect

1887, DESTROYED

Alfred A. Kendall (1855–1910) was a partner in the Portland wholesale clothing firm of Chadbourne & Kendall, which was founded by his father and B. F. Chadbourne on Middle Street in the 1850s. In 1888 Kendall built this $2,000 cottage on Great Diamond Island from designs by Antoine Dorticos. Shingle Style features included an encompassing gable roof with a rounded front porch and rear corner tower. Like many of Dorticos's Shingle cottages, it had clapboard siding on the first story with wood shingle above.

At the time their cottage was built, Alfred Kendall and his wife, Mary Buzzell Kendall, lived at 10 Henry Street, Portland, just off Deering Street. Their two-and-a-half story brick Second Empire style home was later absorbed into the expanded Columbia Hotel on Congress Street. Alfred Kendall and his family returned to their summer island home each season until it burned in the fall of 1905. At that time Kendall probably asked Dorticos to plan a larger replacement cottage, which was constructed during the summer of 1906 and remains in use today. The gambrel roof and attached gazebo porch of the second Kendall Cottage bear a strong resemblance to Dorticos's nearby George H. Libby Cottage of 1902.

In the much more ambitious Kendall Cottage, Dorticos has extruded a curved piazza roof from the base of an all-enveloping steep gable, which can trace its origin to Bruce Price's Chandler House in Tuxedo Park, the house Frank Lloyd Wright used as the model for his own house in Oak Park, Illinois. The drama of the big, simple roof and thrusting piazza is very successful.

Dorticos weakens the concept by adding the upstairs balcony without tying it back into the main roof. The octagonal side bay is more successful, as it turns the back corner and masks the appurtenances on the rear.

The interior has the familiar arrangement of rooms around the central chimney. Here the chimney has two corner fireplaces, and each has its seat, or settle. The dining room nook is especially cozy, and this device will appear repeatedly in the Shingle Style cottages.

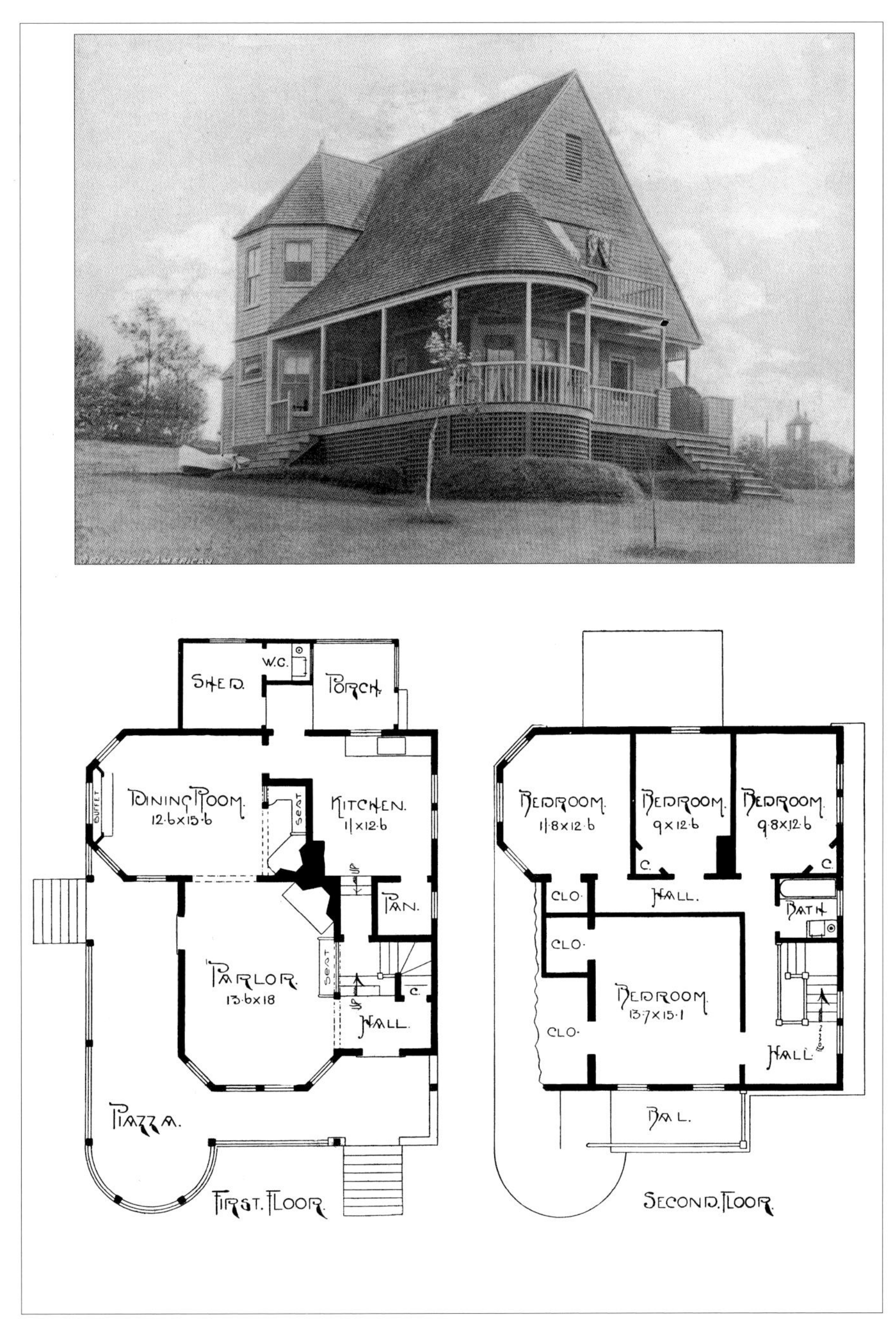
SHED
W.C.
PORCH
DINING ROOM 12·6×15·6
BUFFET
SEAT
KITCHEN 11×12·6
PAN.
PARLOR 13·6×18
SEAT
C
HALL
PIAZZA
FIRST FLOOR
BEDROOM 11·8×12·6
BEDROOM 9×12·6
BEDROOM 9·8×12·6
C.
C
CLO·
HALL
BATH
CLO·
BEDROOM 13·7×15·1
CLO·
HALL
BAL.
SECOND FLOOR

Edwin L. Goding Cottage

Great Diamond Island, Casco Bay

Antoine Dorticos
Architect

1892, EXTANT

Edwin Lyford Goding was the treasurer and manager of the Shaw, Goding Shoe Company, whose Portland workforce of 150 employees manufactured footwear that was sold as far west as the Rocky Mountains. Shaw, Goding and Company eventually operated additional factories in Freeport, Lewiston, and Sanford. Goding was born in North Livermore, Maine, before the family relocated to Portland, where his father was a successful wholesale grocer. By 1873, 22-year-old Edwin Goding was a salesman at Walden and Shaw Shoe Company while still residing at his father's St. Lawrence Street home. In 1882 he married Marion S. Longley, and from 1883 through 1888 they resided at 39 Cushman Street in a two-and-a-half story wood-framed house. In 1889 they moved to a larger brick house at 107 Pine Street, where they remained until at least 1896. By 1900 the Goding family was residing in Sanford, and it is likely that Goding was managing the company's shoe factory there. In 1912 and 1913, the family lived in Mountain View Park, Cape Elizabeth, and then moved to 333 Ocean Avenue in Portland, where they remained through 1918, by which time Mr. Goding was treasurer of the Pliasole Company. In 1919 they moved to 135 Lincoln Place in Brooklyn, New York. The 1920 U.S. Census shows them there with his occupation listed as "shoe manufacturer." Interestingly, the three Goding daughters—Florence, age 36; Emily, 34; and Margaret, 29—are all single and living with their parents. Their occupations, respectively, are school teacher, YWCA secretary, and bank clerk.

In October 1886, Goding approached Antoine Dorticos to design a cottage for him on Great Diamond Island, at the same time that the architect was working on a plan for George W. Beale. Both the Goding and Beale cottages were built in the spring of 1887, but Goding's burned five years later in the grass fire that also destroyed Ansel R. Doten's first cottage. Like Doten, Goding returned to Dorticos for a new design.

Built in the spring and summer of 1892, Edwin Goding's second cottage was the architect's largest Great Diamond Island project, costing $2,500. Here Dorticos was given free rein to create a classic Shingle Style composition of the dramatically sloping saltbox roof, broken by a broad gabled balcony and terminating in a rounded porch. A fanciful Queen

Anne touch is found in the attenuated corner tower at the rear. As the *Scientific American Building Monthly* commented in 1895, "The design presents a very picturesque exterior, with several features that give the building an artistic effect. The spacious and well shaded piazza, balconies, chimney and tower are some of the features."

The 1924 Portland tax records show that Marion Goding owned a cottage on Spring Avenue on Great Diamond Island, and the Dorticos-designed Goding Cottage was then owned by Sarah B. Rollins. The 1930 U.S. Census shows Mr. and Mrs. Goding residing in Norwalk, Connecticut, and his occupation listed as "retired shoe manufacturer."

Dorticos' magnum opus—and final appearance in the pages of the Scientific American Building Monthly*—is the Goding Cottage. It continues some of his more successful ideas, such as the long front roof punctuated by the gable and balcony. The roof plan here is extended to form a curved end of the piazza.*

The plan forsakes the central chimney in favor of a tall exterior chimney for the living room fireplace and nook area. Possibly this was to enliven the side elevation, which appears to be the entrance elevation. Probably the kindest thing to say about that elevation is that there are too many good ideas, and taken together they compete rather than cooperate.

The arched entrance is reminiscent of H. H. Richardson's work. It is a nice modification of the arched opening to accommodate a bench. The spiked bay on the corner is left over from Queen Anne town houses, and it interrupts the flow of the roofs, as does to a lesser extent the projected bedroom gable. The two spider-web oval windows look like afterthoughts. The other elevation has similarly unresolved elements: the back gable in the rear bedroom and the combined window between the upper front bedroom and bath are not centered over the dining room bay. These fussy elements detract from the otherwise generous and well-proportioned front elevation.

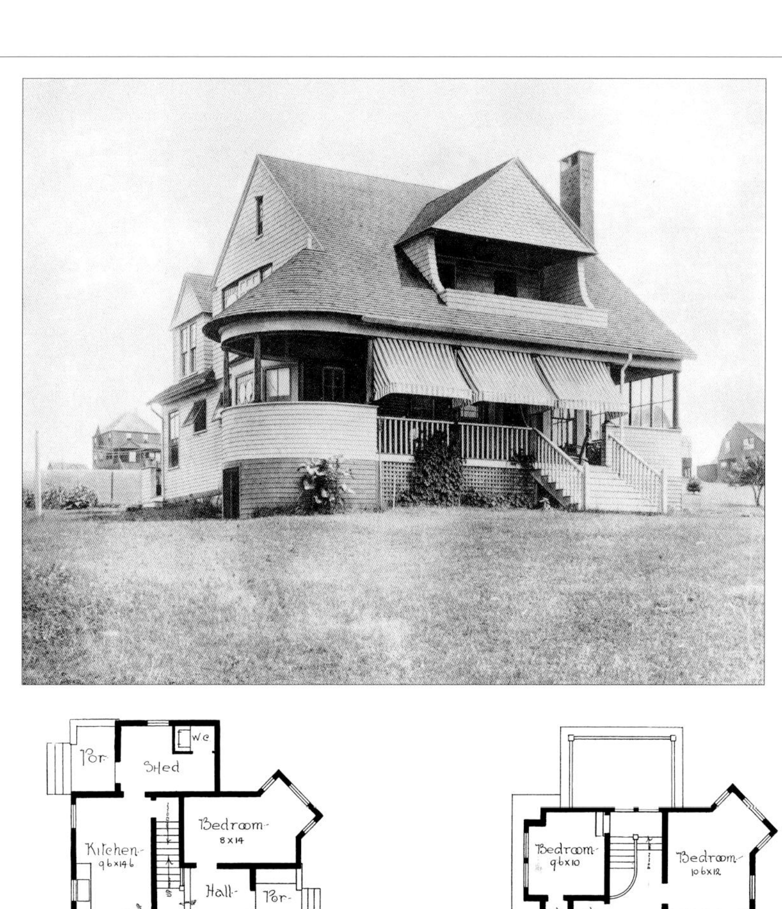

Walter Woodman Cottage

Great Diamond Island,
Casco Bay

Fassett & Stevens,
Stevens & Cobb,
Richards & Richards
Architects

1883, 1889, 1891; EXTANT

During the summer of 1883, noted Portland businessman and civic leader James P. Baxter built one of the first five homes on land acquired from the Diamond Island Association. The architect of this modest saltbox-roofed Shingle Style cottage was John Calvin Stevens, then the partner of Francis H. Fassett. In 1885 Baxter purchased Mackworth Island in Casco Bay, and two years later he constructed a large Shingle cottage there from designs by Stevens. At the same time he sold his Great Diamond Island property to Dr. Walter Woodman, a descendent of a prominent Buxton, Maine, family.

In March 1889, Woodman employed John Calvin Stevens and his partner Albert Winslow Cobb to plan an enlargement of the cottage, which included an arched porch addition to the left façade. By 1892 the Woodman Cottage had assumed its present appearance through a third building campaign designed by the Boston father-and-son architectural team of Joseph R. and William P. Richards. The Richards firm extended the second story over the Stevens porch at the left, enlarged the balcony, and completed the Stevens porch on the right side of the façade. These additions resulted in the pleasing Shingle Style composition of a broad

sloping saltbox roof punctuated by a large off-center porch dormer and a Richardsonian eyebrow window. Five symmetrically placed arches march boldly across the first-story front porch. Woodman's cottage was treated in the *Scientific American Building Monthly* of August 1892 as a complete work by J. R. and W. P. Richards rather than as a summer home that had evolved in three stages.

The piazza wraps three sides of the lower level, from an unusual bedroom off the living room to the blind wall of the pantry. Next to that blind wall is a fully circular moon window, which frames the view from the dining room. Upstairs the generous layout provides six bedrooms, two opening to the loggia. The third front bedroom has an eyebrow dormer.

Many of the island cottages have a balcony cut into the roof of the front porch. The Richards solution to the balcony involves setting the rail at the height of the point where the balcony wall intersects the roof and then dropping the front rail to improve the view. The curve of the drop echoes the curve of the dormer roof bracket, creating a lively interplay of curves.

Overall, except for the unavoidable darkness of the living and dining rooms, this plan is very successful.

Franklin H. Morse Cottage

Great Diamond Island, Casco Bay

Fassett & Tompson, **Architects**

1889, DESTROYED

During the post–Civil War period, the islands of Portland's Casco Bay became increasingly popular summer destinations. In 1882 Captain Elbridge G. P. Smith formed the Diamond Island Association to sell cottage lots on Great Diamond Island. On September 21, 1882, the association issued 210 $100 shares to 108 investors, each share representing a quarter-acre of land. By the summer of 1885, twenty-six cottages had been built on association land, and the summer population had reached two hundred.

Franklin H. Morse (1833–1914) was one of the many Portland businessmen attracted to Great Diamond Island in the 1880s. A partner in the Morse & Pinkham Insurance Agency at 9 Exchange Street, Morse lived at 197 Newbury Street when his cottage was designed by Portland architects Francis H. Fassett and Frederick A. Tompson in 1889. In addition to his career in the insurance industry, Morse was among the incorporators of the Maine Real Estate Investment Company and the Portland and Yarmouth Electric Railway Company, both in 1893. Ansel R. Doten was an incorporator of both the real estate company and the railway as well. He and another railway incorporator, Edward L. Goding, also had Great Diamond Island cottages that were published in the *Scientific American Building Monthly*. In 1910, at age 76, Morse would be a founder of Morse, Payson and Noyes Insurance Agency, which remains in business in 2014.

In contrast to the island's many Shingle Style cottages by John Calvin Stevens and Antoine Dorticos, Fassett & Tompson provided Morse with the plans for a Queen Anne summer house whose elevated design, vertical massing, and spacious wraparound porch ornamented with spindle work gave it the appearance of a suburban residence of the period. Unlike a typical suburban residence of 1889, which would have been finished on the interior with plaster walls and ceilings, hardwood floors, and molded trim, the Morse Cottage interior featured narrow bead board on walls and ceilings, stained pine floors, and natural finish pine trim. The cottage cost $2,500. After remaining substantially unchanged for 117 years, the cottage was destroyed by fire in 2006.

While some architects were Boston sophisticates trying on different summer costumes in their cottages, Frances Fassett remained a serious local architect experimenting with the freedoms of the cottage plan. This early exercise is notable chiefly for its wraparound piazza. The apparent complexity of the plan disguises its basic simplicity as a large rectangular box with one ell and one corner bay. In the plan we see the opening between the dining room and living room as the only freedom from the generally rectilinear organization, and we see the shared front and back stair arriving at a common landing, which was a feature of houses that had servants but not enough budget to provide them with separate stairs. Upstairs the plan is weakened by a tunnel-like hall with no light at the end of the tunnel.

The house is a cottage, but one that has not really left town yet.

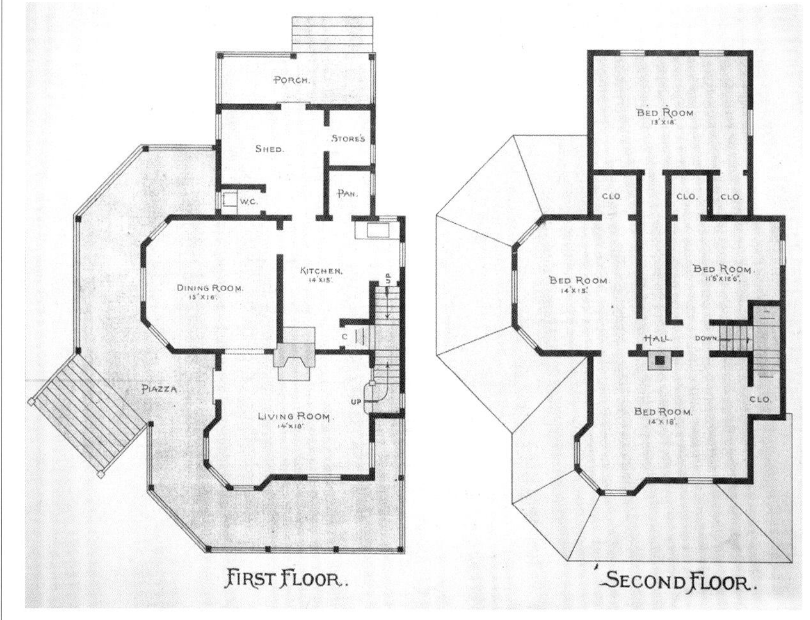

"Moorings," The Reverend Edward L. Clark House

Ocean Avenue,
Kennebunkport

Henry Paston Clark
Architect

1887–88, DESTROYED

Descended from the Lord family of Kennebunkport, the Reverend Edward L. Clark (1838–1910) served as the minister of churches in New York and Boston from 1873 to 1902. During the summer months, he left the city for his ancestral village of Kennebunkport, which had become a popular summer resort. In 1887, Reverend Clark spent $5,000 to build a stylish frame Queen Anne cottage on Ocean Avenue, only to have it burn to the ground after one season. Undaunted, he commissioned his son, Boston architect Henry Paston Clark, to plan a more substantial cottage in the form of a romantic stone castle.

Construction of the "Moorings" was underway by December 1887, and Reverend Clark was in residence by August 1888. Much of the cottage's frame construction was faced with rubble stone gathered from local beaches. In contrast to its rockbound exterior, the cottage featured gracious Colonial Revival interiors, including an entrance hall, drawing room, library, dining room, and kitchen on the first floor and four bedrooms and a study on the second floor. In 1891 Reverend Clark added a stable, which was connected to the main house

by an arched passageway on the first level and a covered walkway on the second.

Reverend Clark returned to his Kennebunkport castle each summer until his death in 1910. Two years later "Moorings," once described as "one of the most picturesque residences along the coast," was torn down by Edwin Robinson of Columbia, South Carolina, to make way for the lawn of his new summer home.

The castle that the Boston architect H. P. Clark built in Kennebunkport for his father takes the opposite tack from the next three houses. If they were conventional, this house is radical. It is a not wholly successful attempt at a German castle, reminiscent of Gillette Castle in Connecticut or Norumbega in Camden, Maine.

From the round tower with its circular study to the flying bridge leading to the carriage house, this is an exercise in the imposition of romantic imagery on a fairly straightforward house plan. It gives itself away as a stage set by using the massive stones only on the scenic sides. Once around the corner of the carriage house or through the portcullis, the walls revert to shingle. Still, it is a vigorous and enthusiastic response to the opportunity the summer cottage provided for flights of imagination.

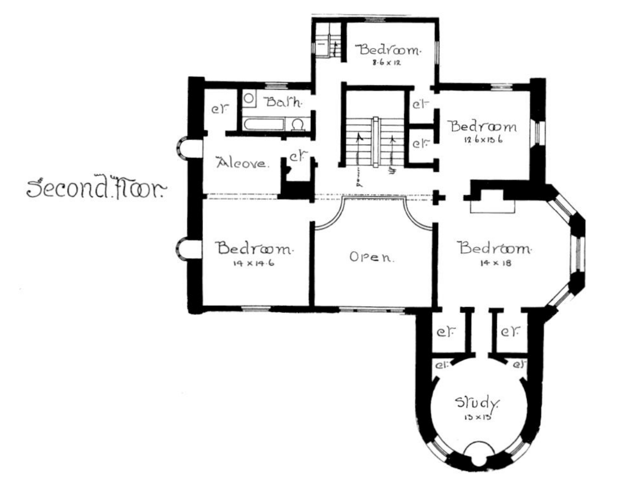

Charles H. Manning Cottage

Ocean Avenue,
Kennebunkport

Henry Paston Clark
Architect

1887, EXTANT

Henry Paston Clark designed this distinctive Shingle Style cottage for Charles H. Manning (1844–1919) in 1887. A native of Baltimore, Manning graduated from Lawrence Scientific School at Harvard in 1862 and served as an engineer in the U.S. Navy from 1863 until 1884, returning to duty in 1898 for the Spanish-American War. In 1884, Manning assumed the position of general superintendent of the Amoskeag Manufacturing Company in Manchester, New Hampshire, which he held until his retirement in 1913.

Kennebunkport was a welcome retreat from the summer heat of industrial Manchester and the job of managing one of the largest cotton mills in the world. In June 1887, Charles Manning purchased his lot on Ocean Avenue for $225, and that fall he built a cottage described as being "after the old New England lean-to roof, giving all the apartments on two floors, with low ceilings and large, open fireplaces."

The Manning Cottage has a medieval stone tower like the one Henry Paston Clark talked his father into, but it is less prominent here—just one floor remains, and Shingle is nearly triumphant. This much more modest effort still tries a little of everything—the tower, gambrel roof on one side, and dormer gable on the other. The piazza is surrounded by arches that repeat the deep entrance porch. The shingled arches are a compromise between the heavy stone Clark himself probably really wanted and the simple summer cottage his clients could afford. Not all clients are as indulgent as one's own father.

This house has the elements that will characterize the Shingle Style: shingles, a low, ground-hugging silhouette within an all-enveloping roof punctuated with dormers, broad piazzas, and porches tying the house to the landscape. The floor plan is not just a set of boxes. The drawing room with its semicircular bay opens to the porch, the dining room, and the entry hall, leaving only the kitchen and service areas cut off by walls with doors. And the stair leads to a generous upstairs hall. Everybody shares the one WC downstairs, however.

That these publications were influential is proved by the construction of a similar but smaller house in another part of the state, with plans by architects Barber & Kluttz of

BEDROOM
10X15
BEDROOM.
14X14
CLO.
CLO.
BEDROOM.
10.6X11.6
SECOND FLOOR
CLO.
CLO.
BAL.
BEDROOM.
10.6X15
HALL
HALL.
CLO.
BEDROOM.
10.6X10.6
CLO.
BEDROOM
12.6X16.6
CLO.

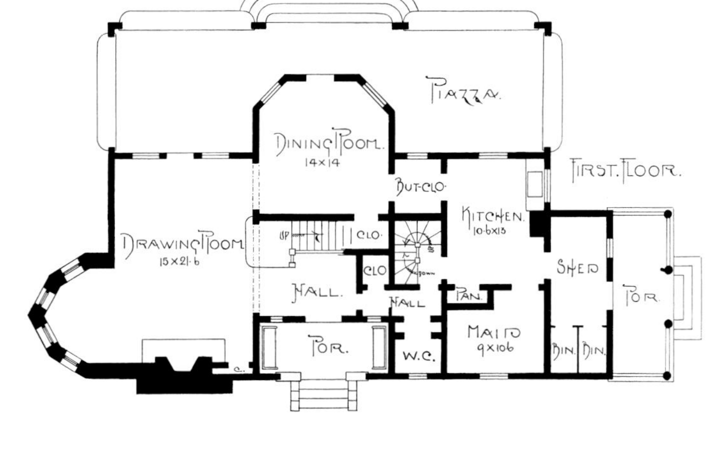
PIAZZA.
DINING ROOM.
14X14
FIRST FLOOR.
BUT. CLO.
KITCHEN.
10.6X15
DRAWING ROOM
15X21.6
CLO.
CLO.
HALL.
HALL
PAN.
SHED
POR.
MAID
9X10.6
POR.
W.C.
BIN.
BIN.

Knoxville, Tennessee. The firm, previously called George Barber & Co., was one of the most successful mail-order architectural plan services of the period, and though they usually provided elaborate Queen Anne houses with a lot of "artistic" ornament, they were obviously not averse to giving a client what he wanted. It is easy to see from its plan that the clients said to the architects, "I want one of those but without the maid's room and back stair."

This house had the same one-story tower and small dormers, but has in recent years been remodeled with larger dormers and a wood-framed second floor to the tower.

"Greywood," Margaret Deland Cottage

Ocean Avenue,
Kennebunkport

Henry Paston Clark
Architect

1887, EXTANT

Architect Henry Paston Clark built this gambrel-roofed cottage in 1887 as a rental property and sold it three years later to author Margaret Deland (1858–1945). Born near Allegany, Pennsylvania, Margaret settled in Boston in 1880 when she married printer Lorin F. Deland. Mrs. Deland published her first collection of poems, *The Old Garden*, in 1886, and her first novel, *John Ward, Preacher*, in 1888.

In November 1890, Margaret Deland purchased Clark's rental cottage and land upon which to relocate it. Within the next two years, the house was enlarged under Clark's direction to include a gambrel-roofed addition to the façade and a service wing at one side.

After Lorin Deland died in 1917, Margaret Deland continued to spend her summers at Greywood until her death in 1945. She is best remembered for her two autobiographies, *If This Be I* (1935) and *Golden Yesterdays* (1941), which deftly depict the social history of her time.

Clark here is designing a small cottage in a more vernacular Shingle mode. It has no stone towers or grand piazzas. Its only romantic gesture is the diamond-paned oriel over the porch. Except for that touch, this could be a fisherman's cottage. The photograph is taken from an angle that emphasizes the large rain barrels, so even the photographer was struck by the casual and unpretentious quality of the design. Of course, that lack of pretension is, in itself, a romantic choice comparable to the general use of the word "cottage" to describe even the most elaborate summer chateau. Here, at least, the term is appropriate.

Por
Living Room
12 x 24
Por
D.w.c.
clt.
Workshop
Shed
Por
Pan.
Kitchen
12 x 13.6
Dining Room
12 x 15.6
Lobby
Por
First Floor
Bedroom
10.6 x 15
clt.
clt.
Bedroom
10.6 x 16
Hall
Bedroom
10.6 x 10.6
Bedroom
10.6 x 10.6
Bedroom
12 x 12
Second Floor

"Point O' View," Burleigh S. Thompson Cottage

Ocean Avenue,
Kennebunkport

Henry Paston Clark
Architect

1894–95, EXTANT

In 1870, nine Massachusetts investors joined forces with two local residents to form the Boston and Kennebunkport Sea Shore Company for the purpose of purchasing Cape Arundel in Kennebunkport and developing it as a summer colony. In 1873, the company started marketing its lots by issuing a plan, which was updated a decade later by the Portland engineer E. C. Jordan. From this plan in October 1894, Burleigh S. Thompson of Kennebunkport selected two adjoining lots on Ocean Avenue and commissioned Henry Paston Clark to plan his summer home on a site "with a commanding view of the ocean and Cape Porpoise." In contrast to his Shingle Style cottages, Clark created an eclectic design for Thompson, the dominant feature of which is the English half-timbered façade supported by rubble stone piers. Since its completion in 1895, Thompson's "Point O' View" has charmed Cape Arundel residents and visitors alike.

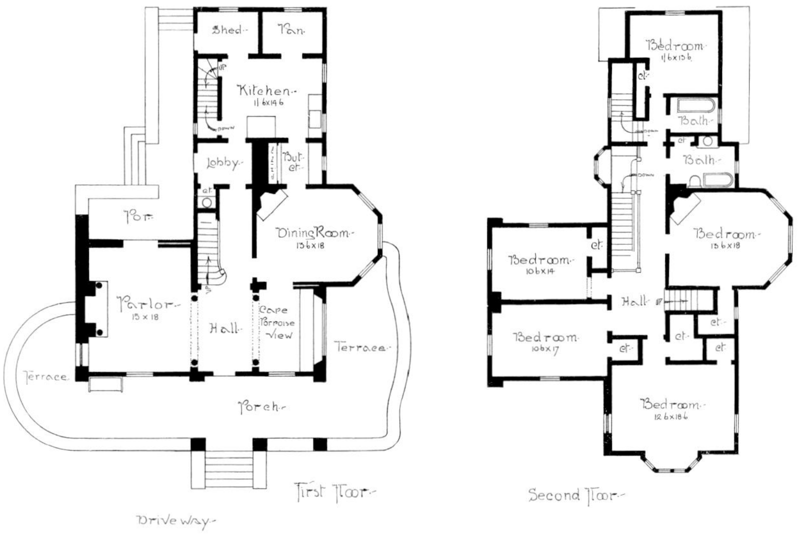
Shed
Pan
Kitchen
11 6x14 6
Lobby
But-
ct
ct
Por
Dining Room
13 6x18
Parlor
15 x 18
Hall
Cape
Porpoise
View
Terrace
Terrace
Porch
First Floor
Driveway
Bedroom
11 6x13 6
ct
Bath
ct
Bath
Bedroom
13 6x18
Bedroom
10 6x14
ct
Hall
Bedroom
10 6x17
ct
ct
ct
ct
Bedroom
12 6x18 6
Second Floor

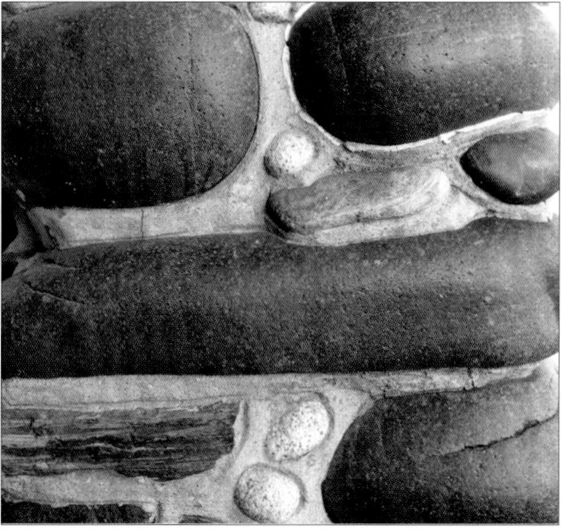

Clark here continues his habit, as with the Reverend Clark House, of including a historical element on the public face—in this case the Tudor half timbering and oriel window—with the other sides being the more usual shingle. Here the shingles end in a rounded pattern, which was then referred to as "fancy butt" but is now more decorously referred to as a "fancy cut." Stone is used only in what will be its usual role as foundation and terrace.

The plan is not that different from the conventional town-house plan, although the front parlor is open to the hall, which in turn is open to a space simply described as "Cape Porpoise View."

The house still exists, though the Tudor elements have disappeared, and it has acquired additions and roof changes. Studying its present appearance can become a game of deciding which surfaces are still the original and which have been modified.

Francis B. Harrington Cottage

Kennebunkport

Henry Paston Clark
Architect

1900, EXTANT

Francis Bishop Harrington (1855–1914) was born in Salem, Massachusetts, and attended local schools. He attended Tufts College from 1873 to 1877, where he was considered one of the school's best football players. Harrington then entered Harvard Medical School, doing his residency at Massachusetts General Hospital and graduating in 1881. The following year he established his practice in Boston and married Abbie J. Ruggles of Fitchburg. From 1889 to 1894 he was an instructor at Harvard Medical School as an assistant in clinical surgery. He would later become a lecturer on surgery at the school as well as an eminent surgeon. In 1905 the Harringtons were living at 201 Beacon Street, Boston. In 1910 the household consisted of Dr. Harrington, his wife, two daughters, and four servants. Following his death in 1914, a 41-page book of tributes to Dr. Harrington was privately published, the tributes having been written by professional colleagues recalling his professional skill and achievements as well as by his friends, including his Kennebunkport neighbor Margaret Deland. The impression that emerges is of an accomplished but modest man who was highly esteemed by colleagues and much loved by patients and friends.

For the Harrington Cottage, architect Henry Paston Clark used several motifs of the Shingle Style that first appeared in the 1880s and may have been somewhat out of fashion by 1900. These features include the double-gabled gambrel roof; pedimented dormers connected by a shed dormer; and a porch deeply recessed under one gable. The cottage is quite reminiscent of John Calvin Stevens' work of the 1880s, except perhaps for the porte-cochère. The conservative design approach may have been at the request of the client, who was noted for not wanting to draw attention to himself. The compact plan wastes little space on hallways. The interiors are done in a combination of Colonial Revival and Craftsman styles that are expected for the period and are nicely detailed by Clark. The exposed electric light bulbs on the beams in the living room are typical of early electric lighting installations. The house was pictured in an advertisement for Cabot Shingle Stains that appeared in the *Ladies Home Journal* in May 1902.

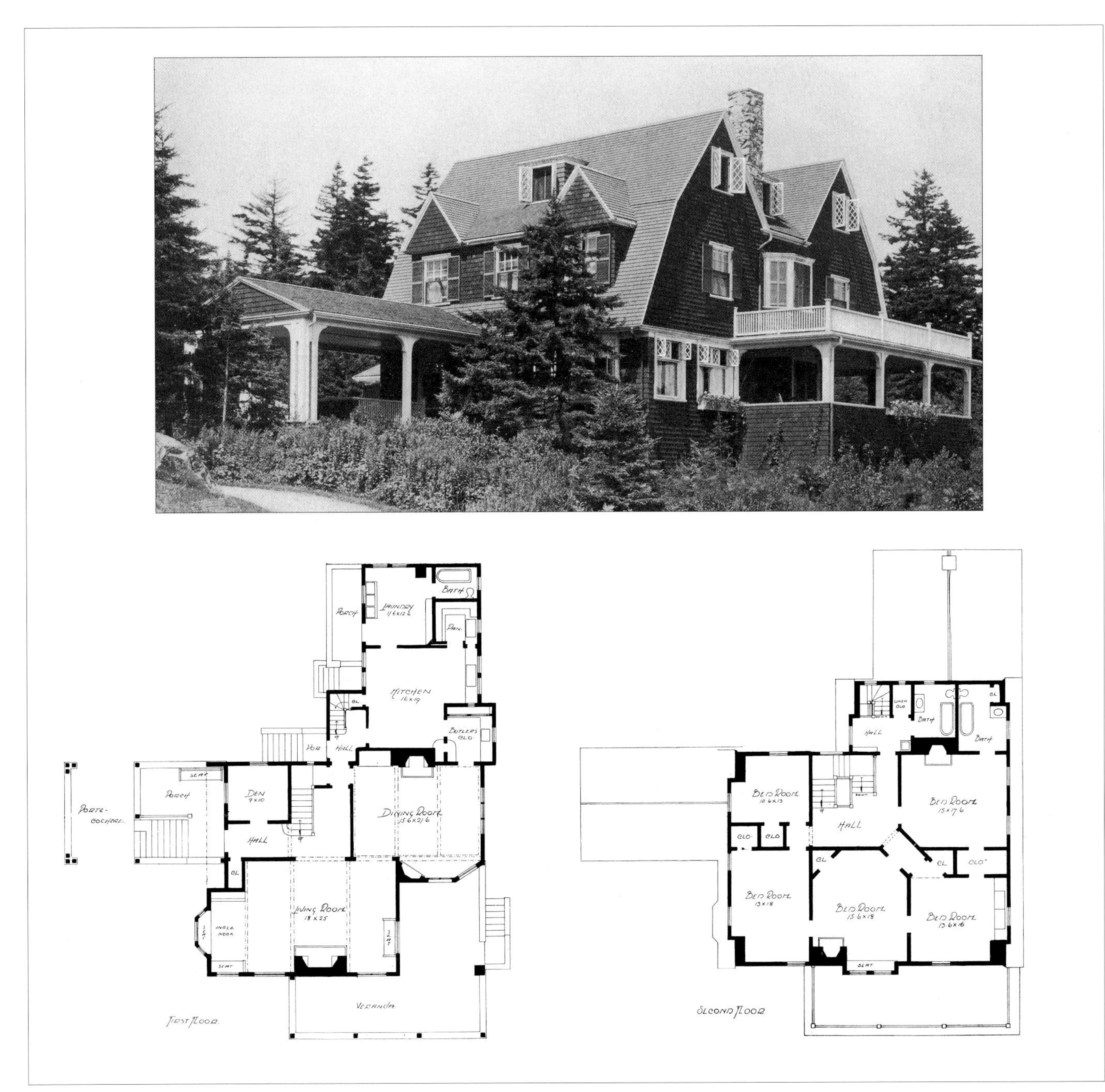
Porch
Laundry
Bath
Kitchen 16 x 19
Butler's Clo
Hall
Den 9 x 10
Porch
Porte-cochere
Dining Room 15.6 x 21.6
Living Room 18 x 25
Ingle Nook
Veranda
First Floor
Hall
Bath
Bath
Bed Room 10.6 x 13
Bed Room 15 x 17.6
Hall
Bed Room 13 x 18
Bed Room 15.6 x 18
Bed Room 13.6 x 16
Second Floor

Clark has here produced a fine example of the Shingle Style, nestling a fairly large plan into its surroundings and reaching out with the porte-cochère and the veranda. The passage through the plan is varied, from the den off the entry, suitable for entertaining business visitors, to the stair hall, hinted at by the bottom steps peeking around the corner. The wide opening to the living room leaves no uncertainty about the destination, but then the opening to the dining room joins those two rooms with a fireplace-to-fireplace diagonal.

Upstairs the stair hall connects to the lower right bedroom with a clever hallway that creates interesting angles in the three bedrooms. The large balcony apparently is reached only from the corner bedroom window, though.

The exterior combines several ideas, with full diamond-paned casements in the attic to English-style upper sash casements, over presumably fixed lower sashes. The second floor has the more usual cottage double-hung windows with muntins in the upper sashes. The entrance side uses the shed dormer between gable dormer motif, and the double gambrel above the veranda could be seen as the same idea writ large. Altogether, this is an assured exercise in an established style, and one that would soon be deemed old-fashioned.

CHAPTER 4

Farewell to Shingle
Revival Styles in Maine

The houses in this chapter represent a movement away from the informal nature of the Shingle Style as the nineteenth century moved into the twentieth and "Revivalism" overtook architectural design trends. The Colonial Revival is the style most represented in these dozen houses, three of which are urban or suburban town houses. Although the Shingle Style had its roots in the rambling early Colonial homes of New England, over time the more formal elements of Georgian Colonial and the Federal styles increasingly appeared, usually as an accent such as a Palladian window in a gable. By the turn of the century, grandly formal and often symmetrical facades composed of elements from the Georgian, Federal, and Greek Revival styles were increasingly common.

This next phase of Colonial Revival architecture is seen in its most formal incarnation in the Frederick Payson House by John Calvin Stevens, and the Perez Burnham House by George Burnham, both in the Western Promenade neighborhood of Portland. It also appears in a more subtle way in the Edwards and Miller double-houses by Frederick Tompson in Portland's Deering neighborhood. Transitions from one architectural style to another are often less than clear-cut, with buildings designed with elements of the style going out as well as the style or styles coming in. The D. D. Walker Cottage in Kennebunkport is an example of this, with a Shingle Style form, a stucco exterior typical of the emerging Tudor Revival style, and a Colonial Revival interior.

Two of the cottages in this chapter are the work of Mount Desert Island's native-born architect of the period, Frederick L. Savage. One embraces the Classical Revival style that was variously called Spanish and Italian during the period. The other is in the Tudor Revival style. Both are located on the island in Bar Harbor. Savage was born in Northeast Harbor and worked as a carpenter as a young man. He worked on some of the first cottages built there, getting to know several of the summer residents and their architects from Boston. His talents for wood carving and drawing were recognized, and he took advantage of an opportunity to work in the Boston architectural firm of Peabody & Stearns as a draftsman. After two years with the Boston firm, he returned to Mount Desert Island and began his career as an architect.

By the time Savage designed the John D. Jones Cottage in Bar Harbor in 1892, he was well established as the leading local architect and had designed dozens of cottages on the island. The Classical Revival Style looked back to Renaissance Europe for its inspiration; the same sources originally looked to for the English houses that inspired Georgian and Federal styles a century or more earlier. By the late nineteenth century, however, American architects were looking past the English copies of European houses to the originals themselves. This movement in residential architecture was paralleled in civic and commercial buildings with the development of the grandly formal Beaux Arts style. Cottages like the Jones Cottage demonstrate the increasing formality of the summer community on Mount Desert Island, being far from the informal fieldstone and shingles of the earlier cottages. Savage's 1903 cottage for himself represents the arrival of the Tudor Revival style, which looked back at English houses of the period just before Renaissance classicism arrived with its more formal and symmetrical character. Savage recognized the changing character of the summer community on the island and demonstrated in the design of his new home that he was fully able to work in the latest mode.

The Sherley Cottage of 1897 retains elements of the Shingle Style, such as the rough stone and gambrel roof form, combined with elements of the Adirondack style more common in the mountainous resorts of New York State. Defying easy stylistic categorization, the Sherley Cottage is a charming example of late nineteenth-century rustic eclecticism.

The two Walker cottages that conclude this chapter were designed by Frazer & Chapman and built side by side on a rocky point of land now known as Walker's Point in Kennebunkport. While the George H. Walker Cottage looked back toward the Shingle Style, the D. D. Walker Cottage reflected the Tudor Revival in its concrete stucco exterior and the Colonial Revival on the interior.

Josiah H. Drummond Jr. House

105 West Street, Portland

John Calvin Stevens
Architect

18891, EXTANT

The Josiah H. Drummond Jr. House of 1891 is one of a group of Colonial Revival residences designed by John Calvin Stevens for Portland's Western Promenade neighborhood between 1885 and 1900. At the same time that Stevens was creating his most advanced Shingle Style homes and cottages in the mid-1880s, he was developing plans for Georgian- and Federal-inspired houses such as the Cyrus F. Davis House of 1885 at 175 Vaughan Street. As Stevens and his partner Albert Winslow Cobb characterized the Davis House in their 1889 book *Examples of American Domestic Architecture*, "Its form is the very simplest that can be devised for an architectural structure. Yet little touches of variety in the shape and disposition of the windows, and some telling detail in the front entrance, relieve the house from any offence of tameness."

The same words could apply to the Drummond House, which is located on a small rectangular lot perpendicular to West Street. This rectangular two-story, hip-roofed frame

house covers the entire lot. Its restrained clapboard exterior is relieved by a parlor bay on West Street and an entrance porch and dining room bay on the west side. The side entrance leads to a central hall with the library and parlor facing the street and the dining room, den, and kitchen at the back of the house. The second floor is devoted to five bedrooms. Echoing Stevens and Cobb's description of the Davis House, the *Scientific American Building Monthly* described the Drummond House in July 1892 as being "in the New England Style, rather modest in appearance, with square outlines that are well broken by many windows and porches, giving it a good effect."

Within a short time, Josiah and Sallie Drummond's growing family of five sons and a daughter necessitated the replacement of the hip roof with a dormered gambrel roof, which created a third story for more bedrooms. At the same time a second story was added to the first-story parlor bay window on West Street.

Josiah H. Drummond Jr. (1856–1921) lived at 105 West Street from 1891 until his death in 1921. A native of Waterville, he moved to Portland in 1860 with his parents, his father being a prominent attorney. The younger Drummond graduated from Colby College in 1877 and joined his father's law practice two years later. An active Republican, Drummond was elected in the 1890s to represent Portland in the state legislature. Drummond specialized in corporate law. As the March 1904 *Board of Trade Journal* noted, "Mr. Drummond has unusual capacity for gaining a clear and correct conception of any case undertaken by him, and so marshalling his evidence and his arguments as to bring out every point of strength in favor of his clients."

During his transition from "the odd cottage style" to the stricter Colonial Revival, Stevens tried to honor the Colonial models while retaining some freedom of expression. The houses he published show this struggle. With the Drummond House he is trying to behave, but he cannot resist modifying the basic box in order to give his rooms something other than strictly rectangular shapes. On the lower floor, three of the four major rooms have a full-width bay that pushes out from under the hip roof. There is a conceptual difference between a room in which the windows have been replaced by a bay that leaves bits of straight wall on each side and one in which the angled walls start at the corners. The latter feels more spacious, as if the room really includes the bay rather than having it added on.

There is another deviation in the plan for an opposite spatial reason: the front library is not as wide as the hip roof allows. It and the bedroom above are set in from the roof edge, and wide brackets are added to make this look intentional rather than accidental. The apparent reason for this is to allow the entry walk to be more prominent by being slightly wider than it otherwise would be. Several of Stevens' houses, including his own, have side entries, and they need to be made more comfortable because of their literal eccentricity. Here, in addition to inset wall and roof brackets, he is able to add a third column to the entry porch so that the arrival is framed by columns on each side. In the Bates House he does not do this, but here he decides it is a gesture worth breaking the box for.

Once through the tiny lobby, the space opens in all directions. Even the den is visible through the screen of the hall bench, and the stairwell landing window adds light from above. Fireplaces are visible in the library and dining room. Upstairs all but one bedroom lose the bay so that Stevens does not have to modify the roof shape. The tops of the bays are given balustrades but no doors, and the entry porch does not even have a window for access; the balustrade falls awkwardly in the middle of the principal bedroom window.

Colonial Revival would win the battle for Stevens' loyalty, and his buildings would become determined by the formal treatment of their exteriors. The freedom of plan and sensitivity to site conditions of the cottage would be disciplined by Enlightenment principles. It would take the modernist revolution and the return to nature of the 1960s for houses to rediscover the cottage idea.

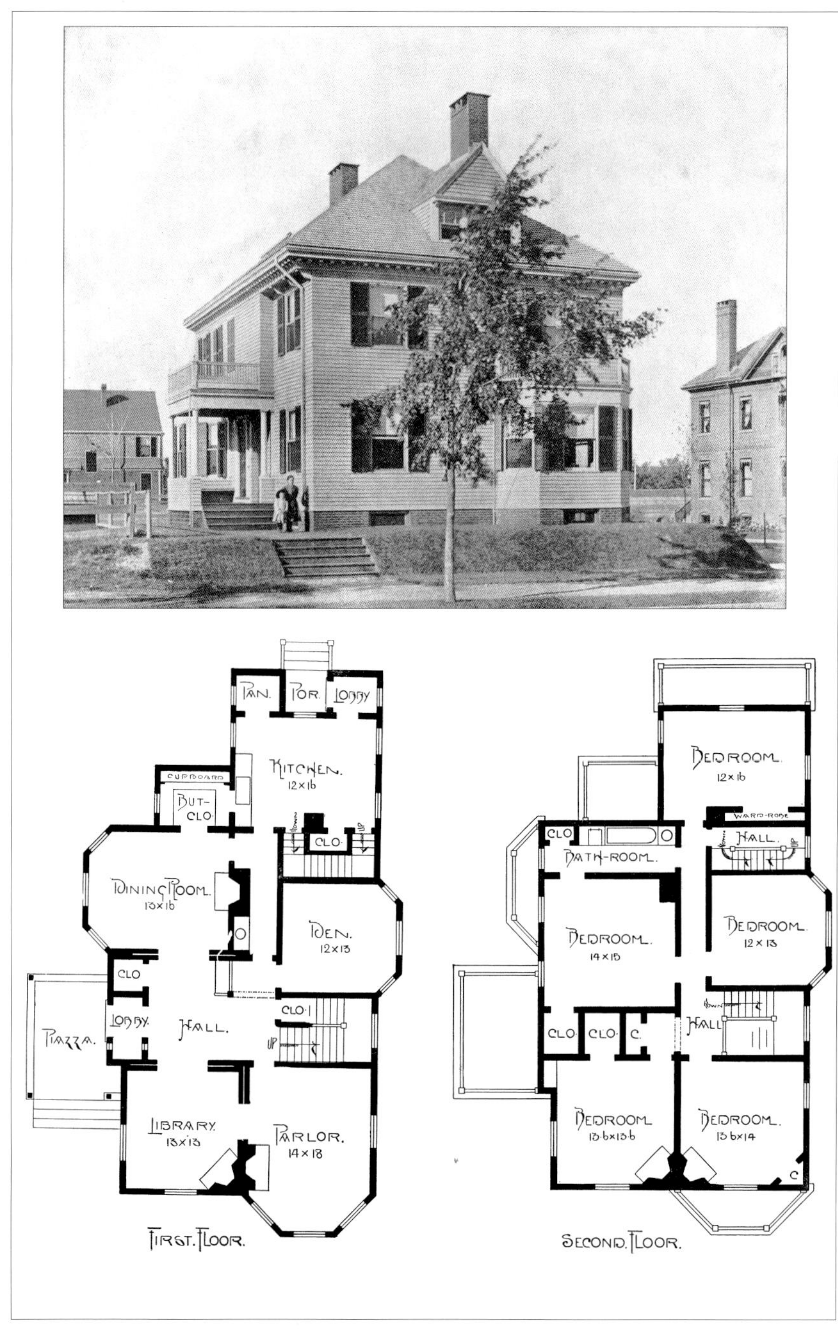

Franklin C. Payson House

28 Bowdoin Street, Portland

John Calvin Stevens
Architect

1901, EXTANT

In 1901 Franklin C. Payson (1856–1930) hired John Calvin Stevens to plan a substantial brick Colonial Revival house in the Western Promenade neighborhood. Stevens and Payson enjoyed a personal friendship that included sporting trips to the Maine woods. Payson was a prominent attorney who had declined a seat on the state supreme court in 1900.

On the Bowdoin Street façade of his home, the formality of the grand Neo-Federal portico and doorway and the forceful symmetry of the gambrel roof are counterbalanced by the asymmetrical placement of the first- and second-story windows. Pink slate is used to sheath the gable ends of the roof. Projecting from the center of the rear wall is a sun parlor, a popular period feature. Stevens' design for Payson's "palm room" appeared in the November 1904 *Scientific American Building Monthly* and in the June 1905 *House Beautiful*. The entire house was illustrated in the *Scientific American Building Monthly* for June 1904. This article included photographs of the spacious Colonial Revival interior and provided the following description of the distinctive central hallway:

"The staircase hall is separated from the entrance hall by an archway, supported on fluted pilasters and columns with Ionic capitals placed on paneled bases. The staircase is of an ornamental character, with white enameled balusters, posts, and risers, and mahogany rail and treads. At the side of the staircase there is an ornamental seat of white enamel treatment with mahogany arms."

The body of the house is pure Colonial Revival, with corner quoining to emphasize its reference to eighteenth-century antecedents. Above the heavy cornice is a gambrel, oddly and not entirely happily set on the long side of the main block so that it rises to a height almost equal to that from ground to cornice. The gambrel and ell gable ends are faced with pinkish slate in an uneasy compromise between brick and shingle. On the rear façade, the living and dining room emerge into full-width bays —identically sized for symmetry, of course— and between them nestles an octagonal conservatory. These are the only spatially ambitious areas in the plan.

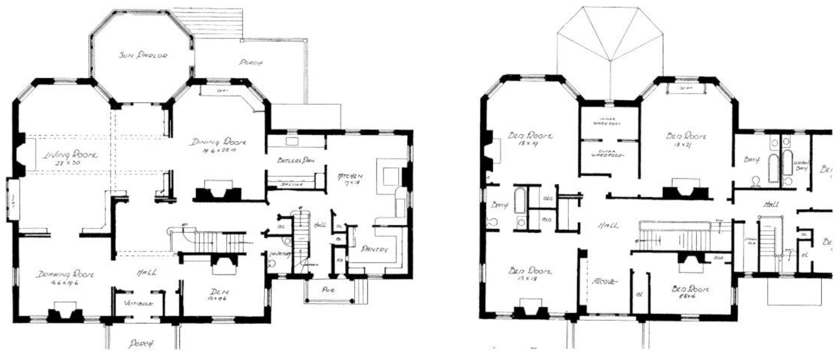

This project is a long distance from the Cushing's Island cottages of only fifteen years earlier. Its enlarged eighteenth-century style would become the fashionable norm for much of the twentieth century, while small cottages would be dominated by the Arts and Crafts and bungalow styles—alternatives for those of lesser means. The original idea of the Scientific American Building Monthly *had been "the presentation in each number of a variety of the latest and best plans for private residences, city and country, including those of very moderate cost as well as the more expensive." The "very moderate cost" end of the spectrum was rapidly losing ground.*

Harry Butler House

1 Thomas Street, Portland

John Calvin Stevens
Architect

1891, EXTANT

During the 1890s, John Calvin Stevens designed several houses in the Western Promenade neighborhood that exhibited an eclectic blend of the Queen Anne, Romanesque Revival, Shingle, and Colonial Revival styles. The E. H. Davis House of 1890, at 6 Bowdoin Street, and the Fred E. Richards House of 1893, at 150 Vaughan Street, are major examples of this trend, as is the Harry Butler House of 1891. Prominently located on a corner lot facing Thomas Street, the Butler House is a large rectangular, two-story brick dwelling with red sandstone trim. The hip-roofed main block of the house is Colonial in origin, while the service wing at the left displays a sloping saltbox roof reminiscent of the Shingle Style, and the semi-detached turret at the right has Queen Anne and Romanesque Revival overtones. Also Romanesque in character is the arched doorway, which is sheltered by a wooden Arts and Crafts porch. In the early twentieth century, the green shingled roof was replaced by the present distinctive red roof tiles, adding an exotic touch to the house.

The first floor plan of the Butler House features a central stair hall. To its right is a living room that includes a semicircular corner formed by the turret. To the left of the hall is the reception room, dining room, and kitchen. Harry and Julia Butler did not have children,

so the second-floor plan consists of a master bedroom with a dressing room and an adjacent bathroom, sewing room, and trunk room. A guest bedroom and a servant's bedroom complete the second floor.

A native of Portland, Harry Butler (1858–1923) attended Phillips Exeter Academy, Harvard, and Harvard Law School. On completing law school in 1881, he took a western trip, returning to Portland in 1882 to begin working for the First National Bank. His decision to pursue banking over the law resulted in a highly successful career in finance and business. By the time of his death in 1923, Butler had amassed an estate worth over a million dollars, much of which he bequeathed to charities and institutions.

This house is a dramatic departure from the other Maine houses published in the magazine. It is tempting to attribute its design to the fact that Harry Butler completed Harvard Law School in 1881. H. H. Richardson's Sever Hall had just been completed in 1880, and Austin Hall, the new law school building, was just beginning construction, so Butler's school years coincided with the construction of two major Richardson buildings. It is easy to see parallels between this house and those buildings. The choice of red brick with stone trim, the great arch around the front door, and the round tower are all elements that echo Richardson. Stevens does insert a couple of his own ideas, notably with the curved walls of the dormers, the doubled square porch posts, and the window seat in the dining room, but overall it is the spirit of old college days that breathes in this house.

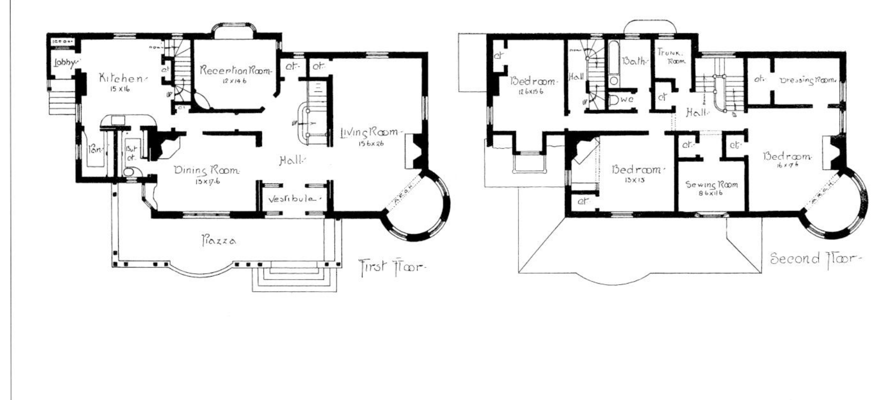

"Edgecomb," Franklin B. and Rosalie Carnes Stephenson Cottage

21 Winslow Homer Road, Prouts Neck

1898–1902, DESTROYED

Most of the coastal Maine summer cottages published in the *Scientific American Building Monthly* were the work of well-known New England architects. "Edgecomb," on Prouts Neck, was the exception, having been built between 1898 and 1902 from designs by the client Rosalie Carnes Stephenson (1855–1920) in collaboration with local contractor Alonzo L. Goggins.

The design of the Stephenson Cottage was dominated by a large gambrel roof, which was pierced by four overscaled, gambrel-roofed dormers, three across the front and one at the side. The gambrel motif was repeated on the attached service wing. The first story featured a generous wraparound porch comprised of a fieldstone base and piers. The entire house was sheathed in dark green shingles.

On the interior a large living room extended across the front of the cottage to take advantage of the ocean view. This spacious room was finished in the period décor of a hardwood floor, a fieldstone fireplace, match-boarded wainscoting, and a beamed ceiling with rough stucco panels. Behind the living room were located the dining room, pantry, and kitchen. The voluminous second floor accommodated five family bedrooms, a bathroom, and a servant's room.

Rosalie Stephenson shared "Edgecomb" with her husband, Dr. Franklin B. Stephenson (1848–1932), and their daughter Catherine. Dr. Stephenson was a career medical officer in the U.S. Navy, retiring with the rank of commander. He is buried in Arlington National Cemetery. In the 1920s Phineas W. Sprague purchased the cottage for his wife's brother, James Shaw. The Shaw family remodeled the house between 1923 and 1925 from designs by Hutchins & French of Boston and renamed it "Clipperways." Always well maintained, the Stephenson Cottage was recently acquired by an owner who demolished it and replaced it with a new summer home.

This is the cottage that was mistakenly published with the plan of the Winslow Homer Cottage. The critic Mariana Griswold Van Rensselaer, describing a cottage by H. H. Richardson, said "its good proportions and the harmonious arrangement of its roof-lines give it

Piazza
Laundry
Kitchen
16x16
Bath
Hall
Butler's Pan
Living Room
24x35
Dining Room
Den
Seat
Piazza
Piazza
Piazza
Piazza
First Floor
Balcony
Bed Room
Hall
Bath
Toilet
Sitting Room
20x30
Bed Room
Bed Room
Bed Room
Bed Room
Bed Room
Closet
Seat
Seat
Seat
Seat

that truly architectural character in which dignity may lie for the most modest building." This house shows what happens when you do not achieve those qualities. The overscaled dormers, which seem to have slid partway off the roof on one side, give way on the other to a timidly underscaled gambrel dormer in the attic, right next to an eyebrow with a truncated window, while the gambrel slope below has a hipped roof dormer and a cut-out access to a balcony the size of a not-yet-invented helipad. The roof offers a little something for everyone except modesty or dignity of design.

The interior landscape of the living room, den, and dining room has two similar fireplaces at right angles to each other. One faces into a space labeled the den, which seems to be a waiting foyer for the dining room. The two sets of stairs are separated on the first floor to keep the servants out of sight, but both stairs arrive at the same spot in the upstairs hall, despite the hall being the size of one of the larger bedrooms. It is of interest that all the bedrooms have connecting doors.

John Calvin Stevens produced some wonderfully scaled, sensitively sited, elegant cottages on Prouts Neck. Mrs. Stephenson's house foreshadows the enlargement of the cottage idea that was replacing the modest seaside cottage with something more on the scale of Newport, as Maine became an ever-more fashionable destination.

George T. Edwards–Charles E. Miller Double House

83–87 Highland Street, Portland

Frederick A. Tompson
Architect

1896, EXTANT

The George T. Edwards–Charles E. Miller House is an example of a popular building type in Portland, the double house. This type of building is actually two houses, usually with mirror-image plans, which abut at the property line between their two lots so as to appear to be a single larger house. From the early nineteenth century well into the twentieth century, these houses were built for Portland residents of all economic levels. Surviving examples range from two-story brick Federal style town houses to small Greek Revival style capes and on to grand Colonial Revival mansions in the Western Promenade neighborhood.

This is an example of the type built for successful middle-class residents like the Edwards and Miller families. George T. Edwards, born 1869, had a varied professional career, working as a clerk for the First National Bank and the Berlin Mills Company and later serving as president of the Williams Manufacturing Company, a woodworking mill, before becoming involved in real estate and development of suburban housing. In addition to his

professional work, he was a noted composer and author, serving as state musical director during World War I and organizing the Centennial Chorus to celebrate the state's one-hundredth anniversary in 1920. The 1900 U.S. Census shows that the Edwards family did not remain in the house long, as another family was in residence by that year. Charles E. Miller, born in 1867, was a traveling salesman for a paint company in 1897 and continued in that business until at least 1915. In 1914 he moved to South Freeport.

It is interesting to note that in the *Scientific American Building Monthly* article, published in December 1896, architect Frederick A. Tompson is credited only with designing the Colonial Revival elevations of the building, working from "plans and suggestions taken from the *Scientific American* by the proprietor." Unfortunately, the text does not identify which published house plan was used as a starting point for this double house. It may or may not have been another Maine house. The plan is similar to that of other published Maine houses, particularly the first floor of John Calvin Stevens' Bates House. Whatever the source, the plan shows that the "living hall" first seen in Shingle Style summer cottages of the 1880s was being used in year-round suburban dwellings by 1896. The cost of the double house, including painting and papering, was $4,500.

While the plan of this house is similar to that of the houses John Calvin Stevens had designed twelve years earlier, the elevations are moving away from references to the cottages and toward Colonial Revival models. The central gable is emphasized by a projecting cornice, and the matching arched windows in the gable are given classical trim complete with keystones. In a backwards nod to the cottage style, only the upper sashes of the gable windows have muntins, while the windows below have no muntins at all. The broad, round bays of the front parlor compensate for the absence of windows on the wall separating the two houses. They have more in common with eighteenth-century Boston bays than with the cottage style. By tucking them under the projection of the upper floor, Tompson avoids having to manage a transition from rounded to linear. The Shingle Style reveled in such transitions. The wall cladding is now clapboards, not shingles. At this transitional period, it was not uncommon to use clapboards without corner boards, imitating the "cottage corners" of laced shingles. Soon the corner trim of full Colonial Revival thinking would return, especially after the mitered or lapped corners of the clapboards began to rot.

The great sweeping front gables, though, are a nod to the cottage style. The tiny dormer that interrupts the sweep serves the purpose of dividing the snow slides and reducing the impact of avalanches on unwary visitors. Despite the functional problem, the entry gable is more welcoming than the square covered piazzas of Stevens' own house and his Gibson House.

Perez B. Burnham House

199 Western Promenade, Portland

George Burnham
Architect

1902, EXTANT

Built in 1902 on the Western Promenade, the Perez B. Burnham House is prominently sited in Portland's most prestigious residential neighborhood. This elegant three-story brick house is an early twentieth-century interpretation of the city's Federal style mansions of a century before.

The client, Perez Burnham (1835–1913), was a partner in the Burnham & Morrill Company, a major canner and distributor of fish, meat, and vegetables. The architect was Burnham's son George, who received his professional training at the Massachusetts Institute of Technology and practiced briefly in Boston and New York before returning to Portland in 1902, the year his parents decided to build a new home in the West End. Like many families before and since, George and Margaret Burnham provided their son with his first significant commission to launch his career in his native city. George Burnham would continue to practice architecture in Maine until his retirement in 1918 due to illness resulting from his service as an officer in World War I.

The *Scientific American Building Monthly* for July 1904 described the Perez Burnham House as "square in form, built of red brick, laid in Flemish bond, with Indiana limestone trimmings, and the wood work is very well detailed, and is painted white. The design is relieved by the ornamental porch and the balustrade which surrounds the roof." The first floor contains an entry hall and staircase, a drawing room, a library, and a dining room, while the two upper floors are devoted to bedrooms and servants' quarters. The third floor features a billiard room.

While Burnham is clearly trying to emulate the great Federal mansions, he seems to be unaware of the rules of proportions they obeyed. The proportion of window area to wall area is ungenerous, and the windows are too short for their width. The lower windows are divided eight panes over one, which is a cottage style not used in the Federal period, when proportion dictated that the correct pattern for windows was six over six or, if the architect was being lavish, twelve over twelve. The third floor is a riot of non-Federal detailing, even with Gothic arches in the bedroom windows.

The entrance porch is indeed well detailed, but it too suffers from awkward proportions. The fanlight over the door is squeezed down by the low ceiling of

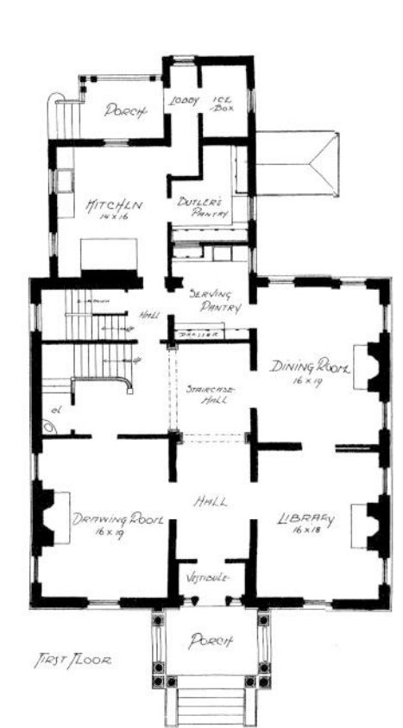

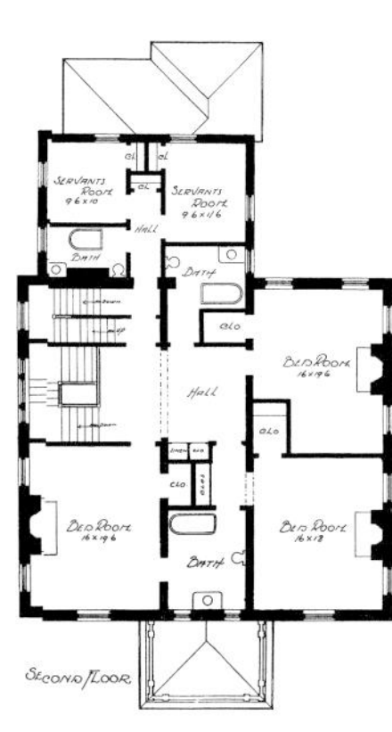

the porch to the point that the tapered bricks at the side of the arch seem to be in pain from the pressure. A similar arch on the stair landing is more comfortable, but seen from outside in the unbroken brick mass, it seems to have slipped from its proper place on the second floor.

The plan is geometric simplicity itself. Four identical spaces, one divided between owner's and servants' stairs, open onto a rectangular hall. Upstairs the plan has to accommodate closets, and it does so by stealing space from one quadrant to serve another.

In his next major commission, Burnham worked with his former schoolmate Guy Lowell on the Cumberland County Courthouse in Portland, and his sense of classical proportion dramatically improved. In later years he would design his family's functionalist bean cannery. But in this early exercise he seemed to be kicking the traces of an uncongenial problem.

"Atlantean," Fred L. Savage

11 Atlantic Avenue,
Bar Harbor

Frederick L. Savage
Architect

1903, EXTANT

Fred L. Savage was Mount Desert Island's home-grown architect of the cottage era. He grew up on the island in Northeast Harbor and developed an interest in building and design at a relatively young age. He was a talented young man in the right place at the right time, as his developing interest coincided with the beginning of tourism on Mount Desert Island. Savage worked as a carpenter on several of the earliest cottages and hotels in Northeast Harbor, where he showed particular facility in wood carving and cabinetmaking. This caught the attention of prominent cottagers such as Harvard president Charles Eliot and led to Savage's relocating to Boston to work as an office boy and draftsman in the architectural firm of Peabody & Stearns in 1885. Savage stayed in Boston for two years before returning to Mount Desert Island to begin his own architectural practice. Training

in an architectural firm without formal training at a school was common at the time. Although he spent a relatively short time in Boston, he had the opportunity to see numerous cottages by America's leading architects being built on Mount Desert Island. He served as local supervising architect during the construction of some of these cottages. With this exposure to the work of other architects, Savage's abilities advanced quickly as he undertook projects for his own family and cottagers from away. Over time, he worked in a variety of styles and on increasingly large commissions.

By 1902, when Savage designed his new home, "Atlantean," in Bar Harbor, he was an experienced architect seeking to demonstrate what he could achieve. With the

symmetrical façade of cut granite on the first story and half timbering and stucco above, sited behind a cut granite block wall in a prominent location on Atlantic Avenue, the house was clearly intended to make a statement about his abilities and his success. If Savage's intent was to appeal to those building ever-more palatial cottages on Mount Desert Island, he succeeded. The following year he designed a 13,500-square-foot cottage for a great-grandson of John Jacob Astor. That much larger house featured the same cut granite first story with Tudor Revival half timbering and stucco above that Savage had used on his own house. Fred Savage continued to be the leading local architect on the island until his death in 1924.

By the time "Atlantean" was published in Scientific American Building Monthly, *Fred Savage has moved beyond his Shingle phase to the Tudor Revival he made a specialty in his later years. While the Tudor Revival style is not known for its symmetry, Savage has designed a perfectly symmetrical façade, with rough granite walls forming a deep entry porch dividing an identical living room and dining room. Above, the two half-timbered gables seem to reach out to keep the central section from falling onto the porch. The straight verticals representing the timber frame are relieved by curved elements that play in counterpoint with the angle of the gables. The design is relentlessly formal and at the same time graceful. From the side, one can see the elegant transition from the front gable roof to the lower-pitched roof between the gables, as an unequal-pitched hip traces their intersection to the main ridge. This is the Stevens trick of hiding a flatter roof between two gables, but Savage lets the joint show, if you know where to look.*

The Gothic and Tudor Revival styles and their companion, the Colonial Revival, were based on finding historical antecedents for each building. In many cases it meant almost literally copying historic buildings, and excellence was judged by the accuracy of the overall design and of its detailing. The freedom and inventiveness of the Shingle cottages was discounted in favor of demonstrated mastery of historic style. Judged by this standard, the island cottages and their informal town-house cousins were seen as naïve attempts to move from the Queen Anne to the more culturally responsible historic styles. Savage was willing to go along, as were most of the architects of his and Stevens' generation.

"Reverie Cove," John Davies Jones House

Harbor Lane,
Bar Harbor

Frederick L. Savage
Architect

1892–93, EXTANT

Dr. and Mrs. John Davies Jones of Washington, D.C., built "Reverie Cove" overlooking the ocean at Bar Harbor between the fall of 1892 and the spring of 1893. The *Chicago Daily Tribune* for July 28, 1895, called the house "the pretty place on the cove." Variously described in period accounts as Italian and Spanish in style, this Classical Revival summer cottage was designed by Fred L. Savage. Local contractor B. W. Candage supervised the construction, and the grounds were planned by landscape gardener Isaac N. Mitchell. The original stucco exterior has given way to shingles.

Savage's interior plan for "Reverie Cove" maximized the use of space in this two-and-a-half-story rectangular house. The first floor features three principal spaces with the living room at the center flanked on either side by a drawing room and a dining room. All three rooms have an ocean view and a fireplace for warmth on foggy days. The living room is actually a living hall, in which a divided staircase, typical of Savage's work, joins at a landing before arriving at the second floor. Three bedrooms line each side of a second floor hall.

Dr. Jones died in 1903, and the following year his widow, May Jones, sold the property to Sarah Hewitt of Ringwood, New Jersey. "Reverie Cove" has been in the family of its present owner since 1962 and is one of the best preserved of Bar Harbor's late nineteenth-century summer cottages.

Savage here continues his penchant for symmetrical facades, even duplicating porches on the front, with one being the entrance porch and the other one the service entrance, complete with half bath. The landscaped drive provides the only clue as to which to use. The house has an Italianate feel from the pure symmetry, the arched windows, heavy cornices with brackets, and the low hipped roof with very low dormers. The shingled curve of the second floor is familiar from the Shingle Style, but here it is upside down compared with its usual use. Perhaps the fact that house was originally stuccoed is the clue: it is another reference to masonry forms such as corbeled cornices or even machicolations.

The absence of a kitchen means that there is a service basement, which seems consistent with the Palladian formality of the building. There is even a pair of Palladian arched windows in the dining room—again with some non-standard muntin patterns that are holdovers from the Queen Anne style.

The grand space of the house is the living room, dominated by a double flying stair that would seem more at home in a hotel lobby than the living room of a summer cottage. A grand arched window based on those in Roman bath vaulting dominates the landing, but only really lights the upstairs hall. A small study with windows low to the floor has taken over the space under the stair. The upstairs is nearly as symmetrically planned as the downstairs. The gem of this floor is the semicircular and grandly named boudoir facing the water. Its balcony looks down onto the terraces descending toward the shore.

Altogether it is a lively house, with inset and projecting balconies breaking up what could have been a stolid box.

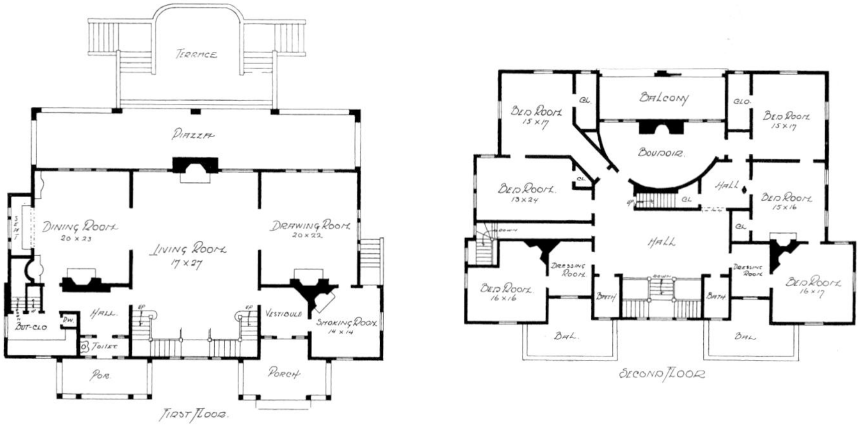

"Back O' Beyond," Catherine Cheyney Bartol Cottage

32 Winslow Homer Road, Prouts Neck

John Calvin Stevens
Architect

1903, EXTANT

When Catherine Cheyney Bartol of Philadelphia commissioned John Calvin Stevens in 1903 to design her summer home at Prouts Neck, the popular Portland architect had been planning cottages at the Scarborough resort for more than two decades. Most of Stevens' work there was in the Shingle Style, but for Mrs. Bartol he provided an English half-timbered design, one of the few instances in his career that he used the style.

John Calvin Stevens achieved a picturesque medieval appearance by creatively employing current building materials and strong Arts and Crafts colors. The first story was sheathed in novelty clapboards that were painted a deep green. The second and half stories were covered with building paper and canvas, upon which were placed planks to form the half- timbered effect. The canvas was painted a deep yellow, the beams a dark green, and the roof shingles a deep red.

The medieval-inspired Arts and Crafts style provides the motif for the interior of "Back O' Beyond." At the center of the first floor is a large hall or living room with an inviting brick fireplace, a beamed ceiling, and a comfortable mixture of Mission and antique furnishings. To one side of the living room is a den, while the dining room and kitchen are found on the other side. Five family bedrooms and bathrooms comprise the second floor, while the servants' quarters and a trunk room were located in the attic. Many original exterior and interior features of the cottage were preserved in a 1980–81 renovation by Portland architect George Terrien.

Catherine Cheyney Bartol was born into an affluent Philadelphia family in 1848. By 1870 she had married Henry W. Bartol, a wealthy Philadelphia merchant. Their marriage, which produced three children, ended in divorce, and Mrs. Bartol spent the balance of her long life living in Pennsylvania, traveling extensively in Europe, and summering on Prouts Neck with family members and fellow Philadelphians.

Stevens seems distinctly uncomfortable in this style. The end gable is almost but not quite even—one side ends slightly higher than the other. That carries around to the downhill side, where that corner becomes a gable that drops down on its right to the front height before being interrupted by a higher gable that is symmetrical. None of the flowing rooflines of the Shingle Style here.

The plan, while competent, does not offer any unusual spaces. Boxy rooms abut mechanically. The whole feels like a design transplanted from the Main Line suburbs of Philadelphia and the designs of Wilson Eyre, but without the enthusiasm for the style that makes Eyre's houses work.

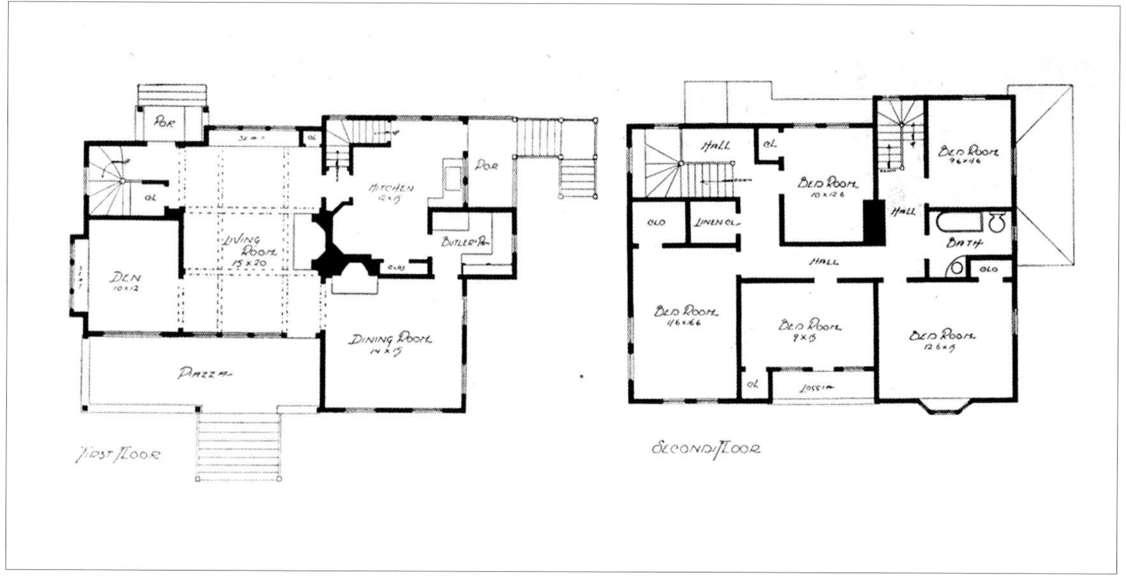

"Birch Nest," Douglass Sherley Cottage

West Street,
Bar Harbor

Douglass Sherley
Architect

1897, DESTROYED

A noted author, journalist, and poet from Kentucky, Douglass Sherley designed and built this distinctive summer cottage for himself in 1897 on Bar Harbor's fashionable West Street. The masonry work was done by Calvin H. Norris and the carpentry by A. E. Lawrence. The structure's rustic stone and log construction was described as "a combination of the New England seacoast and the primitive Kentucky backwoods type." These picturesque motifs were applied to the interior as well, where vernacular wood, brick, and stone features were found in abundance. Furnishings and decoration ranged from the whimsical to the bizarre.

In 1912 Douglass Sherley disassembled "Birch Nest" and paid $20,000 to ship its parts by rail to his family farm near Louisville, Kentucky. There, Sherley reassembled the cottage, siting it next to two farmhouses already on the property. At Sherley's Crest Farm, "Birch Nest" attracted as much attention as it had in Bar Harbor. After nearly a century in its second location, the Maine summer cottage that became a Kentucky farmhouse was torn down.

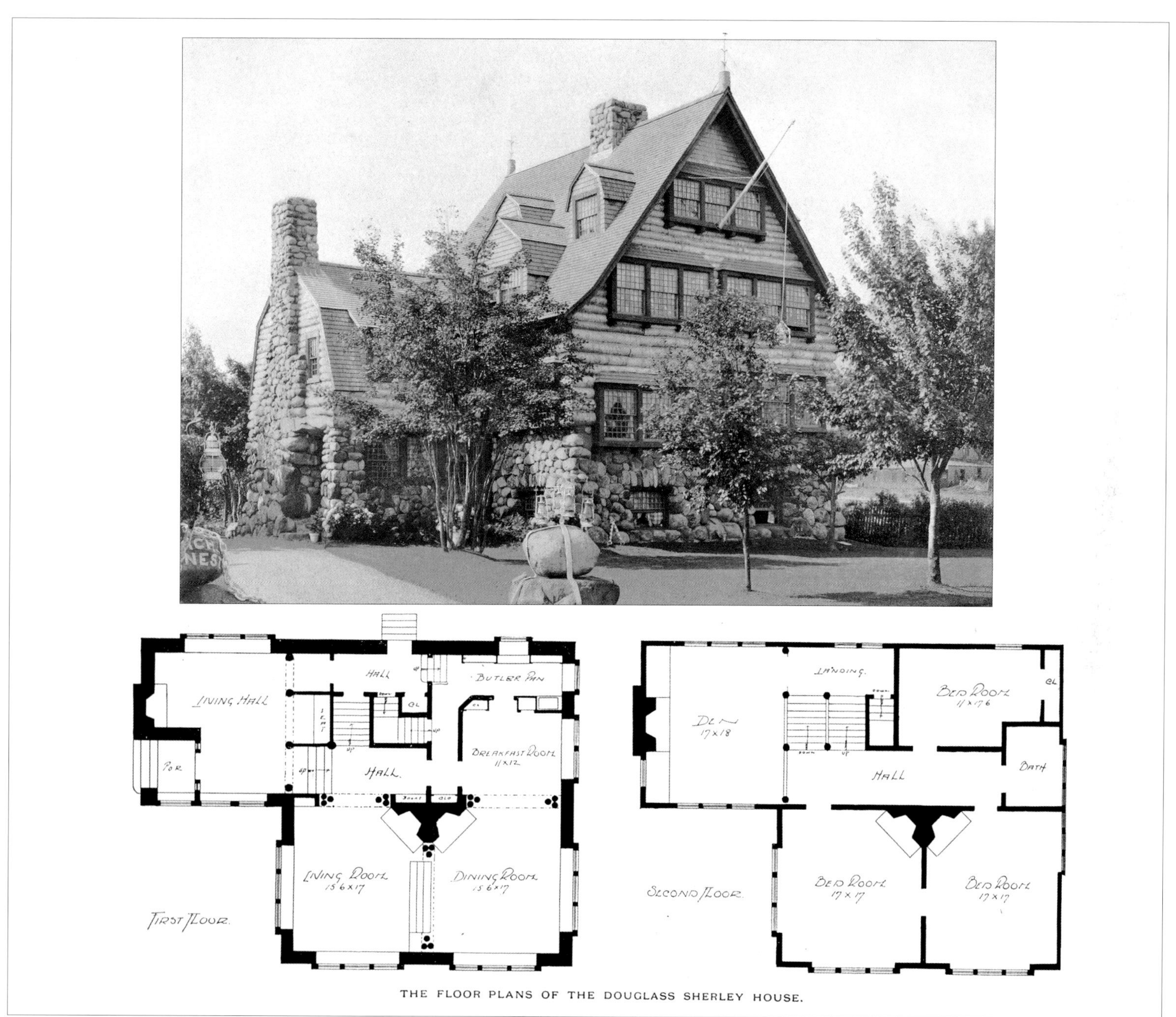

THE FLOOR PLANS OF THE DOUGLASS SHERLEY HOUSE.

Aside from the incredible profusions of rough stone and birch bark logs, the Sherley Cottage has a novel floor plan whose organization would not be seen until much later in the split-level ranch house. The main entrance is through the ell, whose floor is four risers below the main floor. The ambiguity of this low-ceilinged entry space is indicated by the label living hall—as opposed to living room—on the main level. A short flight of steps goes up to the den on the landing level of the stair, after which the stair goes up to the bedroom level and an attic level after that. For all its visual complexity, the house has a clear and workable plan. As for its overall impression, the words eccentric and enthusiastic only begin to describe it.

David Davis Walker Cottage

Walker's Point, Kennebunkport

Chapman & Frazer Architects

1902–03, DESTROYED

David Davis Walker (1840–1918), a successful St. Louis, Missouri, dry goods merchant, built his summer cottage adjacent to that of his son, George Herbert Walker, on land his son purchased from the Sea Shore Company in 1902. Like his son, he hired the Boston architectural firm of Chapman & Frazer to design a large cottage for the rocky site. The architectural firm was established about 1892 by Horace Frazer and J. H. Chapman and did extensive residential work in the Boston suburbs. In Brookline alone, the firm designed at least sixty-seven houses between 1890 and 1916, including the home of partner Horace Frazer (1862–1931). These houses ranged from mid-sized homes for middle-class professionals to large estates for wealthy clients.

Frazer graduated from the Sheffield Scientific School at Yale before studying architecture at MIT. He worked as a draftsman for Cabot & Chandler before moving on to Peabody & Stearns and then Longfellow, Alden & Harlow. He worked independently for a year before establishing a partnership with John H. Chapman (1848–1895). Chapman had also studied at the Sheffield Scientific School at Yale as well as the Royal Academy at Stuttgart, Germany, before training in the architectural office of Ware & Van Brunt about 1880. By 1883 he was working independently as an architect in Boston. Chapman died only three years after the establishment of the firm with Frazer, but his name was retained. The Walker cottage was built by William Keller, a West Newton, Massachusetts, contractor, and cost $25,000.

Like the plan used for George Herbert Walker's "Rock Ledge" cottage, the architects created a large main block with a wing that extended from the main block at an angle. Unlike the rather modest wooden entry porch opening directly into the living room of the G. H. Walker Cottage, D. D. Walker's cottage had a projecting

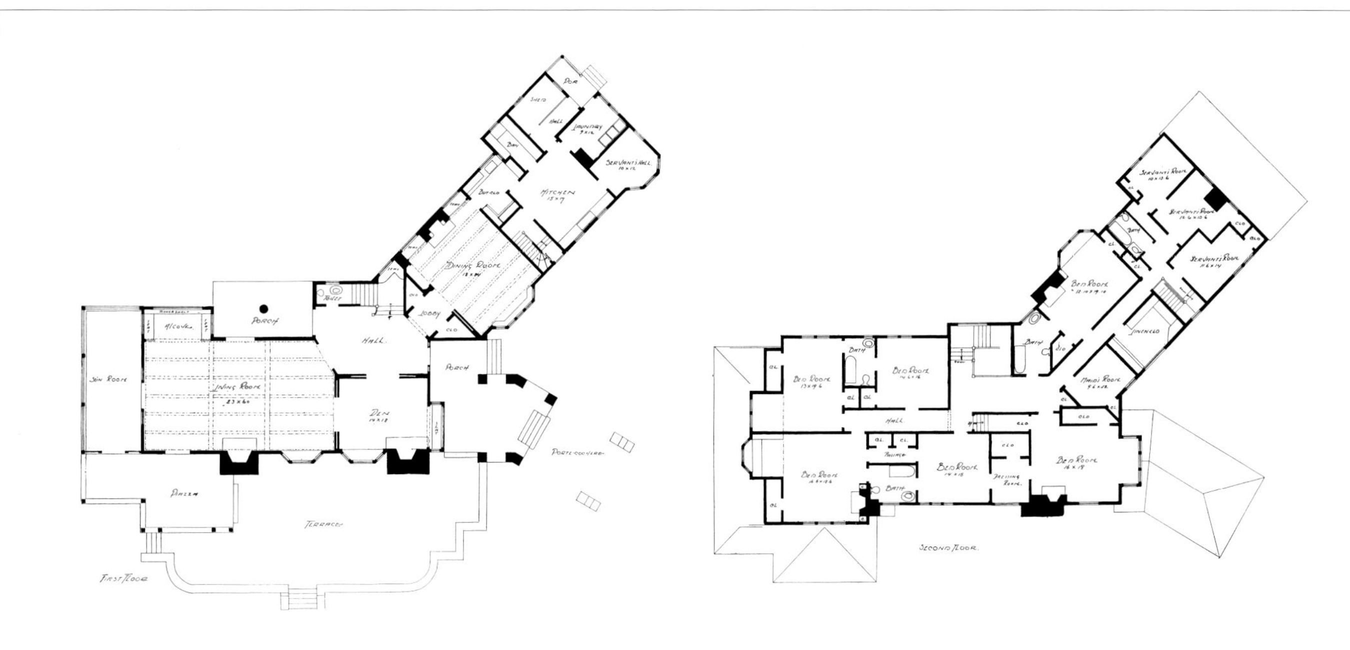
Laundry
9 x 12
Servant's Hall
10 x 12
Kitchen
15 x 17
Dining Room
18 x 24
Porch
Alcove
Toilet
Hall
Lobby
Sun Room
Living Room
23 x 60
Den
14 x 18
Porch
Porte-cochere
Piazza
Terrace
First Floor
Servants Room
10 x 13 6
Servants Room
12 6 x 13 6
Servants Room
11 6 x 14
Bath
Bed Room
Linen Clo
Maids Room
9 6 x 12
Bed Room
13 x 19 6
Bed Room
14 6 x 16
Hall
Bed Room
Bed Room
14 x 18
Dressing Room
Bed Room
16 x 18
Second Floor

port-cochère supported on rough stone piers opening into a sizable entrance hall. Rough stone from the site was also used for the chimneys and large open terrace that faced out to sea. The first floor contained a large living room, a den, dining room, kitchen, and service areas. An enclosed sunroom opened off one end of the living room. The second floor contained multiple bedrooms for family, several bathrooms, and rooms for servants. The interior was done in the Colonial Revival style. While the cottage had the rambling form and varied roof forms typical of the Shingle Style, its exterior was clad in concrete applied in three coats over wire lath. The voluminous roofs were clad in wood shingles.

In addition to being published in *Scientific American Building Monthly* in March 1905, the D. D. Walker Cottage was illustrated in *Concrete Country Residences*, published in 1906 by the Atlas Portland Cement Company, and in the company's advertisements for several years. It appeared in the *Architectural Review* in 1904 and in an article on exterior plaster as a substitute for wood in the February 1906 issue of the same magazine.

The D. D. Walker Cottage was demolished in the 1960s, leaving the G. H. Walker Cottage alone on the point now commonly known as Walker's Point. That cottage is perhaps the best-known Maine summer cottage today due to its associations with Walker's grandson, President George Herbert Walker Bush, and great-grandson, President George Walker Bush.

This was among the last houses published under the Scientific American Building Monthly *aegis, in March 1905. In July of that year the magazine changed its name and format. By this time the magazine's focus had narrowed from a broad array of houses small and large to a preoccupation with the more elaborate and expensive end of the spectrum, and this is a case is point. More like an inn than a family house, the plan separates the living areas from the dining wing with its kitchen, and upstairs the family bedrooms are separated from the servants' rooms above the kitchen.*

"Rock Ledge," George Herbert Walker Cottage

Walker's Point, Kennebunkport

Chapman & Frazer
Architects

1903, EXTANT

George Herbert Walker (1875–1953) was the son of a St. Louis, Missouri, dry goods merchant. He became involved in banking, starting the banking and investment firm G. H. Walker & Co. in 1900. After 1920 he was involved in numerous corporations controlled by financier W. Averill Harriman. At various times he was president and a director of W. A. Harriman & Company and served as a director of Harriman Fifteen, American International Corporation, Georgian Manganese Corporation, Barnsdall Corporation, American Ship and Commerce Corporation, Union Banking Corporation, G. H. Walker & Co., Missouri Pacific Railroad, Laclede Gas, and the New Orleans, Texas, and Mexico Railroad. His interest in golf led to involvement with the United States Golf Association, where he served as president. The USGA Walker Cup tournament is named in his honor.

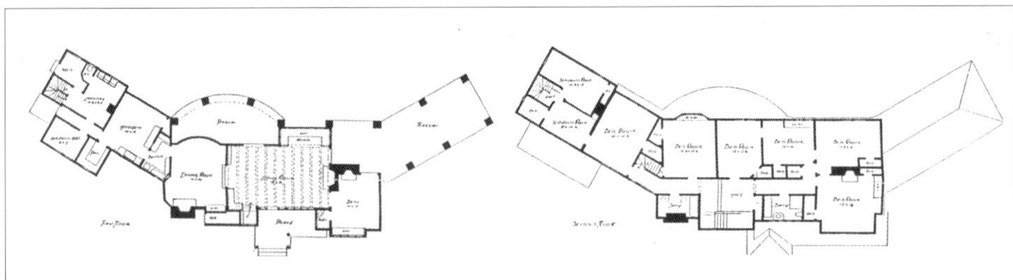

In August 1902, Walker purchased Damon's Point, now Walker's Point, in Kennebunkport from the Sea Shore Company, which had been formed to develop a summer cottage colony at Cape Arundel. He hired the Boston architectural firm of Chapman & Frazer to design his cottage for the rocky site. The firm was also designing the adjacent cottage for his father, D. D. Walker.

The plan used for Walker's "Rock Ledge" cottage created a sheltered entrance front with a modest porch tucked between and below projecting gabled dormers connected by a shed dormer on the second story. This same arrangement of elements was used by the firm for the entrance front of the suburban Randolph F. Tucker House in Chestnut Hill, Massachusetts, circa 1905, and for "Burleigh Brae," a summer cottage for Edwin Webster in Holderness, New Hampshire, 1910–11. The Tucker House was in the Tudor Revival Style, while "Burleigh Brae" shared the Walker Cottage's combination of Shingle and Craftsman styles on the exterior. "Burleigh Brae" also used nearly the same floor plan as the G. H. Walker Cottage, with large, open rooms for the family opening to extensive covered and open exterior terraces and a service wing angled off to one side. The second floors contained multiple bedrooms for family, several bathrooms, and rooms for servants. The Walker Cottage interior was finished in a combination of Craftsman and Colonial Revival motifs. In addition to being published in *American Homes and Gardens* in July 1905, the Walker Cottage was illustrated in advertisements for Cabot Shingle Stains for several years and appeared in an article in the magazine *American Suburbs* in February 1912.

The house has seen numerous changes, including the loss of its service wing and construction of a lower addition in its place, the enclosure of the covered piazza, and the relocation of the entry porch. The most significant change to the site was the demolition of the D. D. Walker Cottage in the 1960s, leaving this cottage standing alone. Several modern service buildings have since been built. The site of the demolished cottage is now occupied by a swimming pool. The surviving Walker Cottage has been severely battered by storms several times in its history, but has always been repaired and continues to serve the descendants of George Herbert Walker.

This house for D. D Walker's son is slightly more modest in scale than the father's cottage from the same architect. It is basically only one room deep, so all the main downstairs rooms are open on both sides to the sea that nearly surrounds the house. The most interesting touch on the exterior is the arched roof between the bedroom gables—a whimsical note that breaks an otherwise fairly restrained exterior.

CHAPTER 5

The End of *Scientific American*

A Mix of Styles in Maine

In the June 1905 edition, the editors of *Scientific American Building Monthly* informed readers that the next issue would be different. It would be called *American Homes and Gardens*, and they promised it would be

> ... a new magazine, new in name, new in size, new in spirit and in form. It will, in short, be a new magazine, published under the same auspices that, for many years, have made the *SCIENTIFIC AMERICAN BUILDING MONTHLY* the leading architectural journal of America, and to which will be brought the experience and knowledge of more than a half century of continuous effort.
>
> . . . Its program will be constructive, not destructive. It will look onward and upward, touching on the past only so far as it is necessary to illustrate the present and the future. This is a definite program, in which we bespeak the cooperation of the many friends who have stood with us in the past, and the many more we hope to win and gain in the future. There is room, and ample room, for a richly illustrated monthly magazine which will treat of the Home from the initial point of architecture. The house is the great essential element of the home life. One needs a house as one needs clothes. Civilization is as impossible without the one as without the other. And from the house proceeds every other form of activity concerned with the home life. The open fields and shady woods, the delights of country sports and occupations, the fascination of the open, all contribute to the charm of outdoor life, but the modern house, with its high development of scientific and artistic equipment makes this life both possible and practical.

What they do not promise is a broad range of house types. The early issues of the magazine had promised "a variety of the latest and best plans for private residences, city and country, including those of a very moderate cost as well as the more expensive." They published plans as well as technical articles on building components intended to be of interest to, yes, architects and builders. By 1905 the renamed *Building Monthly* had realized that its most important readers were the clients, not the builders, and they redesigned the magazine to be "at once of architecture and of the home; and it will be of value and of interest to every one [*sic*] who has a home, to those who hope to have one, to those who wish to improve their homes and make them more attractive, and to those who appreciate the harmony that should exist between the house and its garden."

The descriptive articles would be expanded from the short paragraph of outline specifications to the kind of chatty guided tour of the house that has come to be expected in writings about houses, with comments about the relation to the landscape and the appropriateness of the furnishings. In short, the editors decided, as they would say today, to move "up-market." They would encourage those who "hope to have a home" as well as homeowners to aim for improvements by offering glimpses of how the wealthy did things. The concept seems very familiar.

What is not known is what *Scientific American* thought of this whole adventure. Its magazine shows nothing that month about the end of its daughter publication. The new magazine says it is published by Munn & Company's "Scientific American Office," but by the end of the run in 1915, all reference is gone.

It is tempting to believe that the changed focus of the *Building Monthly* was no longer what had interested *Scientific American* in the joint venture in the first place, which seemed to have been the application of critical and, yes, scientific thinking to the problem of housing the expanding nation. Its cover showing the U.S. Capitol Building hints at its ambition, just as the last cover, with a picture of a large summer house, shows the focus of the new enterprise.

Examples and advice for those of modest means and ambitions would be supplied by the *Craftsman*, a magazine begun in 1901; by precut house suppliers such as the Aladdin Company, founded in 1906; and of course by the Sears catalog, *Sears Modern Homes*, founded in 1909. These publications, in turn, would champion the suburban houses of the mid-century and manufactured or modular housing in later years.

"Fouracre," Alexander J. Cassatt Cottage

Eden Street, Bar Harbor

Chapman & Frazer
Architects

1902–03, DESTROYED

"Neither a palace nor a mansion, but a really fine type of the seaside cottage," was how the July 1910 issue of *American Homes and Gardens* described "Fouracre," Alexander J. Cassatt's sprawling Bar Harbor summer home. A man of the post–Civil War Gilded Age, Cassatt devoted his career to managing major railroads, becoming the president of the Pennsylvania Railroad in 1899. Three years later he broke ground for a "great rambling summer home" measuring 150 feet long and standing two and a half stories high. Inspired by medieval vernacular architecture, Chapman & Frazer designed a house with a brick first story covered in layers of stucco and plaster. The upper stories were of frame construction sheathed in dark stained shingles. The restrained design that characterized the exterior was carried to the interior as well, where the decoration and furnishings were thoroughly Craftsman in style. Such major spaces as the hall, the living room, and the den were elegantly fitted out with Mission and wicker chairs, settees, and tables complemented by period wall coverings and paneling.

The gardener's cottage.

Constructed between the fall of 1902 and the spring of 1903 under the supervision of architect Fred Savage, "Fouracre" served as Alexander Cassatt's Maine vacation retreat for only four seasons, for he died on December 28, 1906. The house was purchased in 1925 by the Philadelphia banker E. T. Stotesbury, who transformed it into "Wingwood House," an immense Neo-Federal style mansion that featured lavishly decorated and furnished period rooms. After the deaths of Stotesbury and his wife in the 1940s, "Wingwood House" was torn down in 1953–54 to make way for the Bluenose Ferry Terminal.

The writer started his description of this cottage with the following: "It is a vast and comfortable dwelling, built, apparently, with a most delightful disregard of the economy often entailed by cost and space, built in a truly rambling way, room added to room, corridor added to corridor, spreading out, if not in every direction, at least in so delightfully extended a way as to seem almost as endless in extent as it is actually boundless in sufficiency and convenience."

He then spends several pages wrestling with how a house on this principle can be reconciled with the frugality of the Maine coastal economy: "Of course it is large, but that is because it was intended to be big; but with all its size no part departs from the true 'cottage' type. In a period when the large seashore house is apt to violate every traditional thought in connection with houses so located, it is something to have a house that so finely illustrates the simple type of architecture, particularly when it does so on extended a scale." This house aptly demonstrates the ironic use of the term cottage.

The publishers gave up on printing floor plans, choosing instead to add a nice generic pen drawing of the seaside. They also added a photograph of the gardener's cottage, whose curved rooflines echo those on the service wings of the main house and which, in a simpler age, might have been the only structure needed.

"Pine Haven," Thomas B. Van Buren Cottage

Kennebunkport

Clark & Russell
Architects

1902, Extant

Thomas B. Van Buren (1866–1915) was a New York City silk merchant who began his career in the silk importing business in Boston after graduating from Yale in 1886. Van Buren's wife, Florence, whom he married in 1889, purchased lot 49 from the Sea Shore Company in Kennebunkport in September 1901. In November of that year, *New England Master Builder* reported that the contract to build a two-and-a-half-story frame residence on the lot had been awarded to Porter & Burnham, Portland contractors. The cottage would include gas and electric lighting and cost $10,000. The architects were Clark & Russell of Boston.

Boston architect Henry Paston Clark was raised on Boston's Beacon Hill but had deep family roots in the Kennebunkport area and was well established as an architect in the community by the time the Van Buren Cottage was designed. In 1899 he formed a partnership with John H. Russell, who had come to work for him as a draftsman in 1883. As a draftsman in his office, it is likely that Russell was familiar with all of Clark's earlier work in the Kennebunkport area, and it is unlikely that his becoming a partner had any significant effect on the designs produced by the firm.

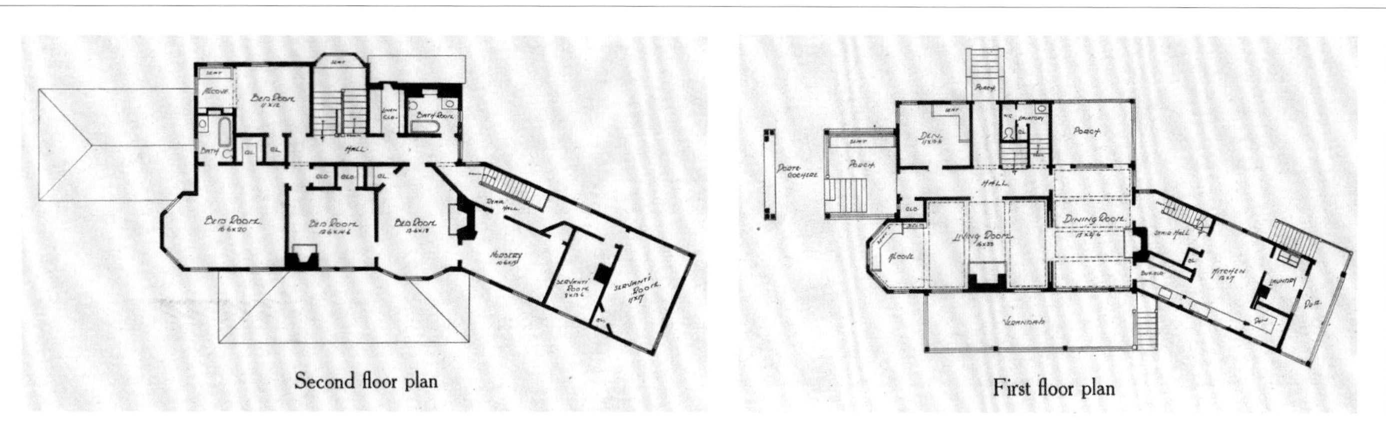

Second floor plan

First floor plan

The plan for Pine Haven places the entrance at one end with a lengthwise corridor extending through the main block, allowing the ocean-facing frontage to be entirely occupied by the living room and dining room. The den and staircase are located on the other side of the corridor, looking toward the wooded side of the site. Porches face in both directions, with the larger porch opening off the principal rooms overlooking the ocean. As is typical of larger Shingle Style cottages, a service wing extends off the main block at an angle. The interiors were done primarily in the Colonial Revival style, with an interesting white painted, carved "colonial" mantel surrounding a fireplace built of large rough fieldstone in the living room.

Here the magazine has to cope with the same issues presented by the Cassatt and Walker houses—how to reconcile vast scale with the Maine environment. This is what they have to say:

> *The charm of this house is its simplicity and its unpretentiousness. In no sense of the word is it a 'show' place, nor can it, on the other hand, be offered as an example of economy in building it. It is, in short, a good, comfortable, summer home, a dwelling of ample size, admirably suited to the demands made upon it by the owner and his family, skilfully designed, and exceedingly attractive in many ways. A house, be its cost of the utmost, could hardly do more than this, could scarce be more serviceable nor more useful.*

Clark & Russell are using the same playbook as Chapman & Frazer: cottage windows and shingles mixed with Tudor diamond panes and barge boards. The house seems less sprawling than that of Cassatt, and its detailing more consistent with local traditions. Granted the market for summer estates of this scale, the Van Buren Cottage seems to do its best to fit in—except for those Tudor touches.

Eben C. Stanwood Cottage

Kennebunkport

Chapman & Frazer
Architects

1900, EXTANT

Eben Caldwell Stanwood (1856–1906) was born in Boston to parents who were both natives of Maine, his father having been born in Augusta and his mother in Alna. His father, also Eben C. Stanwood, became a successful wholesale grocer in Boston and was also involved in sugar refining before dying at age 43 in 1866. He apparently left his widow and children in secure circumstances, as Mrs. Stanwood continued to live at 66 Chester Square in the fashionable South End and reported an estate of $50,000 for the 1870 census. Eben C. Stanwood II attended the English High School where he was a colonel in the school regiment, graduating in 1874. He started his business career as a clerk for James L. Little & Co., dry goods commission merchants, before becoming involved in banking. He established the banking firm of E. C. Stanwood & Co. in 1895 with partner George S. Stockwell. Stanwood married Annie Wincher of Quincy, Massachusetts, in 1879, and the

couple had two daughters. From 1902, they resided at 480 Commonwealth Avenue, Boston. Stanwood died while vacationing with his family on the Isle of Wight, Hampshire, England, in August 1906. His wife and a daughter later had a cottage at York Harbor, Maine, and continued to live at the Commonwealth Avenue house until Mrs. Stanwood's death in 1942.

Stanwood purchased lots 59 and 60 from the Sea Shore Company in September 1899. By late October of the same year, the *Industrial Journal* reported that the W. H. Glover Company of Rockland had the contract to build the Chapman & Frazer–designed cottage for $15,000. A month later the *Journal* reported the cost to be $10,000. The Stanwood Cottage has much in common with other houses and cottages by Chapman & Frazer at Kennebunkport and elsewhere. The entrance façade, with two projecting gabled bays flanking a low entrance porch, would reappear nearby on the G. H. Walker Cottage two years later and at "Burleigh Brae." The interior plan features a large entry hall with an adjoining stair hall that does not quite qualify as a living hall, lacking the requisite fireplace and inglenook. The living room and dining room flank the hall on the ocean side of the house. The den, lavatory, and service spaces occupy the remainder of the main block toward the driveway. A service

wing extends from the house at an angle in the usual way, to minimize its impact on the views from the main house. Two covered porches and an open terrace face onto the water views. The interior is done in a combination of styles including Colonial Revival and Gothic/Tudor Revival. The exterior was clad in wood shingles left to weather naturally, and the roof in shingles stained a dull green.

The cottage was published in *American Homes and Gardens* twice, first in April 1910 and again in June of the following year, when it received an expanded treatment with additional photographs.

A close cousin of the George Walker Cottage, the other Chapman & Frazer house nearby, this effort has the strange distinction of being published twice in close succession. The second time, in June 1911, there is no mention of its having been published as recently as April of the preceding year. The photographs are different but not more lavish, and the text is by the same author and covers much the same ground. It might even be that the author

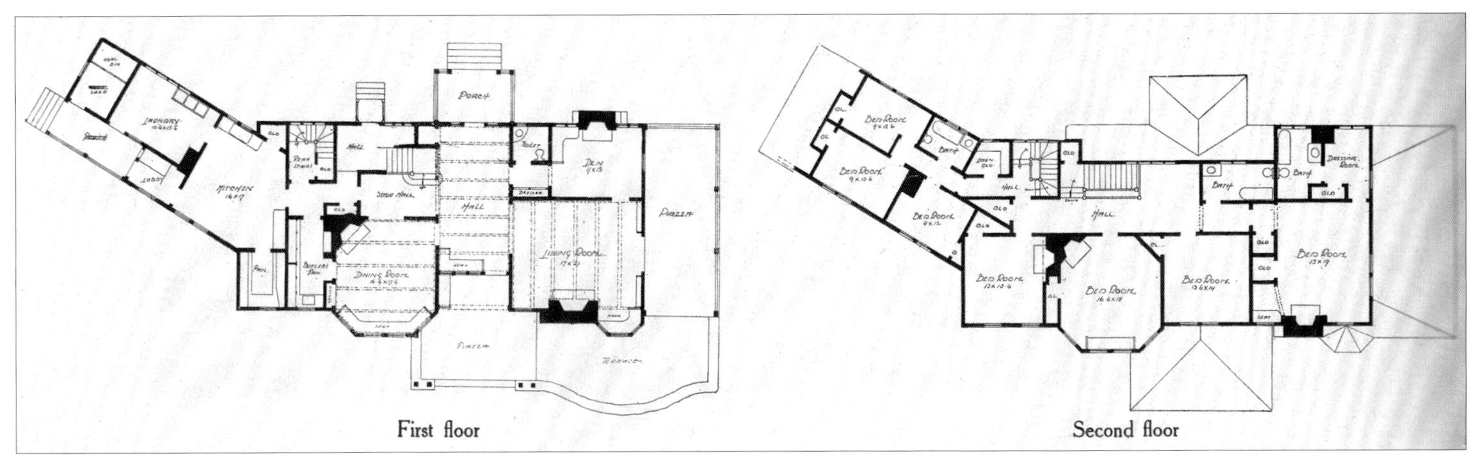

First floor

Second floor

submitted the new text and different photos to see if he could get away with a second try. If so, it would seem he succeeded. He does in the later article address the landscaping around the house, saying, "The grounds about the estate are naturlesque, and have been left in their primitive manner, and are in keeping with the ruggedness with which the Maine coast abounds."

The house itself has the same virtues of natural shingles and cottage windows as the George Walker Cottage, and the same vices of diamond panes and Tudor bargeboards. The wide hall running through the house to the piazza and terrace is nice, especially the way it opens to the living and dining room partway along, giving a hint of the expansive sea view to be revealed. Upstairs, the wide stair hall and the octagonal bedroom provide generous spatial experiences.

The origins of the Shingle Style have been traced to Boston architect H. H. Richardson and the country cottages he designed in the 1880s. His biographer, Mariana Griswold Van Rensselaer, described one of them by saying, "Its foundations follow with delightful frankness the variations of the ground upon which it stands, while its good proportions and the harmonious arrangement of its roof-lines give it that truly architectural character in which dignity may lie for the most modest building. It is so appropriate to its surroundings that it seems to have grown out of them by some process of nature, and it is equally appropriate to its purpose. It explains itself at once as a gentleman's summer home, but with a simplicity which does not put the humblest village neighbor out of countenance." Somewhere along the way, Shingle houses had outgrown their original simplicity, and the concept of a "naturlesque" landscape treatment seems almost a parody of Van Rensselaer's comments regarding growth "by some process of nature." Here the landscape is encouraged to follow the house rather than the other way around.

Russell W. Porter Chalet

Port Clyde, Maine

Russell W. Porter
Architect

C. 1910, EXTANT

Russell W. Porter (1871–1949) was born in Vermont and studied architecture and art at the Massachusetts Institute of Technology before embarking on a widely varied career as a polar explorer, artist colony developer, and noted optical engineer and amateur astronomer. Following his years of arctic exploration, he purchased fifty acres of land from fisherman Alfred Marshall on Marshall Point in Port Clyde, Maine, in 1906. He renamed the property "Land's End" and undertook to develop an artists' colony there. His development plan for the colony survives at the nearby Marshall Point Lighthouse Museum. The artists' colony failed to materialize, but Porter built fourteen cottages on the lots he had laid out and rented them seasonally, eventually selling all of them to summer residents. Porter married Alfred Marshall's daughter, Alice, and in 1911 he constructed an observatory at Land's End. Astronomical observation had been among his duties in the arctic, and the making of optical telescopes became a major focus of his interests after 1911. This interest eventually led the Porters to leave Port Clyde so that he could pursue his interests and education. By the time of his death in 1949, Dr. Porter was famous for his work in the field of optics and telescopes.

In writing about the chalet-style cottage in *American Homes and Gardens*, Porter (misidentified with the middle initial *F*) creates a fanciful story of an "artist builder" (himself) addressing the needs of a client who may have been merely a literary device, since it is known that Porter built the cottages at Land's End as summer rentals. As built, the chalet was compact in plan, with only a living room, kitchen, and bedroom on the first floor and a single bedroom above. Within this small space, he manipulated the floor levels and materials, creating a greater sense of space. He also managed to incorporate an inglenook at the fireplace, an expected architectural feature in a summer cottage of the period. Although the dark stained shingles and natural cedar bark of the original exterior have been replaced with a colorful paint scheme, and the building has been added to and altered over time, the cottage illustrated in *American Homes and Gardens* in March 1912 is clearly recognizable today.

Porter was later a frequent contributor to *Popular Astronomy* and *Scientific American* on the subjects of astronomy and telescopes. In 1915 he returned to MIT as professor of architecture, where he remained for four years. He returned to Vermont in 1919 to work as an optical engineer. There he was among the founders of Stellafane, an annual gathering of telescope makers and enthusiasts that continues to this day. Porter moved to Pasadena, California, in 1929 to work as an associate in optics and instrument design on the Mt. Palomar Telescope, the world's largest telescope with a 200-inch lens. Porter's work on the telescope continued until its successful completion in 1948, a year before his death.

This little folly was published in 1912 and stands in sharp contrast to the magazine's usual run of large complexes. In May 1907 the newly named magazine had republished on facing pages a couple of Stevens' small cottages, the Murray cottage "Bird's Nest," originally published in 1904, and the third Ottawa cottage, published in 1896. The last even reused the decorative borders and sketches of the original. The article limits its verdict to saying that the "Bird's Nest" is "a remarkable illustration of economic building."

The chalet probably appealed to the editors in the same way, and they surely enjoyed Porter's self-deprecating description with its fantasy of the "summer pilgrim." Porter sums up its appeal by saying:

"Here the weary city worker sleeps the clock around and absorbs the heavy balsam odors against another year of toil among the cliff dwellers. Here he looks over the tumble of ledges with its natural bath tub, looks out across the Atlantic Ocean, with nothing between him and Spain but the heaving deep. The outlook is hardly that of a Swiss chalet, hardly suggestive, perhaps, of anything approaching Alpine scenery by reason of the sea taking the place of mountains, but the cottage itself seems remarkably at home in its surroundings."

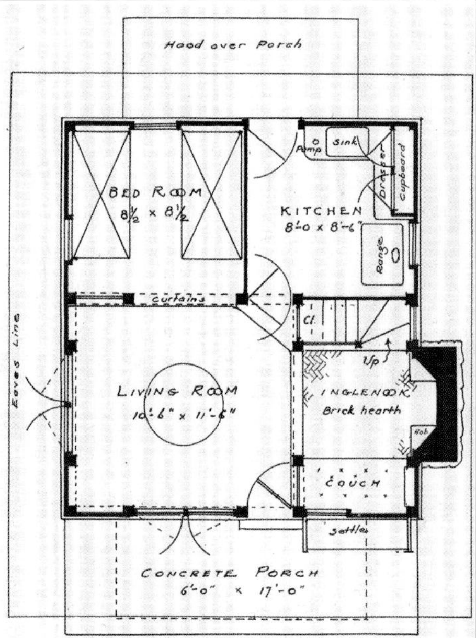

"The Bunk," Henry Paston Clark Cottage

Kennebunkport

Henry Paston Clark
Architect

1885, EXTANT

Boston architect Henry Paston Clark (1853–1927) was the son of a prominent Boston doctor who was a native of Kennebunkport. Clark had an interest in his family's history, and according to historian Kevin Murphy, his "ancestry was central to his identity and inspired his strong affinity for the colonial revival." Clark studied architecture at MIT from 1870 to 1871 and then worked as a draftsman at 18 Pemberton Square, where several architects had offices. It is not clear which architect he worked for. In 1874 he moved to Paris and continued his studies there. By 1878 he was back in the United States, designing a hotel in Kennebunkport.

Clark's interest in his family's history coincided with a developing interest in America's historic buildings by a number of architects in the late 1870s. Architects such as William E. Barry and Arthur Little began publishing sketches of old New England houses, usually from

the seventeenth or early eighteenth century. Often these were shingled buildings that had been added to over the years and had suffered long neglect, giving the buildings a picturesque character with their gambrel, saltbox, and lean-to forms appearing to be thrown together without any plan. These published sketches were the beginning of the colonial revival in architecture, leading first to the Shingle Style that became popular in the 1880s. Eventually interest would shift to the more formal Georgian and Federal style buildings of the late eighteenth and early nineteenth centuries, leading to a more formal Colonial Revival style in the early twentieth century.

In 1882 Henry Paston Clark purchased a lot with frontage on the Kennebunk River for $125, and in 1885 he constructed a rustic shingled building on his lot. As built, the first floor was given over to the storage of a thirty-foot rowing scull, with primitive accommodations for "camping out" in the attic. Setting the little building apart from a typical vernacular outbuilding was a cleanly cut recessed entry porch at one corner, a modern feature for the time. The building came to be called "The Bunk." The first additions to the building were completed in the spring of 1890, perhaps as a result of Clark's marriage in 1888. The attic space may not have suited the young bride as well as it had the bachelor architect. Further additions were made in 1905, resulting in a rambling building with a gambrel-roofed section, lean-tos, and dormers. It was similar in character to the seventeenth-century New England houses admired by the architects of the 1870s. Its plan, however, was not of the seventeenth century, featuring large open spaces that flowed together and a large porch and sleeping balcony overlooking the river. An interesting detail of the interior was the use of stair balusters that had been salvaged from a Federal style mansion that was being demolished. Salvaged historic house parts were used by some Colonial Revival architects to introduce "authentic" character into their new buildings.

"The Bunk" was the last Maine cottage to be published by American Homes and Gardens, *in September 1911, three months after the second appearance of the Stanwood Cottage. The contrast could not have been greater. Stanwood was typical of the palatial estates the magazine had been running. "The Bunk" harked back to the first issues of the magazine, especially to the little exercise for Margaret Deland that architect Henry Paston Clark had designed around 1890. It evoked the same kind of ironic nostalgia that the chalet's author had displayed. What was particularly evocative was that Clark himself wrote the accompanying article. "The Bunk" was his own summer place, an unpretentious riverside camp derided by the locals and summer people alike.*

Clark had gone on to a successful practice, with masterful versions of the prevailing styles and building programs of his time. He had begun with the romantic stone castle for his father, had helped define the cottage style with the Manning Cottage and foreshadowed Tudor in the Thompson Cottage. The house for Dr. Harrington was an assured exercise in the double-gambreled shingle style, and his own palatial exercise of the Van Buren Cottage was right up there with the Walkers or with Stanwood in luxurious rustication. The Van Buren dining room even had a rough fieldstone fireplace surrounded with classical brackets supporting a dentiled mantel. This was the context is which he submitted his description of "The Bunk" and linked it to the appeal of the Maine Coast, with its history stretching back to the shipbuilding days and from there to the Native Americans, but most of all its natural beauties.

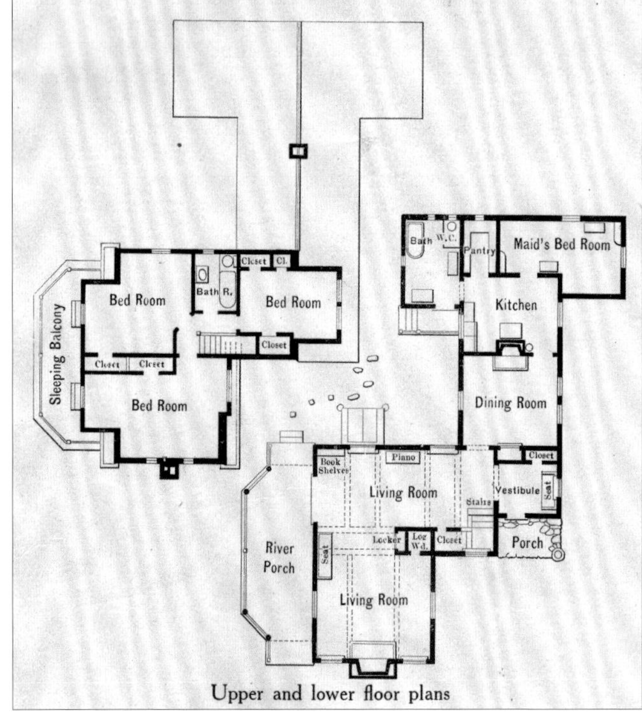

Upper and lower floor plans

His essay is in effect a summary of the whole enterprise of the development of the Maine Coast as a summer destination, the process illustrated by the articles in the variously named magazine. The early response to the environment, as defined by Frederick Law Olmsted, had set the goal of building houses that grew out of the landscape and used shingles and the local fieldstone, "without paint or gingerbread work," and above all did not seek to impress by conspicuous display. This impulse had been translated into cottages using gambrels and broad gables instead of profusions of ornamental detail, not only on the coast itself but in the new residential neighborhoods of the cities, in the hands of architects like John Calvin Stevens. This new style claimed descent not only from nature but from the ideals of the

founding fathers of the nation, and was thus politically and morally a rebuke to the follies of the Gilded Age.

Even as these houses attracted the wealthy and grew to proportions undreamed of in colonial days, there was still the claim of simplicity in their use of materials and their informal siting among the "naturalesque" features of the landscape. The coming generation would reject this simplicity in favor of accurate reproduction of European models, and it would require a new revolution to recover an architecture that would claim its origin in nature rather than culture.

Here, then, by way of conclusion, is William Paston Clark's description of "The Bunk":

"The Bunk," Kennebunkport, Maine

By W. H. P. Clark

THE "Bunk," built for the needs and comforts of bachelor days and ways, by gradual shifting of partitions and by additions has grown into a cottage.

It was first built for the housing of boats and as a place for "bunking." It is placed on the Kennebunk River bank, where the channel runs near it, and where there is a small cove for the mooring of sailboats. The bank is edged with willows and wild roses.

When the Bunk was first built it was looked upon with frank contempt by the natives; it was "too low to the ground," the front faced the river instead of the river "road," and it was shingled like their barns. The water-supply was from the roof, with gin-pipes painted white for storage.

The original Bunk had on the ground floor a large room. On the end toward the street was an entrance-porch which was half the width of the building, and a "galley" with bunkers along one side, a stove, and a "hurricane." The length of the building was fixed by the length of a shell which was hung from the ceiling and which obtruded its nose into the galley, being some thirty odd feet long. On the river end of the building was a veranda and a bridge to a pier on the channel's edge, so that boats could be got off at the lowest tide. The space above the roof consisted of one large room reached by companionway steps fitted with brass step-plates. This was strung with hammocks, not from the "rind of the hammack tree," but of canvas, battens, and clews. The salt air from the near-by ocean, the kerosene of the "hurricane," the tarred clews and the sound of the rote, gave these bunking quarters a genuine flavor of the deep sea.

Turning from the river road now, we approach the Bunk through a rustic gate, almost concealed by wild rose-bushes, and the path spread with white beach gravel is bordered on either side by perennials. Here bachelor's-buttons give their touch of color, there poppies sway in the summer wind, and a fringe of asters yields promise of autumn flowering.

There is something in the very entrance-porch, with its flat stones, cement laid, that suggests hospitality, and one feels certain that the lifting of the brass knocker will bring its welcoming response.

The door opens into a small reception-hall, whose harmony of color immediately attracts; then through a wide opening one enters the living-room, with high windows facing north, and there are glimpses of glowing color from the window-boxes outside. On the left is the stair shown in the photograph. The balusters, some hundred and fifty years old, were taken from the Prescott Mansion at Newcastle, New Hampshire, when it was torn down about twenty years ago. On the wall hangs a quadrant, used in 1835 on the old clipper ship *Rasselas*, Stephen Jarvis master. On the piano is open music, and a violin just laid down, for both the wife and daughter have marked talent, and music is one of the many charms of the Bunk.

Beyond the staircase is a ten-foot opening into the other portion of the living-room, with windows on three sides, and the fireplace at one end, with an old-fashioned settle, and the leathern buckets, dating back to 1825, speak of the owner's New England ancestry. The fireplace is of Philadelphia face brick and the hearth is laid with red unglazed tiles.

This room is paneled with wide, unplaned spruce boards, and the ceiling beams are cased with the same material, and they are stained a warm gray. The ceiling between the beams and in the diamond-shaped panels over the fire-place is plastered with cement plaster with a rough finish. The mantel, window-casings, stair-treads, and floor-boards are of red birch, oiled and waxed. The floor is a much darker gray than the walls. Some of the panels are doors to closets where are kept canoe paddles, tennis racquets, golf clubs, croquet mallets, and the many things that tell of the varied summer life of the family.

Wide double-sash doors open from the living-room on to a covered veranda, one end of which shows in one of the outside views. The roof is supported by rustic posts and, like the trimmings, they are painted ivory white. The rugs, tables, and cushioned chairs make a charming outdoor room where an early caller may find the family at breakfast, and where the dog "Rascal," hesitating between his loyalty to the family and his longing for a morning swim in the river, barks his welcome.

Kaleidoscopic are the pictures that one sees from the veranda at low tide of early morning, when the river is a narrow thread of blue, scarce moving between the dull browns of the flats, where a solitary clamdigger gives the only bit of life, and as the tide comes in new scenes appear from the clubhouse beyond, from the creek which recalls the old Indian massacre, and from the "wading-place" where the Indians had their tents, canoes and launches. For flash of paddles has succeeded the steady stroke of oar, and swift motor-boats churn the water into white foam, but there is still the glimpse of old wharves in the distance and weather-beaten ways that tell of shipbuilding days, when a century ago a granduncle of the owner was collector of the port.

Beyond is the spire of the village church, gleaming white against the flaming colors that flood the sky as the sun loses itself in the water in the place, to which the Indians, moved as we are by its glory, gave some unpronounceable name that means Sunset Cove.

The living-room was refinished last spring. As the old ground floor was a little low-studded, being some inches less than seven feet in the clear, the entire second story was raised so as to get in the beams shown in the photograph, and with a height of eight feet from the bottom of these to the floor. Over this living-room are three bedrooms and a bathroom. In the one-story wing, which is at right angles with the old Bunk and the part described, is the dining room, which finishes up into the roof.

The walls above the dado of painted duck are covered with tapestry paper; opposite the fireplace and mirror shown in the photograph is a china-closet with sash doors having diamond-shaped lights. Here one notices especially a dining-table darkened with passing of time, around which gathered members of the family in days gone by in one of the old historical Lexington houses, and at which Hancock and Adams were frequent guests, and old pewter and china that have been in the family since Revolutionary days.

Beyond is the kitchen, a good-sized pantry, shed-room, maid's bedroom and a bathroom. There is a small cellar under a portion of the living-room. The outside of the building is shingled, the wall shingles are stained a gray-brown color, the roof shingles left to the weather. The outside chimney, which shows in the photograph with a dove-cote, is laid with common bricks with bench headers, flemish bond. The tops of the chimneys are cemented. The sashes are painted white and there are casement windows throughout. The cottage is now lighted by electricity and supplied with town water.

The Bunk has stood a silent sentinel to the passing of the birch-bark canoe, the tholl-pin dories, the "hurricane," the gin-pipes, and the flannel shirt, while the cottage will stand to the coming of the new order of paraphernalia.

Afterword

The houses this book has shown demonstrate the discovery of a new way of thinking about how to design spaces in which to live. Starting from conventionally planned assemblages of rectangular rooms stuffed into packages decorated with the latest fashions, the architects of these Maine cottages explored how their houses could fit with the landscapes of which they were a part, by choosing roofs that seemed to swell up from the ground around them and by opening the house to the landscape with porches and balconies and carefully placed windows and doors.

The same thinking then "went to town," creating neighborhoods of inward-looking houses that do not concentrate on presenting an imposing, historically based front to the street, but rather on enclosing a flowing interior with inglenooks and built-in furnishings made of materials that retain their connections to the trees and quarries of their origins.

The collection goes on to show how these houses are gradually overtaken by the resurgent conventions of eighteenth-century design—symmetry, proportion, white paint, rule-following—and by designs that try to summon the romance of Tudor England. Larger plans call for more impressive houses, and wealth has its way.

But while it lasted, the short reign of the Shingle Style left us a vision of houses that sit lightly on the land, celebrating their humble materials and providing their owners with open and comfortable landscapes for their lives. It was a good way of building, and a good way of living.

Appendix

The Original Magazine Descriptions

1. THOMPSON HOUSE, pg 8

A DWELLING FOR $1,900
Scientific American Architects and Builders Edition, March 1892

The engraving illustrates a dwelling of low cost, erected for Mr. John W. Thompson, at Gardiner, Maine.

Dimensions: Front, 27 ft. 6 in; side, 58 ft. Height of ceilings: First story, 9 ft.; second, 8 ft. 6 in. The underpinning is built of brick, with a foundation of stone. The building is sheathed, clapboarded, and painted light olive green, with dark olive green trimmings. Blinds are painted similar. Roof shingled and painted red. There is a cellar under whole of house containing the necessary apartments. The interior throughout is trimmed with white pine. The trim in hall and parlor is finished natural. The hall windows glazed with cathedral glass. Parlor is provided with a neat wood mantel. Living and dining rooms are treated in colors respectively. The trim in the kitchen is finished natural. Kitchen is wainscoted and fitted up with sink, with closets under same, and a large pantry. The shed is not plastered. There are three bed rooms on third floor, besides store room. These apartments are painted in colors. Cost, $1,900 complete.

2. D.W. EMERY, pg 10

A DWELLING AT AUGUSTA MAINE
Scientific American Architects and Builders Edition, February 1892

We publish a dwelling of low cost, erected for D.W. Emery, Esq., from plans prepared by the proprietor. Dimensions: Front 33 ft., side 49 ft. Height of ceilings: Cellar 7 ft., first story 9 ft., second 8 ft. 6 in., third 8 ft. Underpinning of granite. The building above is of wood, with the exterior framework sheathed and then covered with paper. The first story is clapboarded and painted light brown, with dark brown trimmings; second story and gables are shingled and painted light yellow. Blinds are painted red. Roof shingled and painted red. The plan is laid out in the shape of a cross, the entrance and hall being at side, while the various apartments are thrown out around same. Hall contains a staircase of unique design, turned out of cherry. This hall and staircase are lighted effectively with stained glass windows, and the former contains a fireplace, built of brick, with hearth laid with same. The interior throughout is trimmed with whitewood. Hall, parlor and dining room are stained cherry, the two latter having bay windows and open fireplaces trimmed with tiles and hard wood mantels. Kitchen and pantry are wainscoted and fitted up complete. There are three bed rooms, den, and bath room on second floor, and two bed rooms and storage on third floor. These apartments are trimmed with whitewood also, and are stained cherry. Bath room wainscoted and replete. Cemented cellar contains furnace, laundry, etc. Cost $3,200 to complete.

3. FIRST BAPTIST PARSONAGE, pg 12

THE PARSONAGE AT GARDINER, MAINE
Scientific American Architects and Builders Edition, January 1892

We publish a design of substantial construction, with a pleasing exterior and a roomy interior, erected as the parsonage of the First Baptist Church, at Gardiner, Maine. Dimensions: Front, 34 ft. 6 in.; side 40 ft. 6 in., exclusive of piazza and shed. Height of ceilings: Cellar, 7 ft.; first story, 9 ft.; second, 8 ft. 6 in., third, 8 ft. Underpinning, brick. The first story is clapboarded and painted light olive green, with trimmings of a darker shad; second story and gables are covered with cedar shingles, stained sienna. Roof, shingled and painted red. The interior throughout is trimmed with whitewood, finished natural. Hall contains an ornamental staircase turned out of ash. This hall, dining room and kitchen have hard wood floors, laid with birch in narrow widths. Parlor and library are separated by double sliding doors, the latter containing an open fireplace furnished with a tiled hearth and a hard wood mantel. Kitchen is wainscoted and contains sink and a large well fitted pantry. This house has the customary shed attached which is so frequently seen in this vicinity. There are four bed rooms, large closets, study and bath room on second floor and one room and storage on third floor, all replete. Bath room is wainscoted with birch. Cemented cellar contains furnace and other apartments. Cost $2,500 complete. Mr. Lewis, architect, same place.

4. WALTER G. DAVIS, pg 14

A RESIDENCE AT PORTLAND, MAINE
Scientific American Architects and Builders Edition, February 1892

Our engraving presents a residence erected for W.G. Davis, Esq., at Portland, Me., from plans prepared by John Calvin Stevens, same place. Dimensions: Front, 47 ft.; side 46 ft., not including front piazza. Height of ceilings: Cellar, 7 ft.; first story, 9 ft., 6 in,; second 9 ft.; third, 8 ft. 6 in. The walls are built of brick of a deep red. Roof is coveted with a dark blue slate. Trimmings are painted a dark bottle green. Windows are glazed with plate glass, except the staircase window, which is glazed with stained glass. Hall is trimmed with mahogany, and it is furnished with a parquet floor, paneled wainscoting, ribbed ceiling, arch with spindle transom and a staircase with carved newels. Parlor and library are trimmed with similar wood and are fitted up complete, with open fireplaces, furnished with tiled hearths and facings and elegant hard wood mantels. Dining room is trimmed with black walnut, and it has a paneled wainscoting four feet in height and colonial columns, with wooden ribs into panels. Kitchen and its apartments are trimmed and wainscoted with whitewood finished natural, and are fitted up in the best possible manner. The servants' hall and staircase are private from kitchen to attic. The second floor contains four bed rooms, large closets and bath room, all of which are trimmed with whitewood finished natural. Fireplaces are built of brick, with hearths laid with same. The bath room is wainscoted and fitted up with tub, bowl and closet complete. Three bed rooms and billiard room on third floor. Cemented

cellar contains laundry, furnace, and other apartments. The cost is $11,000, including plumbing, furnace, gas fixtures, grading, etc.; in fact, complete in every respect.

5. EDWARD T. BURROWES, pg 16

A RESIDENCE AT PORTLAND, MAINE
Scientific American Architects and Builders Edition, February 1892

We present a very attractive residence recently erected for E.T. Burrowes, Esq., on the Western Promenade, at Portland, Maine, from plans prepared by John Calvin Stevens, architect, same place. The underpinning is built of selected brick and the building above is of wood, with exterior clapboarded and painted a mellow brown, with trimmings of a darker shade. Gables are filled in with carved panels. Roof covered with red slates. Dimensions: Front, 43 ft.; side, 56 ft., exclusive of piazza and porch. Height of ceiling: Cellar, 7 ft. 6 in.; first story, 10 ft.; second, 9 ft,; third, 8 ft. 6 in. The interior arrangement is excellent and the rooms are well located for light, convenience and comfort. Vestibule has a tiled floor. Hall is trimmed with antique oak. It has a paneled wainscoting five feet high, a ribbed ceiling, and it contains and ornamental staircase, with carved newels, which is lighted effectively with stained glass windows. A toilet is provided under this staircase. One of the most novel and attractive features is the arcaded effect in hall – the pilasters with carved capitals supporting arch. Floors are laid in oak and are highly polished. Parlor, spacious, is treated in a delicate manner with old ivory white, and is provided with an open fireplace, furnished with onyx tiles and a mantel of exquisite design. Library and dining room are trimmed with quartered oak, and each have fireplaces, with tiled hearths and old colonial carved mantels, with beveled plate mirrors. Library is provided with book cases built in, while the dining room has a paneled wainscoting and buffet. The rear hall and staircase are private from cellar to third floor (attic). The kitchen is isolated from the rest of the house and is trimmed with ash, finished natural. It is provided with numerous pantries, well fitted up in the best improved manner. Second floor contains four bed rooms, den and bath room. These apartments are trimmed with whitewood and treated in colors. Each apartment is provided with a large closet and two of them have stationary wash bowls. Bath room is wainscoted with ash. Three large bed rooms and storage on third floor. Cemented cellar contains furnace, laundry and other necessary apartments. Cost, $9,500 complete.

6. JOHN K. ROBINSON, pg 18

A STONE COTTAGE
Scientific American Architects and Builders Edition, March 1892

We publish a unique cottage which has been recently erected for Francis Cushing, Esq., at Cushing's Island, Maine. The building is constructed of rock-faced field stone, laid up at random. There are several bay windows thrown out with latticed window effect. The gables are built of wood, and covered with shingles and stained sienna. The roof is covered with slates. Dimensions: Front, 48 ft.; side, 41 ft., not including piazza. Height of ceilings: Cellar, 8ft.; first story, 9 ft.; second, 8ft. 6

in.; third, 8 ft. There is a cemented cellar under the whole building, and it contains kitchen, laundry, pantries, and all necessary apartments, fitted up in a first-class manner. The hall is finished in cherry, and it contains an ornamental staircase turned out of similar wood. The archways between hall and the other apartments have spindle transoms. The parlor, library and dining rooms are also finished in cherry, and have hardwood floors. Library is furnished with an open fireplace, built of brick with facings of same and hearth of slate. Bookcases are built in on either side of fireplace. Dining-room is provided with a cozy nook with seats. The second floor contains four bedrooms and large closets, while the third floor contains two bedrooms and trunk room. Messrs. Fassett & Tompson, architects, Portland, Maine.

7. SIDNEY W. THAXTER, pg 22

A SUMMER RESIDENCE IN MAINE
Scientific American Building Edition, January 1895

We publish illustrations of a summer residence recently erected for S.W. Thaxter, Esq., at Cushing's Island, Maine. The design presents an excellent example for a summer home, and it has many attractive features, including a spacious and well-shaded piazza, loggia and balcony, and also a bay window with seat. The underpinning is built of rock-faced field stone laid up at random, while the building above is built of wood, and the exterior walls sheathed and covered with shingles, and stained a mahogany color. The roof is shingled, and painted red. Dimensions: Front, 36 ft.; side, 39 ft., not including piazza. Height of ceilings: Cellar, 7 ft.; first story, 9 ft.; second, 8 ft 6 in.; third 7 ft.. 6 in. The living room is a unique apartment. The studding to walls and the ceiling timbers are left exposed to view, and are stained cherry, the space between being plastered and treated in olive yellow. All woodwork is finished in cherry. The newel post at staircase extends to ceiling, and the space between is provided with a screen filled in with spindlework. The nook is a special feature, with corner seats and an open fireplace built of brick, with hearth laid of same and a mantelshelf of wood. Dining-room has a bay window, paneled divan and an open fireplace. Kitchen and pantry are ceiled up with narrow beaded yellow pine, finished natural, and are furnished replete. The second floor is plastered, and all woodwork is stained and finished in cherry. This floor contains four bedrooms and bathroom. Third floor contains two bedrooms and storage. The cellar has an entrance from kitchen, and one from the outside thereto. Cost, $3,100 complete. Mr. John Calvin Stevens, architect, Oxford Building, Portland, Me.

8. OTTAWA HOUSE COTTAGE #1, pg 25

A COTTAGE AT CUSHING'S ISLAND, MAINE
Scientific American Building Edition, February 1895

We publish a Colonial dwelling, which has been erected for Francis Cushing, Esq., at Cushing's Island, Me. The design is unique and picturesque, and an ideal model for a summer home, and for which it is intended. The underpining and balustrade to piazza are built of field stone laid up at

random. The exterior framework is sheathed, covered with shingles, and painted Colonial yellow. The roof is shingled and stained a moss green with mottled effect. Dimensions: Front, 32 ft. 6 in.; side 29ft 6 in., not including piazza. Height of ceilings: Cellar, 6ft.; first story, 9 ft.; second 8 ft. The interior throughout is trimmed with spruce and finished natural. The walls and ceilings are ceiled up with narrow beaded stuff. There is no plastering on the interior. The living room contains an open fireplace built of brick, with facings and hearth of same, and a hardwood shelf. The staircase has turned newel balusters and rail. Parlor and dining-room are well lighted and ventilated. Kitchen and pantry are well fitted up and are complete. The second floor contains toilet, large closets and four bedrooms. The third floor or attic contains ample storage. The cellar is merely a rough cellar for storage, and it could be improved at a small expense. Cost, $2,000 complete. Mr. John Calvin Stevens, architect, Oxford Building, Portland, Me.

9. OTTAWA HOUSE COTTAGE #2, pg 27

A SUMMER DWELLING AT CUSHING ISLAND, MAINE
Scientific American Building Edition, June 1897

We present herewith a summer dwelling recently erected for M.S. Gibson, Esq., at Cushing Island, Me. The design is a combination of good elevations and well arranged plans. The building is erected on cedar posts, and the exterior framework is sheathed and then covered with shingles, and painted chrome yellow. The roof is also shingled, and painted a moss green. Dimensions: Front, 36 ft.; side, 37 ft., not including piazza. Height of ceilings: First story, 9 ft,; second, 8 ft. The interior is trimmed with whitewood, and finished natural. The walls and ceilings are ceiled up with narrow beaded stuff. Hall contains an ornamental staircase. Living-room is provided with window seats, and a large open fireplace, trimmed with tiles, and mantel. Parlor has a similar fireplace. Dining-room is provided with a large pantry. Kitchen is wainscoted, and furnished with the usual fixtures. Second floor contains four bedrooms and large closets. Cost $2,000 complete. Mr. John Calvin Stevens, architect, Portland, Me.

10. OTTAWA HOUSE COTTAGE #3, pg 29

A SUMMER DWELLING AT CUSHING ISLAND, MAINE
Scientific American Building Edition, August 1896

We publish a cottage recently erected for Francis Cushing, Esq., at Cushings Island, Me. The design presents a unique example for a summer home, containing pleasing elevations, well shaded piazza and balcony, and an interior arrangement conveniently fitted up. The building is erected on cedar posts, with stone footings. The cellar is ceiled up with narrow beaded stuff, and it has an outside entrance thereto. The building above this is sheathed and then covered with shingles. It is painted a dull shade of olive green, while the roof is shingled and painted red. The columns at piazza and balcony are turned out of rough cedar posts, dressed and finished natural. The chimney is a feature in itself, and is built of rock-faced stone laid up at random. Dimensions: Front, 33 ft. 6 in.; side, 29ft. 6 in.; not including piazza. Height of ceilings: First story, 9 ft.; second, 8 ft. The interior throughout is trimmed with spruce, finished natural. The walls and ceilings are not plastered, but are left with the beams exposed to view. These beams are dressed and finished natural. The reception hall is provided with an open fireplace, built of brick, with hearth of same, and a neat wood mantel. It is separated from staircase hall by an archway. The staircase is fitted up with ornamental newels, balusters, and rail. Parlor is well lighted. Dining-room is provided with a large butler's pantry, with shelves, drawers, and cupboards. Kitchen is wainscoted and furnished with the usual fixtures. Second floor contains four bedrooms, den, and toilet; the latter complete. Cost, $1,950 complete. Mr. John Calvin Stevens, architect, Portland, Me.

11. J.W. DEERING, pg 32

A SUMMER HOME AT
KENNEBUNKPORT, MAINE
Scientific American Building Edition,
November 1896

We publish the summer home of Captain J. W. Deering, at Kennebunkport, Me. The engravings present a gambrel roof house, of modern treatment, with the lines of the elevations well broken by many good features, executed in an excellent manner, and they include the loggias, the spacious piazza, and the tower and outlook. The underpinning is built up with rock-faced field stone, laid up at random. The superstructure is covered on the exterior with shingles, left to weather finish natural, and the trimmings are painted white. Dimensions: Width, 76 ft.; length, 45 ft., not including piazza. Height of ceilings: Cellar, 7ft. 6 in.; first story, 10 ft.; second, 9 ft.; third 8 ft. 6 in. The interior throughout is trimmed with spruce, finished natural, and oiled. The main hall, broad and long, is arranged as the principal living room, and it contains two pleasant nooks, with paneled seats, and an open fireplace, built of brick, with hearth and facings of same, and a wood mantel. The staircase is an ornamental one, with massive columns rising to ceiling. The reception room is conveniently located, and it contains an open fireplace, built of brick, and provided with a dainty mantel. Dining-room, of irregular shape, is furnished with a paneled wainscoting, 4 ft. in height. The walls, above this wainscot, and ceiling are beamed, forming panels, which are filled in with plaster work. The arched nook, with its seat, and fireplace build of brick, and provided with mantel shelf, and paneled over mantel, is a good feature. The floors are of hard pine, laid in narrow widths, and oiled. Kitchen and pantries and also rear hall are wainscoted with narrow beaded stuff, and these apartments are furnished with the best modern fixtures. The second floor contains a large, open hall, communicating with seven large bedrooms and bathroom, the latter being wainscoted and fitted up complete, with exposed plumbing. Third floor contains three bedrooms, and ample storage. Cemented cellar contains furnace, laun-

dry, and other necessary apartments. Cost $8,500 complete. Mr. John Calvin Stevens, architect, Oxford Building, Portland, Me.

12. JOHN H. DAVIS, pg 36

A COTTAGE OF MODERATE COST
Scientific American Architects and Builders Edition, August 1893

The engraving illustrates a cottage erected for J.H. Davis, Esq., at Portland, Me. The building is constructed in a thorough workmanlike manner. The underpinning and first story are built of various kinds of rough stone, laid up at random, with brick trimmings. The second and third stories are covered with shingles and painted a dull red. Roof shingled and painted similar. Cemented cellar, under whole of building, contains laundry, furnace, and other necessary apartments. The interior throughout is trimmed with whitewood, the first floor being finished in cherry. Lobby and hall have paneled wainscotings and ceiling beams. Hall also contains a paneled divan and staircase of unique design, which is lighted by delicate stained glass windows. Parlor has a bay window and fireplace trimmed with tiles and provided with a cherry mantel. Dining-room has a wainscot in panels, and a pleasant nook with seats and fireplace built of brick, with hearth of same. Kitchen and pantries are fitted up in the best possible manner. The trim on the second floor is treated in the natural color. This floor contains four bedrooms and bathroom, the latter wainscoted and furnished complete. The third floor contains two bedrooms, tank and trunk rooms. Dimensions: Front: 31 ft.; side, 44 ft. 6 in. Height of ceilings: Cellar, 7 ft.; first story, 9 ft. 6 in.; second, 9ft; third, 8 ft. 6 in. Cost, $3,400 complete. Mr. John Calvin Stevens, architect, same place.

13. JOHN CALVIN STEVENS, pg 40

A COLONIAL HOUSE
Scientific American Architects and Builders Edition, January 1892

We present a house, colonial in treatment, erected for John Calvin Stevens, Esq., at Portland, Maine, from plans prepared by the proprietor. Dimensions: Front, 30 ft.; side, 40 ft., exclusive of front porch and platform. Height of ceilings: Cellar, 7ft., first story, 9 ft.; second, 8 ft. 6 in.; third, 8 ft. The design shows a very odd and tasty bit of rural architecture. The first story is built of brick, which protrude at random, giving dots of shadows, playful in their effect. Above this brickwork the walls are shingled and left to weather-stain. Roof shingled. Within the rooms are varied in their treatment. Vestibule has Dutch doors. Hall and library are trimmed with whitewood, deepened slightly in color. The hall contains a very handsome staircase, with colonial columns extending to ceiling. The space between these columns is filled in with spindle work. Parlor is finished in old ivory white. The walls are in grayish blue, while the ceiling is in light olive brown. Dining-room is stained a deep mahogany. This room has a paneled dado five feet in height, and the walls and ceiling above are colored with burnt sienna. The fireplaces are fitted up complete, with tile hearths and hard wood mantels. Kitchen is wainscoted and trimmed with yellow pine, finished natural. It contains range, sink, wash trays, large pantries and lobby large enough to admit ice box. Second floor contains four bed rooms, large closets and bath room, trimmed with white pine finished natural. Bath room is wainscoted and is fitted up replete. Cemented cellar under whole of house, containing furnace and necessary apartments. Cost, $3,800 complete.

14. MONTGOMERY S. GIBSON, pg 44

A COTTAGE OF MODERATE COST
Scientific American Architects and Builders Edition, March 1892

We present a cottage of low cost, erected for Mr. M.S. Gibson, at Portland, Me. Size of structure, 30 x 48 ft. 6 in., exclusive of piazza, porch, and bay windows. Height of ceilings: Cellar, 7 ft., first story 9ft., second 8 ft. 6 in., third 8 ft. The design is quaint and picturesque, and it presents a pleasing bit of suburban architecture. It has a pleasant piazza, a tower and a triangle bay window extending up two stories. Underpinning brick. First story clapboarded and painted pearl gray. Second story, gables, and roof are shingled and stained sienna. The interior is quite roomy and comfortable. Hall, spacious, is trimmed with oak and is entered through a vestibule. This hall contains a staircase of unique design, which is lighted by stained glass windows, and a nook with seat and fireplace, built of brick, with hearth laid with same. Parlor is trimmed with clear white pine and is treated with old ivory white in a delicate mantel. The fireplace has a tiled hearth and facings and a mantel of exquisite design. Dining room is trimmed and wainscoted with antique oak, and is fitted up with nook and fireplace. Kitchen and pantries are wainscoted and trimmed with whitewood, finished natural, and are fitted up replete in every respect. There are four bed rooms, with large closets and bath room, on second floor. These apartments are trimmed with whitewood finished natural. Bath room is wainscoted. Three bed rooms and storage on third floor. Cemented cellar contains furnace and other apartments. Cost $3,500 complete. Mr. John Calvin Stevens, architect, same place.

MONTGOMERY S. GIBSON, pg 44

A CARRIAGE HOUSE
Scientific American Architects and Builders Edition, August 1892

We present a stable of low cost, recently erected for Mr. M. S. Gilson, at Portland, Me. The underpinning is built of local stone laid up at random. The building above is sheathed, clapboarded and painted colonial yellow, with ivory white trimmings. Roof shingled and painted red. Size of structure 23 x 34 ft. The interior arrangement is excellent. It provides a large carriage room, 22 x 22 ft., and a stable well lighted and ventilated, containing two stalls furnished with the usual iron fixtures. The interior throughout is trimmed and ceiled with narrow beaded Georgia pine, finished natural with hard oil. Carriage room is provided with a glass harness case. Stairs from stable lead to man's bedroom and hay loft. Cost $700 complete. Mr. John Calvin Stevens, architect, Portland, Maine.

15. ARTHUR L. BATES, pg 47

A COLONIAL HOUSE AT PORTLAND, MAINE
Scientific American Architects and Builders Edition, March 1892

We present a dwelling, colonial in treatment, erected for A.L. Bates, Esq., at Portland, Maine, and from plans prepared by John Calvin Stevens, architect, same place. Dimensions: Front, 35 ft. 6 in,; side, 55 ft. 6 in., exclusive of front porch. Height of ceilings: Cellar, 7ft, 6 in.; first story, 9 ft. 6 in.; second 8 ft. 6 in.; third, 8ft. The underpinning is built of local brick, while the superstructure above is built of wood, with the exterior framework sheathed, shingled and left to weather stain. Blinds painted bronze green. The design has the appearance of comfort and convenience, while the interior contains many large, well lighted rooms, that are varied in their treatment. Hall is trimmed with laurel. The broad, low staircase, with carved newels, the pleasant little den beneath this staircase and the arch supported on fluted pilasters with carved capitals, are the features of hall, while the old casement window, with seat, and the antique mantel in dining room, are in keeping with the several spindle transoms that carry out the colonial effect. The hall and staircase are lighted effectively with windows glazed with stained glass. Parlor is finished in a delicate manner with old ivory white, while the library is trimmed with cherry and dining room with mahogany, the latter having a paneled dado five feet high and a china closet with beaded glass doors. Fireplaces have tiled hearths and facings and mantels of colonial style that correspond respectively with the trim of each room. The floors are laid with brick in narrow widths and highly polished. Kitchen is trimmed and wainscoted with whitewood, finished natural, and it contains well fitted up pantries, sink, range and private stairs to third floor. There are four spacious bed rooms, large closets, dressing room and bath room on second floor, and two bed rooms on third floor, besides ample storage. These apartments are trimmed with whitewood, finished natural. Bath room is wainscoted and it contains tub, bowl, closet and linen closet, replete. Cemented cellar contains laundry, furnace and other apartments. Cost $3,800 complete.

16. H.M. BAILEY, pg 49

A COTTAGE AT GREAT DIAMOND ISLAND, MAINE
Scientific American Building Edition, March 1895

We present herewith a cottage recently erected for H.M. Bailey, Esq., at Great Diamond Island, Maine. Dimensions: Front, 28 ft.; side 39 ft., exclusive of piazza. Height of ceilings: First story, 9 ft.; second, 8 ft. The design is a unique example for an island cottage, provided with abundant piazza room, well shaded, and a tower with outlook at second story. The rooms are so arranged as to give the best possible comfort and convenience. The staircase rises up to second floor from dining-room, thus avoiding draughts if placed in living room. The living-room is provided with an open fireplace built of brick, with hearths and facings of same and a neat wood mantel, and is separated from dining-room by an archway with spindle transom. Kitchen is provided with dressers, sink and a large pantry. Servant's bedroom is conveniently located. Bathroom is fitted up replete. Shed contains ample space for storage, with entrance hereto. Second floor contains four bedrooms, large closets and balcony. The walls and ceilings throughout the interior are not plastered, but left with the beams exposed to view and finished natural. The trimmings and casings are turned out of spruce, the doors of pine, and the floors are laid with yellow pine in narrow widths. The cellar under building is inclosed with narrow beaded stuff, with latticed windows. The building is supported on cedar posts with stone footings, and the cellar has an outside entrance. The building above is sheathed with spruce, and the first story is covered with clapboarding and painted olive yellow, while the second and third stories are covered with shingles and stained sienna. Roof shingled and painted red, Mr. John Calvin Stevens, architect, Oxford Building, Portland, Maine.

17. C.J. CHAPMAN, pg 51

A SUMMER HOUSE AT GREAT DIAMOND ISLAND, MAINE
Scientific American Building Edition, May 1897

We present a most unique summer dwelling which has been recently completed for C.J. Chapman, Esq., at Great Diamond Island, Portland, Me. The building is erected on cedar posts, with stone footings. The superstructure is built of wood, with the exterior framework covered with shingles (cedar), and left to finish their natural reddish brown color. Roof shingled and painted red. The elevations are very attractive, and they have many good features, including a broad, well-shaped piazza, towers, balcony, loggia and bay windows. Dimensions: Front, 50 ft.; side, 50 ft., not including piazza. Height of ceilings: First story, 10 ft., second 9 ft. The woodwork used in trimming the interior is of yellow pine and finished natural. The walls throughout have a wainscoting three feet high: the space above this point and the ceilings are covered with burlap, put on with excellent effect. The living-room is provided with a paneled divan, ceiling beams, forming deep panels, and an open fireplace build of brick, with facings and hearth of same. The staircase is furnished with newel posts, spindle balusters, and a broad landing with window seats. The reception room is finished similar to living-room. Dining-room is provided with a fireplace, same as the one already described. The first room, kitchen and its apartments, furnished with the usual fixtures, respectively. The second floor contains a large, open hall, large closets, and five bedrooms. The fireplaces are furnished with the usual fixtures. The attic gives ample room for storage. The cellar being inclosed same as main story, ample space is provided for storage. John Calvin Stevens, architect, Oxford Building, Portland, Me. Cost $4,500 complete.

18. FREDERICK L. JERRIS, pg 55

A SUMMER COTTAGE AT DELANO PARK, CAPE ELIZABETH, MAINE
Scientific American Building Monthly, May 1905

The illustrations shown present the summer home of Frederick Jerries, Esq. at Delano Park, Cape Elizabeth, Maine. It is erected on cedar posts with stone footings. The underpinning is formed with framework enclosed with matched sheathing and clapboards, which are painted gray. The first and second stories are covered with shingles and are left to weather finish. The roof is also shingled and treated similarly.

The interior throughout is planned with a view to securing every available space for use, and of a treatment of the same in a simple manner. The living and dining rooms occupy the entire front of the house, and both are treated with a Flemish brown effect. The walls and ceiling timbers are exposed to view, and the side walls are ceiled up with cypress battens. The stairway rises out of the living-room, and at the side of the stairway are placed paneled settles. The open fireplace is built of brick, with the facings and a hearth of brick laid in herring-bone fashion, and a mantel shelf.

The pantry and kitchen are fitted complete, and the walls and ceilings are made up with narrow-beaded stuff. There are also one bedroom and a lavatory on this floor. The second floor contains five bedrooms, a bathroom, and one servant's bedroom. The bathroom is furnished with porcelain fixtures and exposed nickel-plated plumbing. A cellar under part of the house contains ample storage space.

Mr. John Calvin Stevens, architect, Oxford Building, Portland, Maine.

19. GEORGE B. SWASEY, pg 57

A SUMMER COTTAGE AT DELANO PARK, CAPE ELIZABETH, MAINE
Scientific American Building Monthly, June 1904

The summer cottage has been erected for Dr. Swasey, at Delano Park, Cape Elizabeth, Maine. It has a broad, spacious piazza and large living-rooms, and is built on cedar posts with stone footings. The entire structure is enclosed with matched stuff and is then covered with white cedar shingles, left to weather finish. The trimmings are painted gray. The roof is covered with shingles and is stained a moss green. Dimensions: Front 37 ft. 6 in.; side 20 ft. 6 in.; exclusive of piazza. Height of ceilings: Cellar, 7 ft.; first story, 9 ft.; second, 8 ft. 6 in.

There is no plaster throughout the interior of the house-the walls, partitions, and ceilings are ceiled up with yellow pine; the floor beams are exposed to view, and also the under side of the upper floor. The living and dining-rooms are wainscoted, and the partition between the two rooms is built of battens to the height of seven feet; the opening above is filled in with ornamental brackets. The entire woodwork is stained and finished in Flemish brown. The open fireplace is built of rock-faced gray stone with the facings of the same rising and supporting a mantel shelf with brackets; the hearth is laid with brick. There are two paneled seats and an ornamental staircase rising out of the living-room.

The kitchen and pantry are fitted complete, and the lobby is large enough to admit ice box. There is one bedroom on this floor and five bedrooms on the second floor, besides ample closet room, and a bathroom furnished with porcelain fixtures and exposed nickelplated plumbing. A cellar, under part of the house, forms ample space for storage and fuel. Mr. John Calvin Stevens, architect, Oxford Building, Portland, Maine.

20. HARVEY S. MURRAY, pg 59

BIRD'S NEST, A SUMMER COTTAGE AT DELANO PARK, CAPE ELIZABETH, MAINE
Scientific American Building Monthly, March 1904

An illustration of Birds' Nest, a summer cottage erected for Mr. Harvey S. Murray, at Delano Park, Cape Elizabeth, Maine. It is a difficult matter to secure a cottage with the combined appointments, as already stated, at so low a cost as $1,500, but this the architect has been successful in doing. The building rests on a side of a hill, thus forming an excellent basement, which is enclosed with matched stuff painted a dark bottle green. The remainder of the building is covered with matched stuff, and then with white cedar shingles, which are left to finish naturally, while the trimmings are painted a dark bottle green. The roof is also covered with shingles. Dimensions: Front, 33 ft..; side, 24 ft., exclusive of piazza. Height of ceilings: Cellar, 7 ft.; first story, 9 ft.; second, 8 ft. 6 in.

The interior throughout is trimmed with white pine, and the studding, floor joists, and all partitions are dressed and exposed to view. The living-room rises up two stories in height, and the second story hall opens into the well, with a balustrade treated with a pleasing effect. This living-room has an open fireplace built of red brick laid in red mortar, with the facings and a hearth of the same, and a mantel of wood. At the side of the fireplace is a paneled seat, over which there is an opening filled in with spindlework. The spindlework forms the partitions between the living and dining-rooms. The pantries and kitchen are fitted up complete with all the modern conveniences. There is but one staircase in the house, placed in the private hall, which forms an access to the kitchen, and is isolated from the living-room. This floor also contains a bedroom. The second floor contains three bedrooms and a bathroom; the latter is furnished with porcelain fixtures and exposed plumbing. The cellar contains the servant's room, laundry and storeroom. Mr. John Calvin Stevens, architect, Oxford Building, Portland, Maine.

21. CHARLES S. HOMER, pg 62

A SUMMER HOME AT PROUTS NECK, MAINE
Scientific American Building Monthly, February 1905

The illustrations present the summer home of Charles S. Homer, Esq., at Prouts Neck, Maine

The building is a very happy combination of interesting outlines and the whole is most artistically treated. There is no cellar under the entire house, and the building rests upon stone footings and cedar posts. The exterior framework, from the grade to the peak, is covered with shingles of red cedar, which are finished and stained a soft brown color, while the trimmings are painted in an ivory white. The roof is covered with shingles, and is stained in harmony with a moss-green effect.

The interior is trimmed with cypress, the first floor being in the Flemish treatment. The living-room, which is the important room in the house, which it should be in a house planned for summer uses, occupies the ocean front of the house, and in an unobtrusive manner the stairs, which are of an ornamental character, rise out of this room for there is no hall. At the side of the stairway there is a seat, and on a line with this staircase is the open fireplace, which is built of red brick, with the facings of the same, and a hearth of red unglazed tile, and a mantel of quaint design. The walls have a high wainscoting, and the ceiling joints are dressed and exposed to view.

The dining-room is treated in a similar manner, and it also has an open fireplace with red brick facings and hearth, and a mantel. The butler's pantry is fitted up complete. The kitchen and its dependencies are fitted with all the necessary conveniences. The shed contains ample space for the icebox, toilet, and a servant's room.

There are six bedrooms, two servants' bedrooms, and a bathroom on the second floor. The large open hall has an open fireplace of brick and a mantel. Each bedroom has a well fitted closet. The bathroom is wainscoted, and is furnished with porcelain fixtures and exposed nickelplated plumbing.

Mr. John Calvin Stevens, architect, Oxford Building, Portland, Maine.

22. WINSLOW HOMER, pg 67

A RESIDENCE AT PROUTS NECK, MAINE
Scientific American Building Monthly, July 1904

The residence illustrated has been built for Winslow Homer, Esq., the painter at Prouts Neck, Maine. The house is built for summer uses, and is constructed in a simple manner. There is no stone cellar under the house, but the building rests on cedar posts with stone footings, and it is so well elevated at the rear that a door opens into the space underneath the building and forms a cellar for storage, etc. The building from grade to the peak is of wood, and the exterior framework is covered with matched sheathing, and then cedar shingles, which are left to weather finish. The roof is also covered with similar shingles. The trimmings are painted white and the blinds light yellow. Dimensions: Front, 41 ft.; side, 38 ft. 10 in., exclusive of piazza. Height of the ceilings: Cellar, 6 ft., first story, 9 ft.; second, 8 ft.; third, 8 ft.

The living-room occupies the entire length of the house, and is provided with an ingle nook, containing an open fireplace built of brick, with facings and a hearth of the same, and a mantel shelf. The stairway, of attractive character, rises out of this room and extends up to the second story. This room, and also the dining-room, is wainscoted from the floor to the ceiling, the latter having beams, which are dressed and exposed to view. The butler's pantry is fitted up with drawers, cupboard, etc., and the kitchen is also fitted complete. The shed for stores and the servants' porch is a convenience. The bathroom is furnished with porcelain fixtures and exposed plumbing, and it is provided with an outside entrance thereto.

The second floor is plastered, and it contains five bedrooms and a servants' room, with private stairway to the kitchen. The attic contains ample storage space. Mr. John Calvin Stevens, architect, Oxford Building, Portland, Maine.

23. A.R. DOTEN, pg 73

A COTTAGE FOR $800
Scientific American Architects and Builders Edition, December 1891

One of our plates illustrates a dwelling erected for Mr. A.R. Doten, on Great Diamond Island, near Portland, Maine. The design is excellent and it combines both beauty and convenience. It has a spacious piazza, a loggia at second floor, and contains eight good sized apartments. Foundation posts on stone footings, inclosed for storage. The exterior framework throughout is sheathed, and then covered with shingles, stained sienna. Roof, shingled, and painted red. Dimensions: Front, 28 ft 6 in.; side, 28 ft. 6 in., exclusive of piazza. Height of ceilings: First story, 8 ft. 6 in.; second, 8 ft. The interior walls and partitions throughout are of beaded white pine, smooth and clear, and finished natural. Living room has an open fireplace, built of brick, with hearth laid with same, and is provided with a neat wood mantel. Hall contains a staircase neatly turned out of whitewood. Dining room is provided with a buffet window glazed with stained glass. Kitchen and pantry are fitted up replete. Second floor contains four good sized bedrooms and closets. Cost $800 complete. Mr. Antoine Dorticos, architect, Portland, Maine.

24. A.R. DOTEN, II, pg 75

AN EIGHT HUNDRED DOLLAR COTTAGE
Scientific American Architects and Builders Edition, November 1894

We publish a cottage built for A.R. Doten, Esq., in Casco Bay, near Portland, Me. The building is designed for a summer home, and is built on cedar posts with stone footings, while the exterior framework throughout is sheathed, covered with shingles, and stained sienna, with bottle green trimmings. The roof is also singled, and painted red. The cellar is inclosed same as building above, and is lighted and ventilated by latticed windows. It has an entrance on the exterior. Dimensions: Front, 26 ft. 6 in.; side, 27 ft. 6 in., not including piazza which is a good feature, broad and spacious. Height of ceilings: Cellar, 6 ft. 6 in.; first story 8 ft. 6 in.; second 8 ft. The first floor contains a large living room, with an open fireplace, built of brick, with hearth of same, and, provided with a neat wood mantel; dining-room has a stained glass buffet window, large pantries and kitchen, furnished with the necessary fixtures. The staircase in living room is turned out of spruce. The second floor contains four bedrooms, closets, and storage. The interior throughout is sheathed, ceiled, and trimmed with clear white spruce, finished natural. The floors are laid with yellow pine in narrow widths. Cost $800 complete. Mr. Antoine Dorticos, architect, Portland, Me.

25. CHARLES M. TALBOT, pg 77

A COTTAGE IN MAINE—COST, $900
Scientific American Architects and Builders Edition, February 1892

We present a dwelling erected for Dr. C.M. Talbot, at Great Diamond Island, Maine. Dimensions: Front 28 ft. 6 in., side, 41 ft., exclusive of piazza. Height of first story ceiling, 9 ft.; second, 8 ft. Underpinning, brick on stone footings. The exterior framework is sheathed and the first story is clapboarded and painted light olive green, with bottle green trimmings; second story, shingled and painted red. Roof shingled. The design is of the Queen Anne style, and it is provided with a wide piazza across the front and side. The interior throughout is trimmed with white pine, finished natural. The walls, ceilings, and partitions are ceiled with narrow beaded stuff. The living room, good sized, is provided with an open fireplace, built of brick, with hearth laid with same, and finished with a neat wood mantel. The staircase is separated from the living room by a column extending to ceiling, the space between being filled in with spindle work. Kitchen is provided with sink and pantry complete. The shed provides ample room for the storage of wood, coal, etc. There are four bed rooms and loggia on second floor. The floors are of yellow pine, laid in narrow widths. Cost, $900 complete. Mr. Antoine Dorticos, architect, Portland, Me.

26. GEORGE W. BEALE, pg 79

A COTTAGE ON THE MAINE COAST
Scientific American Architects and Builders Edition, April 1892

We publish a summer cottage, erected for Mr. G. W. Beale, on Great Diamond Island, near Portland, Me. Dimensions: Front, 43 ft.; side, 27 ft. 6 in., not including front piazza. Height of ceilings: First story, 9 ft.; second, 8 ft. The design is very picturesque, and the plan is excellent. The spacious piazza and balcony are the features of the exterior. The building is erected on brick piers with stone footings. The first story is clapboarded and painted light olive green, the bottle green trimmings, and the second story is shingled and stained sienna. Roof shingled and painted red. The interior throughout is trimmed with white pine, finished and natural. All the partitions, furrings, and ceilings are ceiled with narrow beaded stuff. The floors are laid with yellow pine in narrow widths. The living room, spacious and well lighted, contains an open fireplace, built of brick, with hearth laid with same, and it is provided with a neat wood mantel. The staircase is separated from living room with posts extending to ceiling, and the space between filled in with spindle work. Dining room, kitchen, and its apartments are fitted up in the best possible manner. Second floor contains four bed rooms and large closets. There is ample room under house for storage. Cost, $1,470 complete. Mr. Antoine Dorticos, architect, Portland, Me.

27. ALFRED A. KENDALL, pg 82

A SUMMER COTTAGE AT DIAMOND ISLAND
Scientific American Architects and Builders Edition, May 1892

Our engraving presents a very attractive summer cottage, recently completed for Mr. Fred. Kendall, at Great Diamond Island, Maine. The plans show a spacious piazza and balcony on the exterior, while the interior contains a convenient arrangement of rooms, well lighted and fitted up in a first-class manner. The house is set on cedar posts with stone foundations, placed eight feet on centers and well braced. The building above is put together in the style called balloon frame, with timbers of good manlike manner. The exterior framework is boarded up and down with spruce sheathing. The first story is clapboarded, and the second story and gables covered with cedar shingles and painted pearl gray with white trimmings. Roof is covered with cedar shingles and painted red. Dimensions: Front, 32 ft.; side, 40 ft., exclusive of front piazza. Height of ceilings: First story, 9 ft.; second, 8 ft. 6 in. Hall, parlor, and dining room are trimmed and wainscoted in panels, 3 ft. 6 in. in height, with whitewood. These apartments also have ceiling beams. The walls above the wainscot are plastered one good coat of brown mortar, which is stamped in a novel fashion, with stamp similar to a butter stamp, but larger and of various designs; the walls being in one pattern and the frieze in another. Hall contains a staircase of excellent design, with newel post extending to ceiling, the space between being filled in with spindle transoms, thus forming a separation from parlor. The opening between parlor and dining room, and the arch over nook in the latter, have similar spindle transoms. Parlor and dining room have paneled divans and open fireplaces, built of brick and furnished with tiled hearths, and mantels. The latter apartment has a buffet built in, with cupboard, drawers, shelves, etc. Kitchen, pantry, and second floor are ceiled with narrow beaded spruce, finished natural. The second floor contains four bed rooms and bath room replete. There is ample space in roof for storage, and the space beneath the house is utilized for this purpose. Cost $2,000 complete. Mr. Antoine Dorticos, architect, Portland, Me.

28. EDWIN L. GODING, pg 84

A SUMMER COTTAGE AT GREAT DIAMOND ISLAND, MAINE
Scientific American Building Edition, July 1895

We publish on pages 5 and 6 a summer cottage, which has been recently erected for Edward L. Goding, Esq., at Great Diamond Island, Maine. The design presents a very picturesque exterior, with several features that give the building an artistic effect. The spacious and well shaded piazza, balconies, chimney and tower are some of the features. The cellar is excavated, and the building is supported on cedar posts with stone foundations. It is inclosed with latticed work, and it has an inside and outside entrance thereto. The

first story is clapboarded, while the second and third stories are shingled. It is painted a silver gray. The columns at front piazza are finished natural with hard oil. Roof shingled, and painted red. Dimensions: Front, 33 ft.; side, 45 ft., not including piazza. Height of ceilings: Cellar, 7 ft.; first story, 9 ft.; second, 8 ft. 6 in. The interior throughout is trimmed with white pine, stained and finished in cherry. The walls of the principal apartments have matting wainscoting, and the space above and ceiling are covered with burlap, put on with mouldings and brass nails. The effect is pleasing, and it gives a cool tone to the interior. The entrance hall, separated by an arch way with spindle transom, is provided with stairway, with turned newel posts and balusters. The living room is furnished with a paneled divan, and a large, open fireplace built of brick, with hearth and facings of same, and a neat wood mantel. Dining-room is well lighted and ventilated. It has a large closet for china, and a pantry with cupboards, and dressers. Kitchen is ceiled up with narrow beaded stuff, and fitted up with the usual necessary fixtures. The second floor contains five bedrooms, large closets, and bath, the latter wainscoted and provided with the necessary fixtures. Third floor contains storage. The floors are laid with yellow pine. Cost $2,500 complete. Mr. A. Dorticos, architect, Portland, Me.

29. WALTER WOODMAN, pg 88

A SUMMER COTTAGE
Scientific American Architects and Builders Edition, August 1892.

We publish herewith, Dr. Woodman's summer cottage, at Great Diamond Island, near Portland, Me. Dimensions: Front, 49 ft. 6 in.; side, 35 ft. 6 in., exclusive of piazza. Height of ceilings: First story, 9 ft,; second, 8 ft. Foundation, brick piers. The exterior throughout is covered with sheathing boards and then shingled and painted light olive green, with bottle green trimmings. Roof shingled and painted red. In the arrangement of the rooms all the space is utilized to the best advantage and the principal feature is the spacious piazza, 10 ft. wide, well shaded and covered by the main roof. The interior throughout is trimmed with whitewood. The living room, spacious, contains a paneled divan and a large open fireplace, built of brick, with hearth laid with same and provided with a hard wood mantel. The staircase, of ornamental design, starts from dining rom. This dining room has a china closet and fireplace. The floors are of hard wood, laid in narrow widths. Kitchen and its apartments are replete. Second floor contains six bed rooms, with large closets and bath room. The latter wainscoted and furnished with the usual fixtures. Cost $3,200 complete. Messrs. J. R. and W.P. Richards, architects, 44 Court Street, Boston, Mass.

30. F.H. MORSE, pg 91

A COTTAGE NEAR PORTLAND, MAINE
Scientific American Architects and Builders Edition, May 1892

We illustrate this month a summer cottage, erected for Mr. F.H. Morse, on Diamond Island, near Portland, Me. Dimensions: Breadth, 31 ft. 6 in.; depth, 44 ft. 6 in., not including piazza. Height of ceilings: First story, 9 ft.; second, 8 ft. 6 in. Although not a large house, the accommodations are generous, owing to the compact arrangement of the rooms. The spacious piazza is the special feature. Foundation, brick piers. First story clapboarded, except the space beneath piazza roof, which is ceiled, and painted light olive green, with dark olive green trimmings; second story shingled and painted olive yellow. Roof shingled and painted red. The interior throughout is trimmed with white pine, finished natural. The walls, ceilings, and partitions are ceiled with narrow beaded stuff. The living room contains an ornamental staircase, turned out of similar wood, and separated with a spindle transom and a fireplace built of brick, with hearth laid with same, and mantel wood, with plate glass mirror. Dining room, good sized, has a buffet window glazed with stained glass. The floors are of yellow pine, laid in narrow widths, and stained cherry. Kitchen, shed, and pantries are fitted up complete. There are four bed rooms, with large closets, on second floor. The piazza is inclosed, and it forms ample storage beneath the house. Cost, $2,500, complete. Mr. F.H. Fassett, architect, Portland, Maine.

31. EDWARD CLARK, pg 93

DWELLING AT KENNEBUNKPORT, MAINE
Scientific American Building Edition, May 1895

We present the country house of the Rev. Edward Clark, D.D., at Kennebunkport, Me. The building as now completed is one of the most picturesque residences along the coast, and it has many artistic features, including the terrace garden, which is a novel idea, giving privacy to the building, and at the same time a place for a quiet rest. It is built of shore rocks, selected from the coast by the proprietor, and are very beautiful in color, showing fine tones in reds, browns, blues, and yellows. The exterior walls of wood are covered with shingles, and left to weather finish. The roofs are also shingled, and left to finish in a similar manner. Dimensions: Front, 53 ft. 6 in.; side, 58 ft. 6 in., not including terrace and porte cochere. Height of ceilings: Cellar, 8 ft.; first story, 11 ft.; second, 10 ft.; third, 9 ft. The hall, 14x16, and 20 ft. in height, is finished in the Colonial style, and is treated in ivory white. It has a paneled wainscoting around both upper and lower halls, and there are fluted pilasters supporting beams, with carved capitals. The ceiling of this hall is paneled with moulded strips, with carved bases. The wall between the paneled and ceiling ribs is painted a light salmon color, and from the centre of this ceiling is suspended a wrought iron chandelier, with other brackets of similar metal, and very artistic in design. The staircase is built with twisted balusters, posts, and a mahogany rail. The drawing-rooms are treated with ivory white in a most exquisite manner. The colonnade effect between the drawing rooms is a pleasing feature, it being composed of archway and columns of a classic order. The ceiling is paneled and beamed, with carved brackets under the beams. The fireplace is built of long Perth Amboy bricks, with a massive carved mantel. The dining-room is trimmed with oak; it has a paneled wainscot, ceiling beams, and

a buffet built in, with leaded glass doors, and a refrigerator under same, with an opening in kitchen for ice., etc. The fireplace is an English grate, ornamented iron and tiled facings, and a carved mantel. There is a large amount of elaborate carving in this room and the other apartments, which has been done by the owner, Dr. Clark, and has been very much admired. Dr. Clark is famous for his beautiful wood-carving, and as a result of his pastime is the balcony and pulpit of the Church of the Puritans, 130th Street, New York, which he carved while rector, and which is the best example of wood-carving of its class in this country. The library is treated in cream white, and is fitted up with paneled wainscot, ceiling ribs, bookcases built in, and an opening out upon the terrace garden. Kitchen, maids' dining hall, and pantries are trimmed and wainscoted with white pine, finished natural. These apartments are furnished with the usual fixtures complete. All window jambs are paneled below window seats and back of same. These window seats occur throughout. The floors are laid with oak, and are wax finished. The bedrooms are finished with white pine, and are treated in colors and some stained work. There are four bedrooms, study, eight closets and bathroom, while the third floor contains the maid's bedroom, store and trunk rooms, and tower room, which is used as a studio. Bathroom is wainscoted and paved with tiles, and is fitted up with exposed plumbing. The cellar contains laundry, furnace, other necessary apartments, and a large cistern, from which the water is pumped into the tank on third floor, and thence supplying the house. The stable is built in keeping with the house, and is connected by a covered way. Mr. Henry Paston Clark, architect, Studio Building, Boston, Mass.

32. CHARLES H. MANNING, pg 95

A SEASIDE COTTAGE
Scientific American Building Edition,
January 1895

We publish a seaside cottage recently erected for C.H. Manning, Esq., at Kennebunkport, Maine. The building is picturesque and is most unique. It is designed after the old "New England" lean-to roof order, giving all the apartments on two floors, with low ceilings and large, open fireplaces. The principal feature of the exterior is the bay-window, chimney and an ell underpinning, built of rock-faced field stone laid up at random. The remainder of the exterior is built of wood and covered with shingles, and stained mahogany color. The roof is shingled and stained similar. Dimensions: Front, 70 ft.; side, 34 ft., exclusive of piazza. Height of ceilings: Cellar, 6 ft. 6 in.; first story, 9 ft.; second, 8 ft. White pine and spruce are the only woods used. The frame is well placed, and covered with matched and beaded stuff throughout the interior. The ceilings are framed with large beams, with small ribs between same; the wall beams are spaced to show in a similar manner. The hall contains an ornamental staircase and a paneled divan. Drawing-room is separated from hall and dining-room by archways with spindle transoms. It is furnished with paneled seat in bay window, and a large, open fireplace, built of long thin Perth Amboy bricks, with facings and hearth of the same, and finished hardwood mantel. Dining-room is well lighted. Kitchen, pantries, closets, shed and maid's room are fitted up with the usual fixtures in the best possible manner. The second floor consists of six bedrooms, and seven closets. Mr. Henry Paston Clark, architect, Boston, Mass.

33. MARGARET DELAND, pg 98

"GRAYWOOD," A COTTAGE AT KENNEBUNKPORT, MAINE
Scientific American Building Edition, July 1895

We present "Graywood," the summer home of Margaret Deland recently erected at Kennebunkport, Maine. The building is treated in the Colonial style, and it shows a picturesque perspective, combined with a well arranged plan. The building is erected on cedar posts, with stone footings. The exterior framework, of wood, is shingled on the exterior, and stained a silvery gray color, while the trimmings are painted bottle green. Roof shingled and stained same as other work. Dimensions: Front, 52 ft 6 in.; side, 28 ft., not including porches. Height of ceilings: First story, 9 ft. 6 in.; second, 9 ft. The interior is trimmed with whitewood, and painted China white. The lobby entrance is paneled. The living-room, which is the principal apartment, is located so as to face the ocean. It has a ribbed ceiling, and is provided with paneled divans, and a large, open fireplace built of brick, with facings and hearth of same, and a Colonial mantel made from special design. Dining-room is well ventilated, and thereby a cool room in summer. It contains entrance to staircase, which rises to second floor. This stairway is separated by a column extending to ceiling, and the space between filled in with ornamental spindles. Kitchen and its apartments are fitted up complete, and conveniently located. The second story contains five large bedrooms, and the third floor contains ample storage. Mr. Henry Paston Clark, architect, Studio Building, Boston, Mass.

34. B.S. THOMPSON, pg 100

A COTTAGE AT KENNEBUNKPORT, MAINE
Scientific American Building Edition, October 1895

We present a residence recently erected for B.S. Thompson, Esq., at Kennebunkport, Maine. The design is treated in the English style of architecture, half timber and stone, and the engravings show one of the most attractive and picturesque residences along the coast. It is situated on a point of rocks, with a commanding view of the ocean and Cape Porpoise. The stonework is built of shore rocks, and are laid up at random. The gables are ceiled up, and painted white, while the trimmings are painted bottle green. The shingle work is round-butted, like tiling, and is painted a tile red. The roof is shingled, and painted similar. Dimensions: Front, 45 ft.; side, 53 ft. 6 in., not including piazza and terrace. Height of ceiling: Cellar 8 ft.; first story, 10 ft.; second 9 ft,; third, 8 ft. 6 in. Hall, reception room (Porpoise view) and a drawing-room are trimmed with white pine, and painted China white in a delicate manner. These apartments are generally

connected, as may be seen by the plan, and are finished with wood cornices, and fluted columns of the Ionic order, supporting an archway, and forming an arcaded effect. Hall contains an ornamental staircase, with oak steps and risers, and balusters and newel, painted same as trim. Parlor is provided with a massive mantel, with columns, and the fireplace is built of red brick, and the hearth is paved with red tiles. Reception room is provided with a paneled divan, placed beneath a large 6 by 8 ft. plate glass window. Dining-room is trimmed with oak, and it has a paneled wainscot, ribbed ceiling, and an open fireplace built of brick, with tiled hearth and facings, and an oak mantel. Kitchen and pantries are well fitted up with the usual fixtures, and are wainscoted with narrow beaded stuff. The doors on first floor are veneered with oak, and the floors are laid with similar wood, and highly polished. The second floor contains four bedrooms, bathroom, and maid's bedroom and bath. These rooms are treated in delicate colors, are well lighted and ventilated, and are provided with large closets. The bathrooms are furnished with the best modern fixtures. There are three bedrooms on third floor, and also a trunk room. Cemented cellar contains furnace, laundry, and other apartments. The house is supplied with gas, water, electric lights and bells. Mr. Henry Paston Clark, architect, Studio Building, Boston, Mass.

35. FRANCIS BISHOP HARRINGTON, pg 104

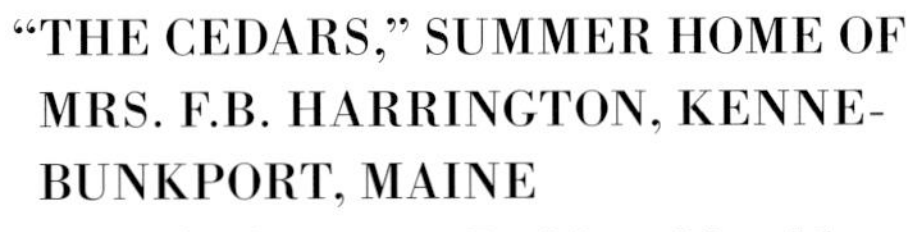

"THE CEDARS," SUMMER HOME OF MRS. F.B. HARRINGTON, KENNEBUNKPORT, MAINE

Scientific American Building Monthly, June 1905

The summer home of Mrs. F.B. Harrington, at Kennebunkport, Maine, is the subject of the illustrations. The house has the entrance at the side, so that all the rooms, so far as is possible, may have a view of the ocean. It is placed among a clump of cedars, from which it derives its name– "The Cedars."

There is no cellar under the house, and it rests upon cedar posts with stone footings. The exterior, from the grade to the peak, is covered with shingles, which are stained a dull brown color, soft in tone, while the trimmings are painted white. The roof is also shingled, and stained a dull green color. The latticed windows and transoms are interesting features of the exterior, and so is the chimney. The gambrel roof further carries out the easy sweeping lines of the house, nearly doubling the proportion of the whole.

A study of the plans shows an admirable scheme. The little den, near the entrance, where the business of the house can be carried on, a large living-room, a dining-room and kitchen form the combination of the first story. The den is trimmed with cypress, stained a Flemish brown, and harmonizes well with the crimson burlap on the walls.

The hall is treated in a similar manner and has a beamed ceiling, and an ornamental staircase, with square balusters and newel posts. The ample living-room is also trimmed with cypress, and is stained and finished in a forest green. Its comfortable fireplace, built of pressed buff brick and terra cotta, and its cozy nooks, with its books and seats, form an ideal place to stay when the cold storms blow in from the Atlantic. The walls of this room are paneled and the ceiling is beamed.

The dining-room is trimmed with cypress, finished with Flemish brown. It is furnished with a paneled wainscoting to the height of seven feet, and finished with a plate rack, above which the walls are covered with a decoration of greenish tones; the ceiling is beamed. There is an open fireplace built of pressed brick, with the facings and hearth of similar brick and a mantel. The butler's pantry is fitted up with a copper sink, drawers, etc.

The kitchen is fitted with all the best modern conveniences. It has a range, large store-pantry, and a laundry well fitted up. Off the laundry there is a servant's bathroom, fitted complete. The rear porch contains a coal and wood bin.

The second floor is trimmed with natural cypress, and it contains five bedrooms with large closets, and two bathrooms; the latter are furnished with porcelain fixtures and exposed nickel-plated plumbing.

The third floor contains the servants' quarters, and ample storage space.

Mr. Henry Paston Clark, architect, Studio Building, 110 Tremont Street, Boston, Mass.

36. JOSIAH H. DRUMMOND, JR., pg 110

A RESIDENCE AT PORTLAND, MAINE
Scientific American Architects and Builders Edition, July 1892

The engravings present a dwelling, erected for J. H. Drummond, Jr., at Western Promenade, Portland, Maine. The design is executed in the New England Style, rather modest in appearance with square outlines that are well broken by many bay windows and porches, giving it a good effect. The foundation is built of stone, while the underpinning is built of brick. The building above is clapboarded and painted colonial yellow, with white trimmings. Roof shingled and painted red. Dimensions: Front, 36 ft.; side, 61 ft. 6 in., not including piazza. Height of ceilings: cellar, 7ft, first story, 10 ft.; second, 9 ft.; third, 8 ft. 6 in. Hall trimmed with oak, contains a paneled divan, with column extending to ceiling and an ornamental staircase. This hall and staircase are lighted by stained glass windows. Parlor is finished in ivory white and it has a fireplace furnished with tiles and mantel of special design. Library and den are trimmed with whitewood, finished natural. Dining room is trimmed with oak and it has a paneled wainscoting and fireplace built of brick, with hearth laid with same. Floors of hard wood. Kitchen and its apartments are trimmed and wainscoted with whitewood, finished natural, and all furnished complete. Second floor, trimmed with similar wood, contains five bed rooms and bath room. Bath room is wainscoted and furnished complete. There are two bed rooms and storage on third floor. Cemented cellar contains furnace, laundry, and other necessary apartments. Cost $5,575 complete. Mr. John Calvin Stevens, architect, Portland.

37. FRANKLIN C. PAYSON, pg 114

RESIDENCE OF FRANKLIN C. PAYSON, ESQ. , AT PORTLAND, MAINE
Scientific American Building Monthly, June 1904

On these pages will be found illustrations of the residence of Franklin C. Payson, Esq., at Portland, Maine. The building is constructed from grade with red brick laid in the white mortar and with Flemish bond. The chimneys are treated likewise. The gables are covered with slate, and the roof is also covered with slate. All the detail throughout is Colonial, and the porches, cornice, and all exposed woodwork are treated with white paint. The blinds are painted bottle green. Dimensions: Front, 78 ft. 8 in.; side 46 ft., exclusive of porch and sun-parlor.

The vestibule has a tiled floor and a paneled wall. The hall is trimmed with pine and treated with white enamel. It has a paneled wainscoting, which extends around the hall, up the staircase, and around the second story hall. The staircase hall is separated from the entrance hall by an archway, supported on fluted pilasters and columns with Ionic capitals placed on paneled bases. The staircase is of an ornamental character, with white enameled balusters, posts, and risers, and mahogany rail and treads. At the side of the staircase there is an ornamental seat of white enamel treatment with mahogany arms. The drawing-room is treated with white enamel, and has an open fireplace furnished with white enameled tiling and a mantel of Colonial style. The den is treated with Flemish brown, and has a book case built in on one side of the fireplace. This open fireplace is built of brick, and has a quaint little mantel with cabinets, etc.

The living-room is trimmed with oak, and is finished in Flemish brown. The ceiling is heavily beamed, and the walls have a paneled wainscoting, except where the book cases are built in, and which occupy mostly the entire wall space. These book cases have leaded glass windows. The recessed window at the side of fireplace, with its paneled seat, book cases over same, and window glazed with leaded glass, forms an attractive feature. The broad open fireplace has a tiled facing and hearth, and a mantel shelf supported on corbel brackets over which there is a painted panel; on either side of the fireplace there are fluted pilasters, which rise and form the framework of the picture.

The dining-room is trimmed with white pine treated with white enamel, and the whole treatment is old Colonial. It has a paneled wainscoting to the height of four feet, and a wooden cornice. The broad, open fireplace has a tiled facing and hearth and a massive, broad mantel with columns, etc. The dining-room, and also the living-room, open onto the sun parlor, which is enclosed with glass and is furnished with a tiled floor. The butler's pantry is fitted up with sink, drawers, cupboards, etc. The kitchen and its dependencies, the immense pantry, rear hall, and stairway are furnished with all the best modern conveniences. The lavatory is conveniently placed.

The second story is trimmed with white pine and is treated with white enamel. This floor contains a large open hall, four bedrooms, and two bathrooms, and also two servant bedrooms and bath. Each bedroom is provided with ample closets, well fitted up, and there are also two linen closets. The bathrooms are paved and wainscoted with white enamel tile, and are fitted with porcelain fixtures and exposed nickelplated plumbing. A novel feature of this floor is the clothes closet with the outer and inner compartments.

The third floor contains a billiard room, three bed-rooms, and bath, and a trunk room. The cemented cellar contains a laundry, heating apparatus, fuel room, cold storage, etc. Mr. John Calvin Stevens, architect, Oxford Building, Portland, Maine.

38. HARRY BUTLER, pg 118

A PORTLAND RESIDENCE
Scientific American Building Edition,
February 1897

We present a residence recently erected for Harry Butler, Esq., at Portland, Me. The building is designed for a town house, and the main walls are constructed of brick, with red shingles and stained a moss green. Dimensions: Front 68 ft. 9 in.; side, 35 ft. not including piazza. Height of ceilings: Cellar, 7 ft 6 in.; first story, 10 ft.; second, 9 ft.; third, 8 ft 6 in. Vestibule is trimmed and paneled with oak. It has a paneled wainscoting and ceiling beams. The staircase is a handsome one, with broad landings, carved newel posts, seat and a cluster of stained glass windows, lighting with good effect. The floor is laid with oak. Reception room is treated with ivory white and gold in a most excellent manner, and is provided with a corner and window seat. Living-room, trimmed with cherry, is provided with an oak floor, a nook with archway and spindle transom, and an open fireplace, with tiled hearth and facings, and a massive carved mantel with columns and mirror. Dining-room is trimmed with whitewood and finished natural, and has a birch floor, window seat and a corner fireplace. Kitchen, pantries, and rear hall are trimmed and wainscoted with whitewood, and each apartment is furnished with the usual fixtures. The second floor, and also third floor, are trimmed with natural whitewood. The former contains three bedrooms, dressing, sewing, trunk and bath rooms, while the latter contains three bedrooms and ample storage. The bathroom is wainscoted and furnished complete with exposed plumbing. The bedroom, over dining-room, has a pleasant nook with paneled divan, and fireplace fitted up complete. Cemented cellar contains furnace, laundry and other necessary apartments. Mr. John Calvin Stevens, architect, Oxford Building, Portland, Me.

39. FRANKLIN B. STEPHENSON, pg 121

"EDGECOMBE," THE SUMMER HOME OF DR. FRANKLIN B. STEPHENSON, AT PROUTS NECK, MAINE
Scientific American Building Monthly,
July 1904

On these pages will be found illustrations of Edgecombe, the summer home of Dr. Franklin B. Stephenson, A.M., M.D., of the United States Navy, at Prouts Neck, Maine. The site upon which the house is situated is one typical to the coast of Maine, and the house is designed and built in

keeping with its surroundings, with its field stone balustrade and columns and the first story of the same, and the second story finished into a gambreled roof. This second story is covered on the exterior with shingles and is stained with shingle stain of a dark green color, while the trimmings are painted ivory white. The roof is also covered with shingles, and is stained in harmony. The triple dormer windows, overhanging as they do, form the principal characteristic of the exterior. Dimensions: Front, 66 ft.; side,; 54 ft., exclusive of piazza. Height of ceilings: Cellar, 7 ft.; first story, 10 ft.; second, 9 ft., third 8 ft.

The interior throughout is trimmed with yellow pine, finished natural. The living and dining rooms and den, which are practically one great room, have a high battened wainscoting, finished with a plate rack and a beamed ceiling. The plaster, which is shown to view, is of rough cast, and is tinted in harmony. The large open fireplaces are built of field stone, laid up at random, with hearths of red brick. There are numerous seats and bookcases built in, and an open staircase built in an attractive manner. The butler's pantry is fitted with drawers, dressers, and sink, and the kitchen and laundry are well fitted with all the best modern conveniences. There is a bathroom on the first floor, which is fitted up with all the necessary conveniences.

The second floor is treated with ivory white paint, and all the rooms are provided with a three-foot wainscoting. This floor contains a large open hall, a sitting-room, six bedrooms, linen closet, large clothes closets, and two bathrooms, the latter furnished with porcelain fixtures and exposed nickelplated plumbing. The open fireplaces, which are shown on the plan, are built of brick, with the facings and a hearth of the same and a mantel.

The third floor contains one room and ample storage space. The house was built from the instructions of Mrs. Stephenson, and by Mr. Alonzo L. Gorgius, a builder of Prouts Neck, Maine.

40. G.T. EDWARDS & C.E. MILLER, pg 125

A DOUBLE DWELLING HOUSE
Scientific American Building Edition,
December 1896

These illustrations present views of the exterior, interior, and floor plans of a double dwelling house, which has been erected for Mr. George T. Edwards and Mr. Charles E. Miller, at Deering, Me. The elevations show a dwelling executed in the modern style, with colonial detail. The plans show the porches placed at either end of the building, providing side entrances, thereby adding a new feature, and departing from the usual scheme of having the entrances at front with adjoining piazzas. The underpinning is built of brick laid up in white mortar. The exterior framework is sheathed, clapboarded, and painted light cream, with light olive green trimmings. The blinds are painted bottle green, and the roof is shingled and painted a reddish brown. Dimensions: Front, 51ft.; side, 45 ft., not including porches. Height of ceilings; Cellar, 7 ft.; first story 9 ft. 6 in.; second, 9 ft.; third, 8 ft. 6 in. The reception halls are the principal features on the first floor. They are trimmed with cypress and finished natural.

These apartments are connected to parlors and dining-rooms by sliding doors, allowing the three rooms to be thrown into one apartment when desired. A good sized fireplace with brick facings and hearth, and a mantel of colonial design with columns and mirror, add much of the beauty of each hall, while the staircases with fluted newel posts extending to ceiling form a unique background for same. The large ornamental windows, overlooking the piazzas, are glazed with stained glass of rose tints. The parlors are trimmed with white pine and treated with ivory white and gold; they are provided with open fireplaces furnished with cream white tiles and mantels of good design; and also bay windows in five sections which form a graceful sweep for one end of the rooms. The dining-rooms are trimmed with cypress, and are fitted up with whitewood and finished natural; the former are wainscoted and fitted up with the usual fixtures. Halls, dining rooms, kitchens, and bathroom have hardwood floors. The second floor, of each house, contains four bedrooms, closets, and bathrooms; the bedroom, over parlor, is treated in ivory white and is provided with an open fireplace with tiled trimmings and mantel. Bathroom is wainscoted and fitted up replete. Third floor of each house contains one bedroom and ample storage. Cemented cellars contain furnace, laundry and other necessary apartments. Cost, including plumbing, heating, painting and papering, $4,500. The elevations were designed by Mr. F.A. Tompson, architect, Portland, Me., and the plans and suggestions taken from SCIENTIFIC AMERICAN by the proprietor.

41. PEREZ BURNHAM, pg 128

RESIDENCE OF PEREZ B. BURNHAM, ESQ., AT PORTLAND, MAINE
Scientific American Building Monthly, July 1904

The illustrations shown on page 7 present the residence of Perez B. Burnham, Esq., which has been erected on the Western Promenade, at Portland, Maine. The building, square in form, is built of red brick, laid in Flemish bond, with Indiana limestone trimmings, and the woodwork is very well detailed, and the whole is painted white. The severity of the design is relieved by the ornamental porch and balustrade which surrounds the roof. Dimensions: Front, 45 ft. 9 in.; side, 67 ft. 8 in., exclusive of the porch. Height of ceilings: Cellar, 7 ft.; first story, 11 ft.; second, 10 ft.; third, 9 ft.

The interior throughout is trimmed with white wood, treated with china white enamel paint. The hall is a central one, reached through a vestibule with a paneled wainscoting, wooden cornice, and a tiled floor. An archway with a pilaster effect separates the entrance hall from the staircase with white enameled risers and balusters, oak treads, and mahogany tail and newel posts. A lavatory beneath the stairway is conveniently located.

The drawing-room has a low Colonial wainscoting and an open fireplace with tiled facings and a hearth, and mantel made from a special design. The library and dining-room are treated similarly, and each has an open fireplace. The principal rooms on the first floor have floors of polished quartered oak. Unusual attention has been given to the butler's and serving pantries, and each is furnished with many cupboards, dressers, sink, etc., complete. These pantries and kitchen are trimmed with brown ash, and the floors are of spruce. The kitchen is fitted with all the best modern conveniences, and the chimney breast is faced with glazed enameled brick. The lobby is well placed, and the ice box is of large dimensions.

The second floor is treated with china white enamel, and it contains three bedrooms, fitted with large closets, and two bathrooms, besides two servant bedrooms and bath, which are placed over the kitchen extension, and are reached by a private hall and stairway, and also from the second floor of the main house. The bathrooms have tiled wainscotings and floors and porcelain fixtures with exposed nickelplated plumbing

The billard-room is trimmed with cypress, stained forest green, and the smoking-room is treated the same, with a fireplace with red brick hearth and facings and mantel. This floor also contains two guest rooms, bathroom, and a truck room. A cemented cellar contains a furnace, laundry, fuel rooms, cold storage, etc. Mr. George Burnham, architect, 120 Exchange Street, Portland, Maine.

42. FREDERICK L. SAVAGE, pg 132

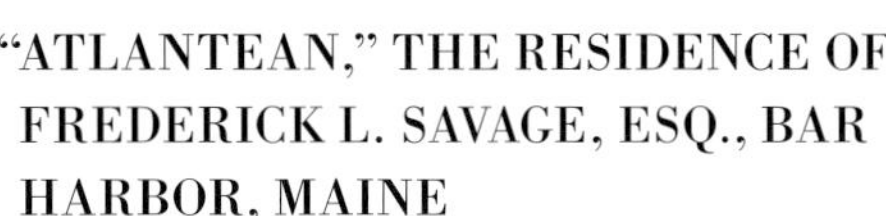

"ATLANTEAN," THE RESIDENCE OF FREDERICK L. SAVAGE, ESQ., BAR HARBOR, MAINE
Scientific American Building Monthly, March 1904

The illustrations present Atlantean, the residence of Frederick L. Savage, Esq., at Bar Harbor, Maine. The underpinning and first story are built of Bear Brook granite, with rock-faced ashlar laid in red mortar. The beams of the second and third stories are treated in a natural state with hard oil and stain, and the spaces between the half-timber work are covered with stucco, which is left in its natural silvery gray color. The roof is covered with shingles and is stained a dull shade of moss green. Dimensions: Front, 55 ft.; side, 53 ft., exclusive of porches. Height of ceilings: Cellar, 7 ft.; first story, 9 ft 6 in.; second, 8 ft, 6 in.; third 8 ft.

The entrance is into a square central hall, which is trimmed with oak and treated in a Flemish brown. The walls have a plate rack extending around the hall at the height of five feet, from which perpendicular strips descend at various intervals to the base, forming wall spaces which are covered in crimson burlap in an effective manner. The wall space above is tinted to harmonize. The open fireplace is built of red brick, laid in red mortar, with a hearth of same, and a recess containing an ornamental staircase, underneath which a short flight of steps descends to the lavatory. The parlor is trimmed with white pine, and is treated with white enamel paint. It contains an open fireplace of brick, and is furnished with a quaint little Colonial mantel.

The second floor is trimmed with white pine treated with ivory white paint, and contains five bedrooms and two bathrooms: the latter furnished with tiled floor and wainscoting and porcelain fixtures and exposed nickelplated plumbing. Each bedroom is fitted with a large well fitted closet, and open fireplace in each bedroom except the bedroom over the kitchen. The third floor contains five bedrooms and a bathroom and a trunk room. The cemented cellar contains a laundry, fuel and furnace rooms. Mr. Frederick L. Savage, architect, Bar Harbor, Maine.

43. JOHN D. JONES, pg 136

"REVERIE COVE," THE SUMMER HOME OF MRS. M.C. JONES, BAR HARBOR, MAINE
Scientific American Building Monthly, December 1904

The summer home of Mrs. M.C. Jones, at Bar Harbor, Me., is located on a high point of ground, sloping to the water's edge. On account of the prominence of the site, as well as its exposure, a special scheme of construction was adopted. The land slopes off rapidly to the sea, and it permitted the placing of the kitchen, servants' hall, laundry and their dependencies in the basement. The house is designed in the Spanish style, and its exterior walls are built of stucco, which is stained a soft yellow color, while the trimmings are painted an apple green. The shingle roof is stained a brilliant red and forms a very happy contrast with the color scheme.

The entrance is into a square vestibule of large dimensions, from which the living-hall is reached. Both are painted in dark Flemish oak, and the latter has a paneled wainscoting and a beamed ceiling. Massive fluted columns form the newel posts to the staircase, and the arcaded effect produced in the living-hall. The staircase rises from either side of the hall to a broad landing, from which a central run rises to the second story, the under side of which is handsomely paneled. A cluster of latticed windows is placed on the landing, and also below the same. The fireplace is built of old gold Roman brick, with the facings and a hearth of the same, and a massive mantel. The smoking-room to the right of the vestibule is finished in a similar manner, and it has an open fireplace built of Roman brick.

The drawing-room is trimmed with pine and is treated with white paint, and has a low paneled wainscoting of Colonial style, and an open fireplace built of white enameled brick, with the facings and hearth of the same, and mantel with fluted pilasters supporting the shelf.

The dining-room is finished in Flemish oak, and has a paneled wainscoting three and one-half feet in height; it also has an alcove with paneled seat, with a buffet built in on either side of the alcove, and an open fireplace with gold speckled brick facings, and a mantel to correspond with the character of the room.

The second floor is trimmed with white pine, finished naturally. This floor contains six bedrooms, boudoir, two dressing-rooms, and two bathrooms; the latter are finished with white enamel and furnished with porcelain fixtures and exposed nickelplated plumbing. The floors, throughout, are of hard wood. The third floor contains the servants' rooms and bath, trunk room and two guest rooms.

Mr. Fred L. Savage, architect, Bar Harbor, Maine.

44. CATHERINE CHEYNEY BARTOL, pg 140

AN INEXPENSIVE SUMMER HOME AT PROUT'S NECK, MAINE
Scientific American Building Monthly, February 1904

This inexpensive summer home has been recently completed for Mrs. Cheney Bartol, at Prout's Neck, Maine. The building is treated in the half-timber style. The house is erected on cedar posts with stone footings, and the exterior is covered with novelty clapboards, and the whole is painted a dark bottle green. The first story above this clapboarding is covered with narrow matched stuff, which is also painted a dark bottle green. The second and third stories are sheathed, covered with two thicknesses of building paper, and then with canvas, and the beamed strips are then placed in position, forming panels, which are painted a deep yellow and the beams a bottle green. The roof is covered with shingles and is stained a deep red. Dimensions: Front, 49 ft.; side, 32 ft., exclusive of porch and piazza. Height of ceilings: Cellar, 6 ft. 6 in.; first story, 9 ft.; second, 8 ft.; third, 8 ft.

The interior throughout is trimmed with cypress, and the principal rooms in the first story are finished in Flemish brown. The living-room has a paneled seat, with a unique little bookcase at one side, and a beamed ceiling; the woodwork, which is stained a Flemish brown, harmonizes nicely with the rough plastered walls, which are tinted in a deep yellow tone. The rough brick fireplace is an attractive feature of this room. The staircase hall is well located, and contains an ornamental stair-

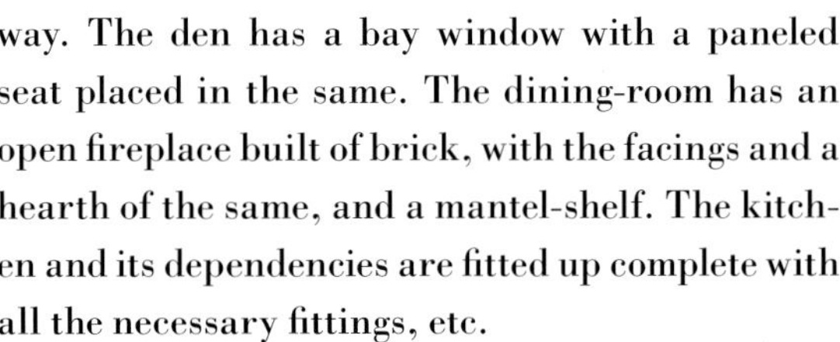

way. The den has a bay window with a paneled seat placed in the same. The dining-room has an open fireplace built of brick, with the facings and a hearth of the same, and a mantel-shelf. The kitchen and its dependencies are fitted up complete with all the necessary fittings, etc.

The second floor contains five bedrooms provided with large closets, and a bathroom furnished with porcelain fixtures and exposed nickelplated plumbing. The third floor contains the servant quarters and a trunk room. The cellar has a laundry and fuel room.

Cost, $3,200 complete. Mr. John Calvin Stevens, architect, Oxford Building, Portland, Maine.

44. DOUGLASS SHERLEY, pg 144

"BIRCH NEST," THE SUMMER HOME OF DOUGLASS SHERLEY, ESQ., AT BAR HABOR, MAINE
Scientific American Building Monthly, August 1904

A very novel and interesting house at Bar Harbor, Maine is that built for Douglass Sherley, Esq. It is built of rock-faced boulders for the first story and chimneys, and birch logs for the second and third stories. The boulders for the stone-work have been carefully selected and have been placed in position with great care, so as to not show the mortar joints. The logs for the superstructure are of birch, and have been cut with the bark on, so as to present the rustic effect which the building now shows and to keep it in harmony with the stone wok and the silvery gray shingled roof. The small lighted windows, the dormer windows, and the stone chimneys are all agreeable features. The main entrance to the estate is provided with gate posts formed of huge boulders, strapped together with iron bands, and ornamented with an anchor and chain which can be stretched across the opening to the entrance, the latter being provided with a cluster of farm lanterns.

The entrance porch is lighted by a nautical lantern, which is hung from an ornamental iron bracket, and the entrance door is formed of rough boards hung with large hinges of wrought iron, which are painted white, while the door is stained a soft brown color.

The interior is unique. The timber, which is rough hewn, is exposed, and the archways and openings between the various rooms in the first story are formed with a cluster of birch logs for columns. The living-hall is stained a soft greenish color, and contains an ingle nook, the walls of which are of stone and exposed to view. The fireplace is built of Roman brick, while the hearth is formed of small cobblestones laid in cement mortar. A short flight of steps leads from the living-hall to the stair-hall, and from which the living room is entered. This living-room is stained a yellowish color, with the windows at the left of the room glazed with green glass, shedding a soft and pleasant light over the entire apartment. There is a stone fireplace in the corner of the room which is built of large granite blocks, with the hearth laid with flat cobblestones laid in a cement mortar.

A short flight of steps from the living-room leads to the dining-room. It is stained a soft green color, and contains a large open fireplace with massive granite facings and a hearth of small cobblestones laid in cement mortar. The breakfast-room has a very attractive cabinet built in for china. The butler's pantry is fitted up with all the best modern conveniences. The kitchen, servant's hall, and all its necessary dependencies are placed in the basement under the breakfast and dining-rooms.

The den is the most attractive room in the building, and is placed over the living-hall. The walls are ceiled to the height of seven feet, and above which the studding and rafters are exposed to view. The space between the rafters and studs is filled in with birch sticks, cut and placed horizontally. The fireplace is built of rough brick, with the facings of brick carried up to the height of nine feet. The hearth, which is of flat cobblestones, is laid one foot above the floor level, and on either side of which are wooden desks built in.

Another short flight of steps leads to the chamber floor, which contains three bedrooms, one of which is stained an olive color, another yellow, and a third red. There is also a bathroom, which is fitted up complete in every respect. The third floor contains ample storage space and the servant quarters. The house was designed and built under the direction of Mr. Sherley. Mr. Calvin H. Norris did the mason work and Mr. A.E. Lawrence the carpenter work.

46. D.D. WALKER, pg 147

THE SUMMER HOME OF D.D. WALKER, ESQ., KENNEBUNKPORT, MAINE
Scientific American Building Monthly, March 1905

The summer home of D.D. Walker, Esq., at Kennebunkport, Maine, is planned in the rambling manner. The terrace wall and chimneys, underpinning and the columns supporting the porte-cochere are built of rock-faced stone laid up at random. The remainder of the house is covered with cement stucco, left in its natural soft gray color. The trimmings are stained a soft brown color. The two chimneys are architectural features in themselves, and the twin gable between the same in the roof is also a good feature. The roof is stained a deep red color.

The entrance hall, which is placed in the angle formed by the intersection of the two wings of the house, has a white painted trim, crimson walls, wood cornice, and an ornamental staircase with painted balusters and posts, and a mahogany rail. A lavatory is conveniently placed under the stairway.

The living-room, of unusually large dimensions, is also furnished with a white painted trim. It has a low paneled wainscoting of the Colonial type, and a massive beamed and ribbed ceiling. The alcove nook is separated by an archway, and is furnished with paneled seats, and a flower shelf in the front of the windows. The fireplace has a brick hearth and facings, and a mantel. The walls are treated in a soft green color, in harmony with the white trim, and very appropriate for a summer house. The draperies are in tones of green, white and red. The den is treated in red and white, and has a fireplace, paneled seat, and a bookcase.

The dining-room is separated from the hall by an attractive archway, with columns at either side of the entrance, and the whole forming a lobby effect. This dining-room is in a combination of green walls and white trim, and has a high paneled wainscoting furnished with a plate-rack, and a beamed ceiling. There is a china cabinet built in, and furnished with doors glazed in latticed form. One end of the room is taken up with an open fireplace with the facings rising up to the ceiling; on either side of this fireplace there are unique little nooks, fitted with leaded glass windows, in front of which there are paneled seats. At the opposite end of the room there is a bay window with a flower-shelf.

The kitchen and its dependencies are planned with a view of providing all the necessary comforts for the servants, which has now begun to form so important a part in the modern house. The pantries are well fitted up, and so are the kitchen and the laundry, and the servants' dining hall.

The second story contains six bedrooms, large closets, dressing-room, three bathrooms, nurses' room, besides a large linen room, and the servant quarters, which are isolated from the rest of the house, with a private stairway, and consist of three bedrooms and bath. The bathrooms have porcelain fixtures and exposed nickelplated plumbing. The third floor contains an open attic for storage, trunk-rooms, etc. There is a cemented cellar under the entire house, containing a heating apparatus, fuel rooms, etc.

Messrs. Chapman and Frazer, architects, 8 Exchange Place, Boston, Mass.

47. GEORGE H. WALKER, pg 151

"ROCK LEDGE," THE SUMMER OF GEORGE H. WALKER, ESQ.
American Homes and Gardens, July 1905

This recently completed house has been built as the summer home of George H. Walker, Esq., at Kennebunkport, Maine. The site is a very rocky and rugged one, from which the name "Rock Ledge" is derived. Its rugged cliffs rise high up out of the sea.

The house has been designed in the style of the modern rambling and elongated type, is built out over the rocks, and rests upon stone footings, which have been built and brought up to a proper level for the foundation. The building, above, is constructed of wood, and is covered on the exterior framework, from the grade to the peak, with cedar shingles, which are stained a soft brown color. The trimmings are painted a dark bottle green. The roof is also covered with shingles and is stained a dull green, with harmonious effect; it blends well into the scheme of color used for the side walls. The columns of the piazza, the terrace wall, and chimneys are built of rock-faced field stone taken from the premises, and are very beautiful in their colors of old gray, blue, green and brown. The house has an average length of 145 feet and a depth of 35 feet.

The entrance has a small porch only, but broad piazzas on the ocean side afford both the view and the privacy needed in a house of this description. The principal living-room, located in the center of the house, with openings on both sides, forms the nucleus of the whole plan, and the den adjoining opens onto a long piazza, for the use of the family, and is so designed and located as to afford ample shelter from the sun, and yet be swept by the prevailing breezes from the southwest. At the other extreme end of the house is the servants' accommodations, which are conveniently placed as to utilize the same breeze to carry off all the cooking odors and smoke.

The living-room is trimmed with yellow pine, treated with stained and finished in a forest green. It has a paneled wainscoting and a beamed ceiling. The staircase, while placed conveniently, is practically isolated from view by the paneled seat with its high back and its ornamental balustrade. On the opposite side of the room there is an ingle nook provided with a paneled seat. The fireplace is built with brick facings and hearth and a mantel. The den has a similar fireplace, and also a window seat. The woodwork is of yellow pine treated in Flemish brown. The walls are treated with battens forming panels, which are filled in with green burlap.

The dining-room, which is placed two steps below the level of the living-room floor, is treated with white enamel paint, and has a paneled wainscoting of the Colonial type. The walls above this wainscoting are covered with a brilliant wall covering, with a white back-ground showing a large green figure, and the whole finished with a molded cornice. The fireplace is built of red brick laid in white mortar, with the facings and hearth of a similar brick and mantel of Colonial style. On one side of the fireplace is a buffet built in, with cupboards below the counter shelf and shelves above, which are enclosed with leaded glass doors and the whole trimmed with bronze furnishings. The circular baywindow at the opposite end of the room is well placed, from which a view is obtained up and down the coast.

The butler's pantry is well fitted with sink, drawers, shelves, etc. The kitchen is planned with ventilation at both ends, and thereby provides a very cool and comfortable kitchen. It is fitted with a sink, counter, range, store pantry, well fitted laundry shed, for the storage of fuel, and a servants' dining-hall, which is a necessary adjunct to the well appointed house.

The second story is treated with white paint, and this floor contains six bedrooms, two bathrooms, besides two servants' bedrooms with a private stairway to the kitchen. A feature of this plan is that the hall is kept to the front so that the principal rooms face the ocean. Some of the bedrooms have paneled seats, open fireplaces, and all are treated with artistic wall decorations. The bathrooms are furnished with porcelain fixtures and exposed nickelplated plumbing. The third floor contains the trunk room, and several extra rooms.

Messrs. Chapman and Frazer, architects, 8 Exchange Pace, Boston, Mass.

48. A.J. CASSATT, pg 159

"FOURACRE" THE SUMMER HOME OF THE LATE A.J. CASSATT, AT BAR HARBOR, MAINE
American Homes and Gardens, July 1910

A house as big as all outdoors and built almost directly on the water, is a terse description of the great rambling summer home build for the late A.J. Cassatt, at Bar Harbor, by Messrs Chapman & Fraser, architects of Boston. It is a vast and comfortable dwelling, built, apparently, with a most delightful disregard of the economy often entailed by cost and space, built in a truly rambling way, room added to room, corridor added to corridor, spreading out, if not in every direction, at least in so delightfully extended a way as to seem almost as endless in extent as it is actually boundless in sufficiency and convenience.

It should not be supposed, however, that all this great upbuilding was done in a haphazard manner or without regard to architectural principles. Mr. Cassatt desired a big roomy house of ample space and ease, a house big enough to live in, in a large and comfortable way, yet of modest and quiet design, suited alike to the situation, to the needs of the house as a place for relaxation and simple living. The program was simple enough, yet it may be admitted without any hesitation, that the problem might have been solved in a more elaborate manner without any wide departure from the elementary conditions. But one may be sure it would not have been so attractive a house, nor one so well suited to meet the wishes of its large-hearted builder.

There are no frills on this house, and none were wanted. It is the highest compliment that can be paid to add that none are needed. It exactly meets the requirements demanded of it, and is exactly what it purports to be. Those who knew Mr. Cassatt would instantly characterize it as precisely the sort of a house he would have desired for this place. Other houses, built and designed in a different way, met his wishes in other localities. But here, in the bracing air of Bar Harbor, this is the kind of a house to build, and the sort of a house to live in.

It is a thoroughly excellent type of the large seashore cottage. It is neither a palace nor a mansion, but a really fine type of the seaside "cottage." Of course, it is large, but that is because it was intended to be big; but with all its size no part departs from the true "cottage" type. In a period when the large seashore house is apt to violate every traditional thought in connection with houses so located, it is something to have a house that so finely illustrates the simple type of architecture, particularly when it does so on so extended a scale.

The house is two stories in height, with great high pitched roofs, a goodly portion of which contains a third story. The first story is built of brick, covered with stucco, with an outer coat of cream white plaster. The second story is frame and shingled and stained dark brown. The roof is shingled and stained like the second story.

As for the design, the house is "just built." It has no architectural façade, no ornamental front in the common acceptance of the word; but it is obviously a house of exceeding comfort and great spaciousness. Where windows are needed they are opened. Where doors are required, they are sufficiently placed. If a bay window is sought to add charm to an interior, it is included in the design. Where expansion is required, it is allowed; and if contraction seems the better thing then that too finds its place in the plan. Both architects and client must have found abundant satisfaction in the seashore home they set about building in this friendly manner; for surely it must have been a friendly work, in which all parties showed a pleasant zest.

Mr. Cassatt's house gives every evidence of a rambling plan, yet this is simply the playful character given it by its architects. It is, in reality, a thoroughly well ordered and carefully studied dwelling, planned with admirable skill and in a thoroughly artistic manner. As usual in large country houses it consists of two parts, the main portion, containing the public rooms and the bedrooms, and a service wing, which is devoted to the servants. As has become much the vogue in later years the last has been deflected at an angle from the main axis, a variation in plan that sufficiently explains its purpose, while giving a welcome mobility to the ground plan and elevations.

The house is entered through a porch that connects with the porte cochere, a simple little pointed roof structure, with stuccoed brick piers and a opened roof frame. Entrance is immediately made to the hall, a large and spacious apartment, comfortably furnished. The ceiling is beamed, but is otherwise undecorated. The walls are hung with yellow grass-cloth-the most cheerful of all colors for a hall. The woodwork is ash, stained to the color of dark weathered oak. The furniture and curtains are of the most part yellow and mahogany figured madras. The stairs to the second story are immediately to the right as the hall is entered.

On the right are two rooms, the first directly adjoining the entrance being the library, while the second, and larger room, overlooking the water, is the living-room. The ceiling has exposed beams, with plan undecorated panels. The wood work is cypress, stained dark green. The walls are hung with gray-green grass-cloth. The furniture is in the Mission style, and the draperies are green figured madras and green velour portieres. The fireplace, which is a conspicuous feature of one side of the room, is faced with green Grueby tile, with a Jungle tile frieze of full greens, yellows, and blues.

The living-room is an apartment of splendid size, and occupying a corner of the house on the water side, is most agreeable situated. Two massive beams divide the ceiling into three great panels. The walls are covered with old gray-blue burlap, and the woodwork is birch stained gray. Exposed vertical uprights divide the wall surfaces into panels which are surmounted by a figured frieze between exposed borders of wood. The frieze represents a "Duc de Guise" hunting scene in wood browns, mahogany and dull blues. An immense fireplace fills the space between two windows on one side of the room. It is faced with rough cherry, red brick laid with gray joints, and is surmounted with a great dull copper hood. A leathern apron depends from beneath the mantel shelf. The draperies are figured madras in shades of blue, and the furniture is, for the most part, of willow, stained gray-green and with covers of figured cretonnes.

The dining-room is the chief apartment on the left of the hall. Once more this is a room of large size. The ceiling is beamed with small panels and the walls are designed with a panel scheme of uprights and horizontals, the latter being arranged to form a frieze at the top. The wall covering is dull blue figured burlap, with draperies of the same material. Immediately in face, as the room is entered from the main hall, is the fireplace. It occupies a recess, lined throughout with cherry red brick, with a hearth of quarry tile that covers the entire recess. The fire opening is arched, and is provided with a copper hood. The woodwork is red birch stained dark mahogany. The furniture is mahogany.

On the left of the main hall is a smaller one that serves as a connecting corridor with the rest of the house. Here on the entrance front, is the owner's office, and immediately beyond it begins the very extensive suite of service rooms. There is, of course, a butler's pantry that connects the dining-room with the kitchen, and which, in its turn, is associated with a larger and a store room. In the deflected service wing is the servants' suite, consisting of a bedroom, servants' dining hall, and kitchen, with the laundry at the farthest end. All of these rooms are reached by a corridor that extends along the entrance front. Mention should also be made of the man's room and the housekeeper's room, both of which adjoin the office.

The gardener's cottage and the stable call for some mention. The former is a pleasant little shingled house, two stories in height, with a low pointed roof, that is carried over the second story windows in gentle curves, giving a characteristic outline. The house is shingled throughout.

The stable is an elaborate structure, built around three sides of an open court, the first, or entrance side of which is enclosed within a solid fence. The gables of the roof are cleverly managed, and form an agreeable grouping. The building is built with a rough sawed frame showing on the exterior, and lined with hard pine planks, planed and varnished on the inside, but left rough on the outside. The whole exterior is stained dark brown.

There is nothing wanting in this place, either in comfort, convenience or luxury; yet it is essentially a "home" house, a simple, unpretentious structure, so far as a house of this size can be designated as simple and unpretentious. Unmistakably a house built for comfort, it avoids in a quite striking degree, any character of pretense, any undue ornamentation, any unnecessary decoration, and unessential enrichment of parts, and very particularly it should be noted, the modern crime of over-furnishing.

It is a comfortable house and therefore a good one. It is comfortable because that was the prevailing thought, the leading motive of its upbuilding. And it is good because this comfort has been given acceptable and graceful form by the architects, who, at every point, have risen to the demands of the problem and have solved each difficulty in a plain, straightforward, direct and satisfying manner.

To a very great extent this is the true essence of house-building. It compels success, because no other end than success can be reached if this path is faithfully followed. "Fouracre" is a place that will well repay study for it amply merits careful scrutiny.

49. THOMAS B. VAN BUREN, pg 163

"PINE HAVEN," THE SUMMER HOME OF THOMAS B. VAN BUREN, ESQ., AT KENNEBUNKPORT, MAINE
American Homes and Gardens, November 1909

The approach is an introduction to a house, and it is so with the summer home of Mr. Van Buren's. It is very happily situated in a group of pines, from which it gets its name "Pine Haven," and which implies a panacea to all ills and creates a restful place.

The house has a stone foundation and underpinning. The exterior is covered with shingles, stained a soft brown color, and the trimmings are painted bottle-green. The roof is also covered with shingles and stained a moss-green. The blinds are painted green. The chimneys are built of fieldstone. The plan is well arranged with a view to light, air and ventilation. Its entrance is placed at the side of the house and is well balanced by a porte-cochere, thus affording an opportunity for the placing of all the principal rooms on the ocean front of the house.

The hall, trimmed with cypress, is stained and finished in a dark Flemish brown. The staircase is of a simple character and is in keeping with its particular style. It has a newel post formed by a column which rises up and supports an arched beam. The walls have a paneled wainscoting and a beamed ceiling. Underneath the staircase there is an inviting nook, with seats and windows. The den at the rear of the living-room is treated in a green weathered oak finish. It has a wall covered with batten strips forming panels. These panels are covered with crimson burlap. There is an open fireplace, with brick facings and hearth and a mantel, at one side of which there is a paneled seat. The dining-room is designed in Colonial style, and is treated with white enamel. The walls have a paneled wainscoting to the height of seven

feet, and the latter is finished with a plate-rack, above which the wall surface is covered with a blue and white wall-paper, the whole rising to the ceiling, which is paneled and beamed. A china closet is built in at the left of the pantry door, with a cupboard beneath the counter shelf, and shelves above, enclosed with glass doors of lattice design. The fireplace has a red brick facing and hearth, and a mantel of Colonial style. The butler's pantry is fitted with all the best conveniences, and the kitchen, laundry and dependencies are provided with all the necessary modern appointments.

The color scheme of the second floor is harmonious and effective. The woodwork is painted white, while the walls of the various rooms are treated in one tone. The master's bedrooms are placed at the front of the hose, so that each one may have a view of the ocean, while the hall from which they are reached is built at the rear of the house. There are two bathrooms, furnished with porcelain fixtures and exposed nickel-plated plumbing. The servants'-rooms and bathroom are built in the extension over the kitchen, and are accessible by a private staircase leading from the first floor. The third floor contains extra guestrooms and bath, and storage space.

The scheme of designing this dwelling was commenced with the conviction that the highest aim in architectural motive was to construct a building that would in every way attain the purpose intended.

50. E.C. STANWOOD, pg 166

RESIDENCE OF E.C. STANWOOD, ESQ., KENNEBUNKPORT, MAINE
American Homes and Gardens, June 1911

The house built for E.C. Stanwood, Esq., at Kennebunkport, Me., presents an excellent example for a summer home, with its large, open, well-ventilated rooms and ample piazzas. The principal feature of the house is its elongated form, low and rambling, which makes it present a picturesque effect. The site on which it is built is well wooded with pines, and the building rests upon a knoll of sufficient height to permit its overlooking the sea. The underpinning, the wall for the terrace and the chimneys are of rock-faced local stone laid up in a rough manner. The exterior walls of the building are covered with shingles and left to weather finish a soft brown, while the trimmings are painted a dull olive green. The roof is also covered with shingles and is painted a dull green with a harmonious effect. The entrance is direct into a central hall, which extends through the house. This hall is trimmed with cypress and is finished in a Flemish brown. It has a beamed ceiling and a paneled wainscoting to the height of five feet, at which point a plate-rack extends around the room. At the entrance front of the house there is a paneled seat, over which there is grouped a cluster of small windows. The staircase is recessed in an alcove to the left of the hall, and has an ornamental balustrade and a paneled wainscoting extending to the second story. The living-room, which forms the principal feature of the modern summer home, is placed to the right of the entrance. The woodwork is of cypress, finished in a soft brown tone. It has a paneled wainscoting, finished with a plate-rack, and a beamed ceiling. The large open fireplace is built of rock-faced boulders for the facings, and it has a hearth of red tile and a mantel at the height of the wainscoting, supported on carved corbel brackets. There is an attractive over-mantel of Gothic design. To the left of the fireplace there is an inviting nook, with seats and windows. The den at the rear of the living-room is treated in a green weathered oak finish. It has a wall covered with batten strips forming panels. These panels are covered with crimson burlap. There is an open fireplace, with brick facings and hearth and a mantel, at one side of which there is a paneled seat. The dining-room is designed in Colonial style, and is treated with white enamel. The walls have a paneled wainscoting to the height of seven feet, and the latter is finished with a plate-rack, above which the wall surface is covered with a blue and white wall-paper, the whole rising to the ceiling, which is paneled and beamed. A china closet is built in at the left of the pantry door, with a cupboard beneath the counter shelf, and shelves above, enclosed with glass doors of lattice design. The fireplace has a red brick facing and hearth, and a mantel of Colonial style. The butler's pantry is fitted with all the best conveniences, and the kitchen and laundry and dependencies are provided with all the necessary modern appointments.

The color scheme of the second floor is harmonious and effective. The woodwork is painted white, while the walls of the various rooms are treated in one tone. The master's bedrooms are placed at the front of the house, so that each one may have a view of the ocean, while the hall from which they are reached is built at the rear of the house. There are two bathrooms, furnished with porcelain fixtures and exposed nickel-plated plumbing. The servants'-rooms and bathroom are built in the extension over the kitchen, and are accessible by a private staircase leading from the first floor. The third floor contains extra guestrooms and bath, and storage space.

The scheme of designing this dwelling was commenced with the conviction that the highest aim in architectural motive was to construct a building that would in every way attain the purpose intended.

Mr. Stanwood wanted a summer home that in arrangement of the rooms, in the design of the exterior, and the building of the porches, would represent the expression of the best thought obtainable for the building of a house that was intended only for summer use, so he employed Messrs. Chapman and Fraser, architects of Boston, Mass., to carry out his work and ideas. That they have succeeded goes without saying, for the house and its appointments meet with all the requirements demanded of it. The grounds about the estate are naturlesque, and have been left in their primitive manner, and are in keeping with the ruggedness with which the Maine coast abounds.

The only development that was thought necessary was the building of a roadway from the highway to the entrance porch, and the service part of the house.

Some planting has been done about the porch, at the entrance, at the side of the building and wherever it was found necessary to soften the curves of the landscape. Shrubs have been placed among the pines that require shady places in which to develop with the best results. Only such shrubs as grow well on the coast have been selected, and these are perennials, planted so as to require as little care as possible, and at the same time to blend with the natural characteristics of the site upon which the house is built amid primitive surroundings.

From the entrance porch, which is built at the rear of the dwelling, a roadway leads to the stable and the garage, which are constructed in the rear of the property, and within appropriate distances from the house. The stable is designed in keeping with the architectural scheme of the dwelling to which it belongs, and is most harmonious in every detail.

Its exterior walls are covered with shingles and left to weather finish a soft brown, while the trimmings are painted a dull olive green. The roof is also shingled and is painted a dull tone of green, which blends well with the color scheme of the trees which overhang it.

The interior of the stable contains a excellent carriage room, and a space large enough to accommodate a number of horses.

Both the stable and the carriage room are equipped with every modern appointment.

The coachman is provided with quarters, consisting of two bedrooms, living-room and bathroom in the second story of the structure. In addition to these there is ample storage and space for hay and feed.

The garage is built separately from the stable and its appointments are all that are required for the service of a modern up-to-date motor house.

In the planning of a country estate it is difficult to secure so delightful a result as is presented in the accompanying illustrations. There is perfect harmony, everywhere, in the relations of each of the buildings, one with the other in their architectural scheme and in the harmony with their surroundings, in the interior decorations and furnishings, and in the whole general scheme and outlined by the owner and his architects.

Plenty of thought has been given to the solution of a problem which in most surroundings of this kind are considered difficult, for it is interesting to note that while this house is very modern in its building, the estate has been a semi-wilderness for many years. Yet thoroughly new as this house is, it fits into the landscape, and forms part of the estate in a thoroughly natural way.

51. RUSSELL W. PORTER, pg 172

A CHALET ON THE MAINE COAST
American Homes and Gardens,
March 1912

A chance summer wanderer to Land's End, late in the season of 1909, was very much taken with a certain spot on the ocean shore where the ledges formed a natural bathtub. By this is meant a depression in the rocks, just below high tide, where the salt water is warmed by the sun, and bathing in cold waters of the Maine coast is rendered comfortable. Twice a day, high tides clear and replenish the reservoir.

"Build me a cottage here," said the summer pilgrim, standing on the raised beach directly back of the bathtub. "Cut no more trees than necessary; construct the building so as to accommodate three or four persons, but make it cozy; reduce household drudgery to a minimum; give me a sleeping-porch and a fireplace, and use whatever style you will. But it must come under six hundred dollars and you must first find me drinking water.

With these requirements on the part of his client, the artist-builder set to work. He was fortunate with the well, over which he had held grave doubts. After all, a sure source of good water is first essential. Fall was then well over, but he knew the value of getting the foundations down before winter set in, for he must lay the sills before the frost was out of the ground the following spring. But the cottage would not take shape, neither in his mind nor on paper, and time went by.

In January he went sketching in Italy. On his flying return across the Continent he passed through Switzerland in the daytime, by the St. Gotthard route. "There," he exclaimed as the train emerged from the long tunnel and pulled up at a small hamlet where the firs and spruces walled in the houses in dense masses of deep green. "There," he exclaimed again, the blue shadows on the snowdrifts making him homesick for New England, "I will build for my summer home a Swiss chalet such as these. The setting will be highly appropriate. Why not a Swiss Chalet, modified to fit the Maine coast?'

As the train wound down through the valley, the artist-builder was busy with his sketchbook, catching fugitive details needed from the brown huts hugging the mountain sides. And so the chalet was born. Bedrock was just under the grass roots, and it allowed him a concrete floor to the porch, also a hearth to the fireplace that completely filled the ingle-nook, at a low cost. Gravel ranging from coarse sand to pebbles the size of hens' eggs was there for the asking, and a few barrels of cement did the rest.

The colossal scale of the gable being the characteristic feature of Swiss house caused the builder some concern, as this construction is entirely honest and the beams are all hewn by the axe. He solved it buying an old nearby barn, tearing it down and using the heavy frame for the living room posts, the floor beams overhead and the roof purlins. A shipyard furnished six huge ship's knees, which amply bracketed out and supported the porch and the roof overhead.

The brown, almost black, color of Swiss beams was obtained by staining them with tar and linseed oil. Cypress shingles laid well to the weather covered the walls down to the line of the window stools, and from there down the walls, after first applying a heavy builder's paper, were covered with spruce slabs, the bark on, their sides edged, and running up and down. This up-and-down treatment permitted the slabs coming clear on the ground and covering the unsightly spaces under cottages supported by piers or posts. More for effect under the gable than for utility, the roof rafters were covered with three-inch strapping, to which the shingles were nailed. Inside, the plan is simplicity itself. It comprises a small low-beamed living- and dining-room and inglenook combined, a bedroom and a kitchen. The living-room is one

step below these other rooms, and has a shelf at the height of a platerail appearing and disappearing between the heavy posts and wall openings. The windows here are small-pane casements and swing outward. A tiny flight of stairs leaves the inglenook for the chamber overhead. Opposite it is a built-in couch with bookshelves handy, and between the firebreast boasts a large metal hood, across which is beaten in, with a nail-set, the legend *Sic Habitat Felicitas*. The face of the fireplace had the butts of clinker brick showing hit-and-miss across the different courses. The glazed leaden surfaces of these bricks contrast pleasantly with their red neighbors. The ample hearth is of brick, laid in herring-bone patter, worthy of the nook.

Above, the large chamber gives through a glass door to the sleeping-porch, tucked up under the gable. Here the weary city worker sleeps the clock around and absorbs the heavy balsam odors against another year of toil among the cliff dwellers. Here he looks over the tumble of ledges with its natural bathtub, looks out across the Atlantic Ocean, with nothing between him and Spain but the heaving deep. The outlook is hardly that of a Swiss chalet, hardly suggestive, perhaps of anything approaching Alpine scenery by reason of the sea taking place of mountains, but the cottage itself seems remarkably at home in its surroundings. And from the water this above, with its Mullein-green roof, its brown and gray walls, and a figure lazily stretched out on the high-backed settle of the porch, appear to be saying, "It is well worth six hundred dollars." And it truly is!

52. HENRY PASTON CLARK, pg 175

"THE BUNK," KENNEBUNKPORT, MAINE
American Homes and Gardens,
September 1911

Editor's note: The write-up for "The Bunk" is presented in its entirety in Chapter 5.

About the Authors and Photographer

A native of Portland, **Earle G. Shettleworth, Jr.,** cofounded Greater Portland Landmarks in 1964. In 1971 he was appointed by Governor Curtis to serve on the first board of the Maine Historic Preservation Commission, and he has served as director of the commission since 1976 and as Maine State Historian since 2004. Earle has lectured and written extensively on Maine history and architecture.

Christopher Glass is an architect practicing in Camden, Maine, since 1974. He taught architectural design at Bowdoin College for twenty years and has lectured widely. He is a former chair of the Maine Historic Preservation Commission, former president of Maine Preservation, and author of two previous books on the architecture of Maine homes.

Scott T. Hanson, an architectural historian with Sutherland Conservation & Consulting in Augusta, has researched and written numerous National Register nominations and Maine Historic Building Record documentation projects in addition to consulting on historic tax credit rehabilitation projects. Scott is the author of one previous book and co-author with Earle G. Shettleworth, Jr., of *The Architecture of Cushing's Island* (2012).

Architectural photographer and Maine native **Dave Clough** is a life-long lover of photography with a special passion for photographing structures of historical significance. His work has been published in Japan and the U.S. Dave lives in the coastal community of Rockland, Maine. This is his first book.